Chuck Pierce is one of those rare individuals who deftly handles the tension between the prophetic gift and ministry—with a practical eye toward implementation of the prophetic.

Frank Damazio
Senior Pastor, City Bible Church
Portland, Oregon

Every generation needs a few Joshuas with the courage and spiritual insight to lead the Church into conquest. I believe Chuck Pierce is one of these Joshuas. In *The Future War of the Church*, Chuck not only sounds the alarm, but he also gives us specific instruction in how to overcome the enemy. This book fanned zeal in my heart. It gave me courage to fight until we see the kind of global spiritual transformation that Jesus said His message would bring to the earth.

J. Lee Grady
Editor, *Charisma* magazine
Lake Mary, Florida

The Future War of the Church is must-reading for all Christian leaders and saints who desire to understand the times and seasons in which we live.

Bill Hamon
President, Christian International Ministries Network Institute
Colorado Springs, Colorado

The authors reveal that even as the darkness in our culture is increasing exponentially, the release of God's people into a fuller dimension of power and victory has never been so near. *The Future War of the Church* summons us to embrace this crucial hour and move forward in our destiny as the Third Day Church. A must-read!

Jane Hansen
President, Aglow International
Edmonds, Washington

Chuck Pierce identifies the strongholds of the enemy, and he tells us how to subdue and destroy them. Chuck is an apostolic prophet with a keen eye and ear toward the future. Put this important, revelatory book on your reading list!

John P. Kelly
Executive Apostle, International Coalition of Apostles
Southlake, Texas

Reading this book will open your eyes to the accuracy of God's prophetic guidance to help us win the war for our nation.

Dutch Sheets
Dutch Sheets Ministries
Colorado Springs, Colorado

Chuck Pierce has an amazing gift and an anointing to hear what God is saying to the Church for the coming hour. *The Future War of the Church* reveals how the shift we are seeing in the Church's governmental order and authority is even greater than that experienced in the days of Martin Luther and John Calvin.

Steve Shultz
Moderator, The Elijah List
Albany, Oregon

Once again, Chuck Pierce is sounding a clear trumpet, rousing the Church to alertness and a place of abandonment to the Lord in these momentous days. With clarity and breadth, this book summons all believers to take their places in the army of God.

Robert Stearns
Executive Director, Eagles Wings Ministries
Milwaukie, Oregon

This book is a clear prophetic window into what God has planned for His kingdom in our generation. The authors have given us a practical strategy manual, showing how the army of God can win victory upon victory in the future war of the Church.

C. Peter Wagner
Chancellor, Wagner Leadership Institute
Colorado Springs, Colorado

THE FUTURE WAR OF THE CHURCH

HOW WE CAN DEFEAT LAWLESSNESS AND BRING GOD'S ORDER TO THE EARTH

CHUCK D. PIERCE
& REBECCA WAGNER SYTSEMA

Regal

From Gospel Light
Ventura, California, U.S.A.

Published by Regal Books
From Gospel Light
Ventura, California, U.S.A.

First edition, 2001
Second edition, 2007

The Library of Congress has cataloged the first edition as follows:
Pierce, Chuck D., 1953-
        The future war of the church / Chuck D. Pierce and Rebecca Wagner Sytsema.
        p.   cm.

    Includes bibliographical references.
    ISBN 978-08307-4414-5 (trade paper)
        1. Church   2. Spiritual warfare.   I. Sytsema, Rebecca Wagner   II. Title
    BV600.3 .P54   2001
    243—dc21

                                                                              2001018575

1 2 3 4 5 6 7 8 9 10 / 10 09 08 07

Rights for publishing this book in other languages are contracted by Gospel Light Worldwide, the international nonprofit ministry of Gospel Light. For additional information, visit www.gospellightworldwide.org.

This book is dedicated to all the intercessors, prophets, apostles and spiritual leaders who have led us through the last season of the Church and paved the way for God's glory to come. May His glory bridge the past to the future and synergize the generations who together will pioneer the next move of God. May we enter this new season of Church history with expectation, joy and strength to overcome. Hope deferred from past defeats will be unleashed as God's presence comes upon His people to fulfill the best He has destined for our lives—individually, corporately and territorially.

EZEKIEL 37

Contents

Introduction

I can still remember the day I got up early and went from our bedroom to the couch. As I lay down and began to meditate and get my mind set on the Lord for the day, an interesting thing happened: *a blackboard appeared before me*. Visions are very interesting. I can't say that I have had many, but the few God has graced me with have been dramatic.

I began to see words appear on this blackboard. The hand of God seemed to be writing before me, just as He wrote in the days of Daniel. I saw the following words: *anti-Semitism, militant Islam, covenant conflict, women arising for My purposes, lawlessness, the transference of wealth, overthrowing thrones of iniquity* and *prepare for war*. "Prepare for war" seemed to be the illuminating cornerstone of the vision.

I said, "Lord, what are You showing me?"

"This is *the future war of the Church*," He said.

I saw one other topic that caused my spirit to leap: *Prayers that outwit the devil*. I have since written a book called *Prayers that Outwit the Enemy* (Regal Books, 2004) to help God's people pray in a more strategic way. The book begins with a look at the game of chess. Much like various pieces in a game of chess, each of us plays a key role in God's end-time strategy or future plan for fullness in the earth realm. Like chess, the only way we can be defeated is to fail to think ahead and anticipate the enemy's moves.

When this blackboard appeared in front of me and I meditated on what God was saying, I knew He was asking me to write something that would help the Body to prepare for the days that lie ahead. I called Bill Greig III, president of Regal Books, and shared with him what had happened. I then went to Peter Wagner, who I minister with, and told him of the vision. They both concurred that this was a message for this hour. After receiving confirmation, I asked Rebecca Wagner Sytsema to assist me in writing the first edition of this book. Rebecca and I worked diligently to write an interpretation of what the Lord showed me that morning when the blackboard appeared.

Even though it has been seven years since I received this vision, this is not a dated revelation. The topics addressed in this book can help us understand the overall covenant conflict in which we are a part. The fullness of the revelation has not been completed. Much revelation continues to unfold on how to advance in the times we are living in.

This book's companion, *God's Unfolding Battle Plan* (Regal Books, 2007), further explains the times we currently face as well as the times to come. We have chosen to publish these books simultaneously, as it would be very difficult to understand all of the revelation and information in *God's Unfolding Battle Plan* without first developing the foundation that is laid in this book.

A Continued Awakening

Rebecca and I finished writing *The Future War of the Church* and turned in the manuscript in October 2000. The book took longer to develop than I had anticipated, and I started to wonder if I was out of God's timing. But the awakening move of God's Spirit had only begun.

As the election of 2000 approached, I was speaking at a conference in Oklahoma. Oklahoma had gone through great tragedies in the previous years and was probably the most mobilized state for prayer in our nation. John Benefiel, pastor of Church on the Rock in Oklahoma City, has been used as an apostle to align pastors and intercessors across the state. Over the past five years, we have had quarterly meetings there.

Most of our quarterly meetings are concentrated on the needs of the state, but sometimes the Spirit of God comes down and gives revelation pertaining to the whole nation. That's exactly what happened on October 27, just as our nation was in an intense time of prayer for the election of 2000. We were in an incredible place of worship, and through a word of wisdom I saw Isaiah 32. I opened

my Bible and read the chapter out loud, and as I did so the Lord
began to speak the following words to me:

> *I am setting My course for judgment upon the states of this land.
> Judgment will come based upon the complacency of the Church
> from state to state to state. You have thought that judgment would
> come based upon the acts of the national government that is now
> in place, but I say to you that instead, judgment will come because
> of the complacency of My people.*
>
> *Remove false judgments, for I am setting a new course of
> righteousness. Those who I am about to put into places of authori-
> ty need to be surrounded with your shields of faith. I long to cover
> them so that a righteousness can be seen that has not been seen
> before in this land. Therefore, they must stay shielded so that they
> might display My righteous judgments.*
>
> *War will now break out in these next 18 months. This will be
> a war of great spiritual magnitude. The war will be over the
> boundaries of the future, for the enemy has shifted boundaries.
> There is a war over the justice of this land. I will establish justice in
> the midst of My people. Therefore there will be war over laws that
> have been established wrongly. Know that you are warring with
> an antichrist system. Therefore, do not fear this supernatural war
> that I am calling My people to be engaged in.*

This word was given to mobilize people to pray now to determine the future of our nation. The word was given in the presence
of leaders from a seven-state region and was sent out to intercessors across the U.S. in the Strategic Prayer Network. The mood of
the Lord was one of encouragement, and His voice released an
awareness of His character of justice and order.

How, Then, Shall We Pray?

For some time, my predominant role in the Body of Christ has been
to use my apostolic anointing to mobilize prayer worldwide. As I
have done this through the years, I have identified some prayer
points that I believe go hand in hand with this word given in

Oklahoma. God wants us to build a wall of fire and protection from city to city and state to state throughout our land. Prophecy is usually given in order to stimulate aggressive intercession.

Before you begin to pray, define the boundaries within which you are praying. Paul says, "[God] has determined their preappointed times and the boundaries of their dwellings" (Acts 17:26, *NKJV*). Some of you will pray for your home with the following prayer points. Others of you will pray for your church. Some of you are called to pray for your city. Some have been called by the Lord to pray for your state. And, of course, some will pray for our entire nation or even beyond. Apply the key prayer points below to whichever regional boundary God has called you to pray.

1. *Ask God to remove complacency from your life and region.* Complacency limits and distorts vision. Pray that the power of complacency will be broken from your church, city or state. Sometimes the enemy sends a spirit of slumber, so declare that the spirit of slumber is broken in your region. Shout, "Awake!" when you are driving throughout your city, and allow that word to go through the spirit realm of your area.

2. *Ask the Lord for the spirit of grace and intercession to fall on your region.* Many times, we have not because we ask not. If intercessors will cry out for a spirit of grace and intercession, God will begin to blanket the people of your region who have never felt the burden to pray. Communion and prayer will begin and changes will be activated. You will probably hear of a spirit of travail coming forth in people throughout your church, city or state.

3. *Pray for the key authority structures in your region.* Ask the Lord to put an urgency in the gatekeepers. Cry out for mercy for the authorities who are now operating in unbelief. Ask for a sweeping gift of faith to fall on spiritual authorities in your region.

4. *Ask the Lord to build up the wall with the correct spiritual leadership for your region.* God raises some up and puts others down. Don't pray from a motivation of control, but release "leadershift" powerfully into the spirit realm and watch this take action in your region. Trust God to work in His timing.

5. *Cry out for corporate worship times to arise in your region.* Pray that not only will 24-hour prayer be established but also that there will be corporate worship times in which the Church will gather just to worship a holy and living God. Pray that what has happened in Cali, Colombia (see chapter 6), will happen in your region as well. True worship tears down idolatrous structures.

6. *As a new level of worship is established in the Church in your region, ask the Lord to break the power of child sacrifice and close down abortion centers.* Ask the Lord for true worship to overthrow powers in the heavenly realm that influence earthly actions contrary to the will of God. Ask the Lord to gather people from all over your region to worship. I see gatherings very much like Promise Keepers, but they will be "state-owned" by the apostles, intercessors, prophets, pastors and spiritual leaders of that region. Stadiums will be filled with people worshiping the living God.

7. *Ask for lawless structures that are linked with terrorist activities to be revealed.* This word was given in Oklahoma, where prior to 9/11 the worst terrorist attack on U.S. soil occurred. Declare that all the hidden evil structures that are governed by false religious principles will be uncovered.

8. *Declare that unjust laws that have been established will be overturned in your region.* Pray that the right judges will

be put in place from region to region and that the Spirit of God will empower the Church with a new coat of armor for spiritual war. This is a day of Esther overturning Haman's decrees.

9. *Ask the Spirit of God to penetrate dead religious structures that are resisting His move in your region.* The Spirit of God is the restraining force that stops demonic powers from expanding their evil works. Declare that those who are speaking out of a mind resistant to the Holy Spirit will be silenced and that the Spirit of God will begin to break out in various places in your city and state.

10. *Do not fear, but cry out for God's perfect restorative grace to take action throughout our entire nation.* Even though this prophetic word mentions judgment, it gives very clear instruction that judgment does not have to come if the Church will rise from complacency now and worship!

It is my prayer that you will allow this and other prophetic words to bring you into a new expectation of the victory God has prepared for the Church in days ahead. This is a *kairos* time for God's people to understand authority, for authority is the key to power. This is a time for us to deal with the spirit of fear that has embedded itself into the heart of the Church. The spirit of fear creates an unsound mind, weakens power and negates love.

God has given us an awesome responsibility. Through the prophets, He has shown us His holy desire for the future of our nation. However, as we see throughout history, God makes the fulfillment of His desire contingent on the obedience of His people. Apostles, prophets and intercessors play a crucial role. If the apostles, acting on the word delivered through the prophets, effectively mobilize the intercessors, and if the intercessors enter into powerful, strategic, prophetic intercession, we in the Body of Christ will truly be praying the future into being. It will be God's best future for us, and our nation will be blessed as never before.[1]

Times and Conflicts Are Escalating

War will now break out . . .
This will be a war of great spiritual magnitude.
The war will be over the boundaries of the future,
for the enemy has shifted boundaries.[2]

The U.S. Global Apostolic Prayer Network always has a meeting in January. We call it "Starting the Year Off Right!" It is a meeting to receive revelation from the Lord so that those in the prayer movement can find their footing to pray during the year ahead.

In the January 2001 meeting, the Lord said, "There will be a *restoration* of the *war mantle* of the Body of Christ." I then began to teach as the Lord instructed me: "This year is the beginning of wars for the next seven years. Great conflict will come to this nation, a conflict you have not known before in your history. By September 18 (2001), this nation will be in war! Pray for these cities: New York, Los Angeles, Miami, Houston, Chicago, Seattle . . ."

I began to share this message, believing that the Body of Christ would want to know what they would be facing in days ahead. Often, I was asked if I thought we would go into a physical war. I always said yes and explained that I felt a physical war was imminent and would occur by September 2001. The response was surprising. The Body resisted the notion of changing times and warfare within our land. It was difficult for people to understand the relationship between spiritual war and physical war. What goes on in a spiritual war many times manifests naturally (see Rev. 12). A corporate spiritual war affects every aspect of natural society: religion, politics (legal and military), economics and education. Therefore, God raises up *worshiping intercessors* in each one of these arenas of power.

Since that time of resistance, we have begun to submit to the discipline of the Lord. From a spiritual point of view, we have seen a shift in society. We have seen the beginning of war.[3]

The Unthinkable Happened

I do not think any of us were prepared for what occurred on September 11, 2001. The tragedy of the World Trade Center and Pentagon attacks were physical manifestations of the season ahead. As the three commercial airplanes approached the World Trade Center and the Pentagon, the world as we know it changed. The fiery crashes, the disintegration of the Twin Towers and the loss of approximately 3,000 lives propelled the United States—and the world—into an unprecedented season of conflict.

The weeks before and after September 11, 2001, Global Harvest Ministries sponsored Future War of the Church conferences. The latter of these gatherings took place in California. At that conference, I stated:

> We have now entered the seven-year war season. The only way we will win this war is through worship. We must learn to ascend in worship and then descend in war. If we will go into the Throne Room and hear our Lord's voice and strategy, we can then walk in the earth realm and have victory in days ahead.

The representatives from Regal Books who were attending the conference asked me to write a book called *The Worship Warrior* to go with *The Future War of the Church*. This is one of the few books on worship that can help you to understand the connection between worship and war. We must learn to open the portals of heaven so that the Spirit of God can have liberty to move and protect us in the earth.

Here is one story from *The Worship Warrior* that demonstrates the worship-war connection:

> Everyone knows that the United States went into trauma and mourning on September 11, 2001. Much of the world mourned with us. On March 11, 2002, we "remembered" this tragic time by an hour of prayer and silence. Also,

where the World Trade Center had stood, two lights permeated the heavens. Bill Yount writes:

"On March 11, as the bright lights were turned on in the darkness representing the Twin Towers, I heard a rumbling in the heavens as though New York City had captured the attention of Heaven—as though the light could be seen from the Portals of Heaven. Immediately I saw Angels beginning to descend down upon these light rays like they were a 'Jacob's Ladder.' As though Angels were waiting in line for the moment the rays of light would be turned on . . . creating an open heaven for Angels on assignment to descend. I heard the Father speak to these ministering Angels. 'These Rays of Light are man's ways of reaching upward to Me. Though they don't know Me they are seeking for a "Ray of Hope" in their darkness. WE MUST GO DOWN!' As these Angels began to descend downward, the 'Twin Towers' of Light eventually became covered solid with Angels from top to bottom. I sensed many of these Angels were the ones that were present on Sept. 11th and had ushered in many of the dying into the presence of the Lord. Now these same Angels were descending downward once again to minister and bring comfort and hope to those who had suffered great loss of loved ones. 'Are they not all ministering spirits, sent forth to minister for them who shall be heirs of salvation (Heb. 1:14)?' There was a definite assignment given to these Angels to war against the hopelessness of life and influence many to turn to Jesus, their only hope. I heard the Father's voice speak Isaiah 60:1 into New York City and America:

ARISE [from the depression and prostration in which circumstances have kept you; rise to a new life]! Shine—be radiant with the glory of the Lord; for your light is to come, and the glory of the Lord is risen upon you! For behold, darkness shall cover the earth, and dense darkness all peoples; but the

Lord shall arise upon you, [O Jerusalem], and
His glory shall be seen on you. And nations shall
come to your light, and kings to the brightness
of your rising.[4]

Now, we are living and maturing in this season of war. One of
the things that the Lord keeps speaking to me is, *"My blessings will
surround you, but you must learn to open the door of heaven so that these
blessings can manifest in your sphere of influence and territory. You must
cooperate with My Holy Spirit and not quench or resist His plan. He is the
only resistor of evil. He is the One who can expose your enemy."*

We can see many blessings manifested on the earth in this season. We have entered into covenant conflict, which means that we
are warring to see those blessings spread throughout the earthly
realm. Psalm 24:1 declares that the "earth is the LORD's, and the
fullness thereof" (*KJV*). God has a plan of fullness, and we must go
to war to see this fullness manifested. When we open the portals
of heaven, blessings that have been shut up and unable to be seen
will be manifested on the earth.

God continues to bring fullness to the vision He gave me
seven years ago. In each chapter, we have included a short update
on God's unfolding revelation since *The Future War of the Church*
was first written. As we continue to wage the covenant conflict,
I pray that the blessings of God manifest in each one of you as you
read this book (see 3 John 2). My prayer for you is the following:

To You I will cry, O LORD my Rock . . . Hear the voice of
my supplications when I cry to You, when I lift my hands
toward Your Holy sanctuary . . . The LORD is my strength
and my shield . . . with my song I will praise Him. The
LORD is their strength, and He is the saving refuge [or
defense] of His anointed (Ps. 28:1-2,7-8, *NKJV*).

I bless you as you read or reread this book. May you gain confidence in our Father who loves us. May you pray and commune like
never before in your life. May you find your place in His sanctuary

and boldly enter the Throne Room of Grace. May you be filled with renewed joy. May all of the trials and discouragement of the past and any hope deferred that has settled in your soul be gone. May your soul rejoice and prosper. May the work of your hands prosper. May He work in you mightily to do His will. May the gifts of God within you be released and activated. May a new anointing arise within you and favor be seen upon you. May He defend His anointed. May your shield of faith be polished and renewed. May you see that you have a good future ahead.

Foreword

Amos spoke about a "famine . . . for hearing the words of the Lord," a time when people "will go to and fro to seek the word of the Lord, but they will not find it" (Amos 8:11,12). The prophet Samuel was born into such a time: "And word from the Lord was rare in those days, visions were infrequent" (1 Sam. 3:1). A shortage of revelation, understanding and prophetic words from the Lord is indeed a curse.

Daniel, on the other hand, spoke of a time when prophetic insight would increase:

> But you, O Daniel, shut up the words and seal the book until the time of the end. Then many shall run to and fro and search anxiously through the Book, and knowledge of God's purposes as revealed by His prophets shall be increased and become great (Dan. 12:4, *AMP*).

Without a doubt, we are blessed to live in a day as seen by Daniel. The increase of prophecy has indeed become great, reaching a point probably best described as multiplication—another meaning of the Hebrew word *rabah*, translated "increased" in the above verse.

When Daniel was allowed to look ahead to a time such as this, he could easily have seen Chuck Pierce, a person who walks in as keen a gift of prophetic revelation as I have ever witnessed. He is a spiritual son of Issachar, one who understands the times and, therefore, has knowledge of what we must do (see 1 Chron. 12:32).

Combine this rare gift with the writing skill and understanding of Rebecca Wagner Sytsema—one who obviously inherited the literary genes of her father, C. Peter Wagner—and you have what you hold in your hand: an incredibly important book for the future of the Church. Perhaps this is why God has given Chuck a national voice so rapidly. We need him!

The Future War of the Church is not an imaginative, Frank Peretti-type depiction of the spiritual realm, with frothing demons and sword-wielding angels locked in lethal combat. Don't get me wrong. I enjoyed *This Present Darkness,* and it may not be that far from reality in the spiritual realm; but this book isn't about that. The conflict Chuck speaks of is not imaginary, nor is it an ethereal attempt to sensationalize spiritual warfare or the prophetic dimension of the Spirit. This is clear scholarly teaching, filled with and substantiated by an abundance of Scripture, brought to a prophetic point of application for a people born for such a time as this. For those who would be truly strategic and progressive in the coming days, *The Future War of the Church* is not optional.

As you read the pages that follow, you'll begin to preach and teach the material if you're a pastor or teacher. If you're an intercessor, you'll begin to pray with greater confidence and accuracy. All of us fortunate and wise enough to read this book will be more victorious, for we will have added the power of prophetic knowledge to our arsenal of weapons. Proverbs 24:5-6 tells us, "A wise man is strong, yes, a man of knowledge increases strength; for by wise counsel you will wage your own war, and in a multitude of counselors there is safety" (*NKJV*).

Because of people of God like Chuck and Rebecca, I have hope for America and the rest of the world. I have confidence that the waiting harvest won't rot before it is reaped. I believe the spiritually barren places of the earth can be healed of their sin-induced sterility. I'm convinced God will win and Satan will lose, and the future war of the Church is going to become, in reality, the future *victory* of the Church.

"Now thanks be to God who always leads us in triumph in Christ, and through us diffuses the fragrance of His knowledge in every place" (2 Cor. 2:14, *NKJV*).

Dutch Sheets
Colorado Springs, Colorado

CHAPTER ONE

Prepare for War

In peace, Love tunes the shepherd's reed;
In war, he mounts the warrior's steed.
SIR WALTER SCOTT (1771-1832)

The war has actually begun! The next gale that sweeps from
the north will bring to our ears the clash of resounding arms!
Our brethren are already in the field! Why stand we here idle? . . .
Is life so dear or peace so sweet as to be purchased at the price of chains
and slavery? Forbid it, Almighty God. I know not what course others
may take, but as for me, give me liberty or give me death!
PATRICK HENRY (1736-1799)

The Future. When most people think of the future, they get a queasiness in their stomachs. "Future" is a word that causes man, woman and child to experience anxiety and fear—particularly those of us born and raised in the twentieth century with its cautionary tales and images of science fiction. But ever since Adam and Eve's banishment from the Garden of Eden, fear of the future has been one of the most prevalent fears in all of human society.

War.

This is another word that creates instant fear in most people. When we hear the word "war," our minds conjure thoughts of destruction, sorrow, grief, loss, conflict and death. However, Jesus said that although we will hear of wars and rumors of wars, "See that you are not troubled" (Matt. 24:6).

Nevertheless, these two words—"future" and "war"—coupled together are not usually related to faith building in the kingdom of God. And yet the title of this book was chosen very carefully: *The Future War of the Church*.

Notice there is one other element in the title: *the Church*. This is the faith factor. If the Church rises up to take its proper place in the days ahead, and if we understand and employ the strategies of spiritual warfare, the future will hold no fear for us.

The Future War of the Church

God is saying this is a time for war. But when we talk about the future war of the Church, what does that mean? Will there be bloodshed in our land? Will our sons be drafted and sent to fight on foreign soil? No. Even though war in the heavenlies can manifest on Earth and result in physical war, we are not referring here to a physical war.

Second Corinthians 10:3-6 provides a very clear picture of what the Lord means when He says there is a time for war:

> For though we walk in the flesh, we do not war according to the flesh. For the weapons of our warfare are not carnal but mighty in God for pulling down strongholds, casting down arguments and every high thing that exalts itself against the knowledge of God, bringing every thought into captivity to the obedience of Christ, and being ready to punish all disobedience when your obedience is fulfilled.

Our warfare is not fought with mere human weapons. Weapons of the flesh will not overcome the dark spiritual forces that we contend with here on Earth. We must war against arrogant philosophies and rebellious attitudes—any ideas that exalt themselves above the mind of Christ. We must be ready to bring those things into obedience of the Lord's ultimate purpose for the earth.

All of what the Church will face in the days ahead has always been part of our spiritual conflict with the enemies of God. However, the *intensity* of the warfare we are facing has increased, and it will continue to escalate to unprecedented levels. The enemy knows his time to reign is growing short, and in his desperation he is fighting with more vicious intent than in days past.

Therefore, this is a time for learning the spiritual dynamics of the escalating war we face. It is a time for equipping God's people in new ways that will carry them through to victory. God is calling His Church to awaken and become alert to the spiritual war around us. We must be prepared to battle the spiritual forces behind ungodly philosophies that threaten to overtake entire societies.

The future war of the Church is, therefore, a spiritual battle to see God's will established on the earth and whole societies turned from satanically inspired philosophies and practices to reflections of God's marvelous power and glory.

The End Is Not Yet

> And you will hear of wars and rumors of wars. See that you are not troubled; for all these things must come to pass, *but the end is not yet* (Matt. 24:6, emphasis added)

If, as Jesus says, the end is not yet, then we must rise up and enter into the *now* of God. Because we have not reached that final time when the culmination of all things has occurred, we must learn to operate in the present—for what we do now will determine our future. Isaiah 46:9-10 says:

> Remember the former things of old, for I am God, and there is no other; I am God, and there is none like Me, declaring the end from the beginning, and from ancient times things that are not yet done, saying, "My Counsel shall stand, and I will do all My pleasure."

When the Lord makes a declaration, you can be sure He already knows the end of the thing. It is the process of that prophetic declaration, or divine promise, that we will look at in this book.

God already knows the end. Recognize that you are on a path of life; it is set before you. You are urged to press along that path and endure that path until you reach the end. There are big boulders and potholes all along the way, and oftentimes the path needs to be cleared before you can even begin. Know that your Father in heaven is going to watch over you from the first step until you reach the finish line, because He already knows the end.

With this reality understood, we should never lose faith or hope along the path. The real issues along the path are who God is and what His purpose is from the beginning until the end. He says, "I am the Alpha and Omega, the Beginning and the End, the First and the Last" (Rev. 22:13). He is saying to you, "I AM. I AM, and I can make you well able to accomplish My purpose here on the earth."

Is Anything Too Hard for God?

Jerusalem was under siege and about to be conquered by the Babylonian forces of King Nebuchadnezzar. The prophet Jeremiah knew that God was handing the city over to Babylon because of Israel's idolatry and its refusal to obey His laws. The land had been defiled, and God's judgment was imminent.

At this time the Lord gave Jeremiah an opportunity to purchase property in the very land that God said would soon be ravaged by war, famine and disease. Jeremiah knew God's voice, and he knew that he was to buy the land and hide the deed in a safe place. Nevertheless, doubt began to creep in. After all, why should he pay good money to purchase property that would soon be in the hands of his enemies?

Jeremiah is perhaps the easiest of the Old Testament prophets for modern man to relate to. Like so many of us, Jeremiah was briefly overcome by what he saw happening around him, and he began to question God. But God spoke to Jeremiah and said, "Is there anything too hard for Me?" (Jer. 32:27).

God then promised to restore the fortunes of the people—that they would one day return to the land, causing fields to again be bought and sold and prosperity to be restored (see Jer. 32:44). When the promise of God enters into our circumstance, things look totally different. Suddenly Jeremiah's deed for this war-torn piece of land did not look worthless but, instead, very valuable.

The future of Jerusalem had been declared by God: One day the Israelites would return to this land and embrace the inheritance God had set for them in that place. Jeremiah's act of faith in buying the property and burying the deed had great significance, illustrating four important principles for our own lives:

1. Jeremiah knew the times in which he lived.
2. He understood the future from the promise of God.
3. He saw a window of opportunity to bridge the present with the future.
4. He obeyed God's will accordingly.

Once again, God's people are at a pivotal point in history. We are faced with continual change, conflict, fear, war, rumors of war, generations battling generations, and generations battling among themselves.

The warfare tactics learned by the Body of Christ in the 1990s will not be enough to overthrow the enemy who will come against us in this new season. To be victorious, we need to grasp the same four principles so clearly understood by Jeremiah. Let us allow God to show us how these principles apply today so that we will be in a position to receive a fresh impartation of overcoming strategy that will carry us into the future with victory.

Knowing the Times

These are wonderful but dangerous times. The Church is maturing, but it's not yet mature. Perhaps more than at any other time in history, the Church is in a crisis of competition for harvest with other organized religious forces, including Islam, Buddhism, Hinduism, and a host of other -Isms.

Confrontations with demonic forces behind opposing belief systems will be the norm for the future, and God is calling His Body to prepare for the warfare we are entering even now. Part of our preparation is to develop an understanding of our role in the establishment of government in the future. Both the Body of Christ and the governments of nations are already changing drastically.

God is transforming our minds so that we can have the mind of Christ, and He is searching out those with a heart to lead the troops in the days ahead. As we enter this new season, here are some guidelines that will assist us in maintaining our spiritual focus.

We must think prophetically. Proverbs 29:18 tells us that without a vision, a people perish. That is to say, without prophetic utterance, we begin to go backward. If Jeremiah had not had the prophetic word of the Lord to give him a vision of the future, he would not have understood anything beyond the fact that Jerusalem was falling to the enemy. The prophetic word of the Lord gave Jeremiah the vision he needed to move forward, despite the signs of doom around him.

During the past few decades, God has brought about a great resurgence of the prophetic. One reason why we have seen this resurgence is because we, like Jeremiah, need vision for the future. Without vision we can't see the provision God has made available to us. If we cannot see our provision, our supply for the future will be easily cut off by the enemy.

Ask the Lord to remove anything that has quenched His Spirit in your past and stopped His prophetic flow in your life.

We must stay alert to activity and anything unusual around us. God is restoring a watchman anointing to His people. In biblical times, though a city had strong walls and double gates, security was not complete without watchmen in their places, shouting, or heralding, anything they saw that was out of the ordinary. Their job was to warn the people of impending danger. They would pay with their lives if they failed to inform the city of an enemy's approach. If the watchmen were not alert, cities could fall, territories could be lost and many people could be slaughtered or forced into captivity.

Today's spiritual watchmen are just as important to the kingdom of God. But the Church has become so familiar and comfortable with the world that our watchmen may not notice when adverse conditions enter our boundaries. In this hour God is saying, "Watch the boundaries I have set for you, so that the enemy does not gain access to your inheritance."[1]

We all must allow the Lord to teach us to have a strong defense so that we can both stay on the offensive and guard that which God has given us.

We must keep our spirits alive and active so that we discern properly. One of Satan's greatest tools of destruction is apathy. That's why the Lord warned the church of Laodicea against falling into spiritual lethargy (see Rev. 3:14-22). If you become lukewarm, you have no passion or strength to move ahead into the best that God has for you. Discernment is a key to defeating apathy and remaining on the offensive.

We must know how to get in touch with each other immediately. Maintaining our connections and relationships with each other is another key to securing our future. God sovereignly connects and aligns us with one another so that we can function effectively. Know with whom God has connected you and how to let them know what God is saying to you. This will keep God's warning system in proper order.

One way that we remain connected is through frequent gatherings. In Genesis 49, we read that Jacob called his sons together and revealed their futures to them. The Lord is using prophetic gatherings today in much the same way. As we come together corporately, God will speak to us and reveal things we may not see on an individual basis.

Another method God is raising up to maintain connections is through organizations like the World Prayer Center in Colorado Springs. The World Prayer Center uses state-of-the-art communications technology to both gather and disseminate information to praying people throughout the world on urgent matters that require immediate, fervent prayer.[2] This is one way God is connecting the Body of Christ in order to secure the future harvest.

We must learn to understand each other's ways and methods of communication. Communication is the vital component to understanding God, prophecy and the future, as Jeremiah did.

To communicate is to impart knowledge, make known, divulge, transmit information and to give or exchange thoughts. It also means to be joined, or connected. As I have worked with intercessors and Christian leaders throughout the world, I have seen a real communication gap among God's people that often keeps us from accomplishing these things.

Intercessors in particular can be very misunderstood. Intercessors are a part of the resurgence of the prophetic. However, they must learn when to pray and when to say. Once they begin to talk about what God is revealing to them, they take on the function of the prophet. The Lord has disciplined me through the years to be patient with someone who is trying to give a prophetic message. If we do not attempt to understand how differently each of us processes the voice of God, we can easily miss God's message of redemption, warning and salvation.

We must not let petty issues distract us; they may be the work of religious spirits. A demonic religious spirit works to get us focused on legalistic rules and regulations to the extent that we miss the overall picture of what God is doing. We can get so busy dotting every *i* and crossing every *t* that we miss the gist of the sentence.

Jesus came to fulfill the Law and the prophets. He did this through love and through the cross. Faith works by love, and faith overcomes. But when we are legalistic with one another, faith is weakened and we fall into criticism and judgmentalism, rather than walking in the love of Christ. This behavior creates an opening for religious spirits to operate in our midst, and they work to keep us focused on what everyone else is doing wrong rather than on the Great Commission. May we all stay focused on the harvest fields of the future and all that we must do to bring in the harvest, rather than harping about how someone else is doing it incorrectly.

Embrace one another. We must be flexible enough to connect with and embrace those who will help us accomplish our mission, even if they are not people we have worked with or have been comfortable with before. Remember this: You do not have all the gifting you need to accomplish your purpose. That is why God has given us each other.

I have seen members of the Body who reject certain gifts (in people and function) and end up failing because they would not embrace the resources God was providing. In the context of a teaching on spiritual gifts, Paul warns us not to reject each other or the gifts reflected in one another: "But now indeed there are many members, yet one body. And the eye cannot say to the hand, 'I have no need of you'; nor again the head to the feet, 'I have no need of you'" (1 Cor. 12:20-21).

Today, more than ever, the Lord requires the whole Body to move forward—together.

Understanding the Future

As we mentioned, the future is a fuel that greatly propels human fear. Not knowing what will happen can produce paralyzing effects in those prone to such fear. On the other hand, the future is also linked with expectations, anticipation or hope for an occurrence, like the birth of a child. These expectations can cause us to have a passion, joy, strength and faith in what God will do.

Building faith and hope is one of the functions of the prophetic gift. Jeremiah was able to obey God in the midst of troubling circumstances because he had been given a picture of the future. We too must be willing to obey God in these troubling times, even if He asks us to do something unusual, knowing that God has plans and purposes far beyond what we are able to see or comprehend—plans for good and not evil, plans for a hope and a future (see Jer. 29:11).

At many points throughout this book, you will encounter prophetic pictures of the future Church. For instance, the coming days will be likened to those of Moses, in which demonstrations of God's power will overthrow today's pharaohs in order to bring about the redemption of entire territories. Numbers 33:3-4 holds a key principle for the days ahead:

> The children of Israel went out with boldness in the sight of all the Egyptians. For the Egyptians were burying all their firstborn, whom the LORD had killed among them. Also on their gods the LORD had executed judgments.

The Egyptians could not stop the Israelites from leaving because they were busy burying their dead. And their gods had been rendered powerless because God had judged them. *In the days ahead we will see God make a path of freedom for His people who have been held captive, and we will see evil forces rendered powerless as God executes judgment on them!*

Our hope is that these and other prophetic words in this book will bring to your life new expectation of the coming victory God has prepared for the Church.

Our Window of Opportunity

Jeremiah understood that the right action taken at the right time would lead him into God's plan for the future. Suppose that Jeremiah had not purchased the land and had not prophesied the future of Jerusalem. When God was ready to fulfill His promise of restoration, Israel may not have possessed the inheritance God intended for them! Instead, Jeremiah saw his window of opportunity and acted and, as we will see, set into motion events many years later that God would use to bring Israel out of their Babylonian captivity.

This is a tremendously important principle for the Church to understand. The Greek word *kairos* is used in the New Testament to describe the opportune, or appointed, time that God has set for a thing to occur. Jeremiah knew the *kairos* time for purchasing the property. Jesus knew the *kairos* time for beginning His ministry, just as He knew the *kairos* time for returning to Jerusalem to be crucified. We must recognize that God has *kairos* times—appointed seasons—for certain events to occur, and we must respond when the opportunity arises.

What happens if we miss our *kairos* time? The children of Israel learned this hard lesson when they came out of Egypt. Despite God's mighty displays of power that had delivered them out of captivity, the Israelites fell into disbelief, which led them into idol worship. As a result, they missed their *kairos* time to enter into the Promised Land and instead wandered in the wilderness for 40 years until the sinful generation passed away. Another *kairos* moment for entering the Promised Land did not occur until a new generation was set in place.

We, the Church, are standing on the threshold of a *kairos* time—a tremendous opportunity to advance the kingdom of God on Earth. But if we do not act in proper timing, the window of opportunity will shut and the harvest of the future will be lost. We cannot afford to wander for 40 years waiting for another *kairos* moment. Millions of lost souls will go to hell if we do not respond to God's leading now!

This book is about the window of opportunity that has opened to the Church for this *kairos* season. Like no other time in history, the Church has the opportunity in the coming days to deal with the spirit of lawlessness, dethrone the powers that sit on thrones of iniquity, and evangelize those caught in the structures of false religions (what we call the "-Isms"). We will also expose the proliferation of "antichrist" weapons, including anti-Semitism, abuse of the prophetic gift, rejection of the godly role of women in the Church, ethnic domination, and perversion.

Again, the warfare we are entering into will require new wisdom and strategy. Like Daniel, we must engage in urgent and fervent prayer, and we need to learn how to pray and discern. We also need to understand the new system of government that God is bringing to the Church to carry us into the future.

The seasons are changing, and we must be willing to change with them. Let us move as the Spirit of God leads us in order to seize the *kairos* opportunities at hand!

The Vision

On December 31, 1985, I (throughout the book, "I" will refer to Chuck) opened my Bible to read and pray in preparation for the coming year. As I went before the Lord, I felt a nudging, or prompting, to shut my Bible. I knew I was to lay aside my prayer list and just wait for God to speak to me. As I waited, God indeed began revealing many things to me. I felt He was showing me how the Church was to prepare for the future.

He began by saying that within 12 years from that time, the government of the Church would change to reflect the pattern given to us when Jesus ascended to heaven (we will discuss this in chapter 3). The Lord then said He would release revelation and gifting for new administrative methods that would cause His people to become influential and victorious in the next season of history. In this visitation God showed me three distinct governmental structures on this earth and their importance for the future of society.

The Existing Church Structure

God first showed me the Church as I knew it. At that time I was a member of a mainline denomination, and I really didn't know any other method of doing church. I had always been open to a move of God, but as far as church government was concerned, I knew only the democratic, congregational form of decision making in church matters. Now that form of church appeared to me as a large building of about 50 stories. Each room was brightly lit and the structure well built, although the building was also flexible at that time.

However, as I watched, the building became more and more rigid and unchangeable. As it grew rigid the lights grew dim, even though there was still some light emanating from the rooms. The structure began to look more like a prison than a flexible organism of change. And God said, "I will have an opportune time when many will come out of this church government and begin to flow into another government structure that will arise."

Other Types of Government

God then showed me two other buildings rising up. The first building was labeled Militant Religious Governments (the -Isms). This building was being constructed rapidly and had great strength. I saw rooms that represented religious systems from nations around the world, including the United States.

The Lord showed me the effects that these religious systems would have on our society in the days ahead. I saw strategy rooms in this building where plans for terrorist activity were being devised. The proposed acts of terrorism were designed to create great fear in the target areas—fear meant to cause people to convert to these religious systems. This fear was also meant to cause wealth that God intended for His kingdom to be withheld and controlled by other religions. I then saw the Lord's heart for those ensnared by, and working in, these religious systems—He longed to see them released and their trapped gifts liberated for Kingdom purposes.

One key religious system God showed me was Islam, which will have great influence on Earth in the days ahead. (One important note on this point: When I refer to Islam, I am not talking about the Muslim people per se, whom God loves and for whom Jesus died; I am referring, rather, to the religious structure of Islam, which is controlled by satanic principalities and powers.) I saw that Islamic religious forces would be positioned in key places throughout the world. The Islamic religion understands the spiritual principle of treading to gain territory (see Josh. 1:3). First, they march militantly to gain control of territories. Then they establish their authority through war, bloodshed or whatever else may be necessary to maintain and secure the ground they've gained.

In this portion of the vision, there was another, smaller building located in front of the -Isms. The smaller building was called Lawlessness. In this building there were hidden lawless forces linked with secret societies such as the Ku Klux Klan and Freemasonry. I saw the influence of this building begin to result in lawless acts of violence and murder taking place in schools, churches, shopping malls and supermarkets.

The building of Lawlessness was actually connected in form and administration to the religious systems located in the -Isms building behind it. I thought this peculiar at first, but the Lord began to show me that the same type of religious spirit controlled both of these entities. I then saw how the governments of the earth were being influenced by these structures and how some of these governments were trying in vain to resist them with their own strength.

The Lord then showed me what the foundations of these two buildings were made of. Words appeared on their foundations: "mammon," "Ashteroth," "Jezebel," "Ahab," "Babylon," anti-Semitic slogans, and Hindu philosophy, among others. God said that if we were to understand how these structures operated, we would have keys for victory in the future when the structures of the -Isms and Lawlessness would rise up and attempt to gain control.

The Church of the Future

God then showed me a third picture. This was of a building that was filled with light. The Lord called it My Future Kingdom Authority. This building was very small. It was just beginning to form and was still lacking in size and shape. Even so, the structure was nothing but light (similar to a hologram) and glory.

Several words appeared on its foundation. They were the five ascension gifts listed in Ephesians 4:11 that make up the government of God: apostles, prophets, evangelists, pastors and teachers. God was bringing order to these five gifts and placing them in the foundation. Every time one gift would be set in order, the light would increase tremendously.

He said that this order would become very visible over the next 12 years. Once the proper order had been established, He would rapidly transfer His people to the new structure. I saw many leaders from the first building (the Existing Church Structure) move their offices from the old building to this new structure. As they turned out the lights of their offices in the old structure, that building grew darker and much more rigid, and it was unable to withstand the -Isms and Lawlessness. However, the Lord's new structure began to arise, and it had the ability to superimpose itself over the -Isms and Lawlessness structures and could overcome their governments.

God then said to me:

This is the government of the Church of the future that will arise and spread My light throughout the world in the latter days. This government will overcome all other governments. When this government is in order, you can then command governments of the earth to come into order.

This will be the government that My latter-day blessings will rest on. This will be the government in which My glory will be seen. This will be the government that truly comes into a double-portion anointing and will dethrone the systems of Babylon on this Earth. This government will not be one of compromise but of determined commitment to My purposes.

As the vision was coming to an end, I asked, "Lord, how in the world will we make the changes necessary to move into this new structure in such a short amount of time?" Here is a list of six directives the Lord gave me to prepare for the future:

1. Understand Authority

Authority is the key to power. No greater faith had Jesus seen in all Israel than the man who understood authority (see Matt. 8:5-13). The Lord showed me that if I would begin to understand and analyze every authority that had influence in my life, I would begin to operate in a new level of faith.

Faith is linked with authority. To the extent that we submit to the authority God has placed in our lives, our faith has the opportunity to be stretched and strengthened. Faith is the overcoming agent that God's people have on this earth (see John 14:12); therefore, if the Church is to overcome, we must understand and submit to proper authority.

2. Deal with Your Greatest Fear

The spirit of fear creates an unsound mind, weakens power and negates love. The Lord showed me that at the end of this 12-year period, a new move of holiness would begin to emerge among His people that would unleash a genuine fear of the Lord. The fear of the Lord releases wisdom, and wisdom will unlock and dismantle demonic forces.

You cannot shout down principalities and powers. They are a structured hierarchy that forms a government, and governments have to be dismantled. Wisdom causes false governments to topple. If we will tear down the spirit of fear that is hindering us and move into a new fear of the Lord, we will topple iniquitous patterns that allow principalities and powers to blind unreached people groups, cities and even entire nations to the light of the gospel.

3. Increase Your Discernment

During my vision, I said, "Lord, I do not have the ability to discern at this level." It was as if the Lord said I did not have a choice. He then said to me, "Discipline yourself in the Word and exercise My Spirit within your spirit, for it will take both Word and Spirit to cause the reality of Me to be seen in days ahead." If we quench the Holy Spirit in our lives or if we do not wash ourselves with the written Word, we fall out of spiritual balance and open ourselves to delusion. Under these conditions we can never reach the level of discernment we will need for the critical times ahead.

4. *Know Who Labors Among You*

The Lord showed me that in the coming days it would be imperative for His people to communicate necessary information to one another efficiently. God said that He was going to start building true unity of purpose and function within His Body from territory to territory. I began to see a network that would form a net. When this net was completed, He would begin to drag it through cities and nations, collecting a great harvest.

I saw that everyone in the regional Body would need to be connected to each other, with everyone working to accomplish God's purposes for that territory. One reason we will need to know each other and be linked together is to help us discern when infiltrators attempt to undermine God's purposes.

5. *Be in the World, Not of It*

The prince of the power of the air rules this earth (see Eph. 2:2). Satan loves to find places in our human nature where he can ensnare us to do his will. To prevent this, Christians often try to distance themselves from the world. They become highly separatist, and the root of this is fear and religious pride. Once we get cleaned up, we are always a little afraid that the temptations of this world will get us dirty once again. But Jesus reminded me that He was in the world but not "of this world" (John 8:23). The Lord is planning for the glory that He is about to release in His

Church to permeate the earth. But we cannot spread His glory if we hide out.

6. Understand Wealth

I believe that the Lord is disciplining us so that He can send us forth without being trapped by the god of mammon (money). "The love of money is a root of all kinds of evil" (1 Tim. 6:10). We must allow purification to come into our lives wherever money is concerned.

God is planning a great transference of wealth to His people. Wealth does not just mean having money but also having strength and the spoils of war (in this case, a harvest of souls). I believe God wants us to understand money and finances so that we will be good stewards to advance His kingdom in the future. If we allow God to purify us and make us holy, He will then be able to trust us with great wealth.

This visitation came at the end of 1985. The 12-year period of bringing the order to the new Church structure ended in 1997. I have come to believe that this new Church structure, the Church of the Future, is what C. Peter Wagner has termed the New Apostolic Reformation, which we will look at more closely later in this book.

The Rest of Jeremiah's Story

When Jeremiah bought the property and placed the deed in a clay jar to preserve it, he was performing a prophetic act—a physical act performed at the prompting of the Lord that illustrates something the Lord is speaking prophetically into a situation.

According to the Word of the Lord, Jeremiah prophesied that the Lord would allow the Israelites to be captured and carried off into captivity by the Babylonians as punishment for their idolatry (see Jer. 25:8-11; 32:28-35); then, after 70 years, God would deliver them out of captivity and heal the city of Jerusalem. Jeremiah went on to declare that the Lord would rebuild the cities of Judah and

Israel, that He would restore their fortunes and bring peace and prosperity to the land once more (see Jer. 32:36-44).

So what effect did Jeremiah's act of obedience have on God's plans for Israel's future? The story is continued in the book of Daniel. Daniel uncovered the prophetic writings of Jeremiah while Israel was still held captive in Babylon. He learned that Jerusalem must lie desolate for 70 years—and now that time had come to an end (see Dan. 9:2). Because of Jeremiah's prophetic declaration, Daniel knew that now was the time to act. Jeremiah's understanding of the future had become a "Now" word for Daniel.

Four specific things then happened that would eventually bring about an end to Israel's captivity:

1. *Daniel prayed and fasted* (see Dan. 9:3). Jeremiah was specific in saying that the Lord would turn a deaf ear to His people for 70 years, so Daniel knew that the *kairos* time had come to beseech the Lord for an end to their captivity.

2. *Daniel repented on behalf of himself and his people* (see Dan. 9:5-16). Daniel confessed and repented, not only for his own sin, but also for the sins and iniquities of the Israelites that had resulted in their captivity in the first place.

3. *Daniel received an angelic visitation* (see Dan. 10:1-14). God sent His messenger Gabriel after Daniel had prayed, fasted and repented for three weeks. Gabriel appeared to Daniel to tell him what would happen to his people.

4. *Daniel received revelation of the future* (see Dan. 11–12).

Daniel understood the same four principles outlined at the beginning of this chapter. Because of Jeremiah's prophecy, he understood the times in which he was living. Because he understood the times, he saw his window of opportunity and began to seek the Lord with great fervency. When he did, he gained an understanding of the future God had for his people; and he learned that through obedience to God's commands, they could begin to move out of captivity.

When the word of God is released through prophecy, it is never forgotten. It is stored in heaven until God is ready to release it back into the earth. As the Body of Christ, we have received many prophetic words, both through Scripture and modern-day prophets, that are about to come to pass. We need to understand the times, seize our *kairos* opportunities and move into the future with victory!

Even though the times ahead may be difficult and will change rapidly, we have great confidence that God will give us the revelation we need to move forward. And should we find ourselves overwhelmed by our circumstances and apparent defeats, we must listen to the Lord speak to us, just as He did to Jeremiah, "Is there anything too hard for Me?"

God's Unfolding Revelation: On the Move

After seven years of war, do we still have a future? I believe the answer is *yes*! Do I believe the war ends just because we have finished this seven-year season? *No.* Do I believe we are more prepared than we were when we began? *Yes!*

We are living in uncertain times that might give each of us a feeling of insecurity, whether personally, corporately or nationally. However, in the midst of these times, we can come to know the power and love of God like never before and become a secured tent peg in a time of trouble (see Ezra 9:8).

The biblical concept of the future is that *we have an end, and our end will be greater than our beginning.* The real issue is that we do not become stagnant but keep moving forward and pressing toward the finish line in every area that God has for us.

How do we stay on the move? We recognize that we are going from one place to the next and that we have a destination.

We are moving from one wineskin to another wineskin. Wineskins represent structure. Peter Wagner says that we have now fully entered the Second Apostolic Reformation (when this book was originally written, we had just entered this season). For too long, the Church has defined all of the foundational spiritual gifts as "pastor." We now recognize that each spiritual gift the Lord gave when He ascended to the Father's right hand is very important.

A name represents a function. During this past decade, the prophetic and apostolic gifts have been defined more clearly than ever before. This allows the functioning power and authority of the Church to be demonstrated. Old structures and methods of administration are not appropriate for the season we are in. As the foundation of the Church continues to be aligned properly and to function efficiently, we will see the harvest for this generation unlocked.

We are moving from religious ritual to a new dimension of glory and from one dimension of faith to a demonstration of true authority. We can no longer say that God is capable without expecting Him to overcome in a chaotic world.

We are moving from "gathered ones" for fellowship to "the gathered one" for war. The *ecclesia* of God is now a group who gather to gain a strategy for their future. We are moving from centralized fellowship to corporate warring and travailing through worship. The atmosphere of our gatherings is changing.

We are moving from decreeing judgment and being a judgmental people to being sons of Issachar who not only understand the times but also know what Israel should do (see 1 Chron. 12:32). Without a prophetic utterance, revelation or restrained boundaries, a people perish (see Prov. 29:18). The prophetic dimension of the Church is changing.

We are moving from hope deferred to new strength. So many times we lost focus as we warred with our prophetic word to bring forth the promises that God had for a certain season. This has produced weakness and sickness in the Body of Christ. We are now shifting so that the deferred hope that is stopping faith from arising can be dissected and removed from our souls. This is causing a new anointing to be released. We are beginning to recognize that we are an anointed people. We are moving from anointing to anointing.

We are becoming sons and daughters of God for this generation. We know that we are a people who have an inheritance, and we are determined not to lose what God has promised us in this generation. Therefore, we are willing to war like never before. A Kingdom people understand God's call to occupy and take dominion of the sphere of authority He has destined for them in their generation. We are that Kingdom people who are now rising up to answer His call.

CHAPTER TWO

Foundations for Future Victory

Efforts and courage are not enough without purpose and direction.
JOHN F. KENNEDY (1917-1963)

It is fatal to enter any war without the will to win it.
GEN. DOUGLAS MACARTHUR (1880-1964)

I n the vision I shared in the previous chapter, the Church was
undergoing a great transition, moving from the Existing
Church Structure to the Church of the Future. In the next
two chapters we will examine that transition to understand
how God is preparing the Church for victory in the war that
lies ahead.

In his book *A Divine Confrontation*, Graham Cooke writes:

These days more than ever we need to pray for a depth of
understanding regarding the purposes of God. We need
the cobwebs of our mind swept away by the Spirit of God.
The Church must be realigned with God's present purpose
and break out of the things that have made us irrelevant in
this day and time. We are in transition now whether we like
it or not—indeed, we are in a process of change whether we
want it or want to avoid it! All change begins in the heart
of God and makes its presence felt in our lives by His hand.
There are times and seasons when God intervenes sovereignly in humanity to bring an end to one thing and a
beginning to another.[1]

God brings change to cause us to profit in a new way. John
Eckhardt says that the Body must see "the benefits of change"

before it will embrace change:

> People will not change if there is no benefit. Why go through all the difficulty of changing if there is not? They need to see the blessing of changing into an apostolic church. They must see the greater blessings and power that will flow through their church as a result of change. Reformation always causes the blessings of God to be released in a greater way. Without reformation, the Church becomes stagnant and eventually loses the full blessing of God. Through reformation, multitudes are blessed and released into their individual destinies. The Church also begins to walk in corporate destiny and release salvation and blessing to multitudes.[2]

The Importance of Preparation

Transition is a time of preparation. During this time of transition for the Church, God is preparing His people to be victorious in the days ahead. When considering a Scripture passage or a word of prophecy, I find it helpful to open the dictionary and review the definitions of key words in order to fully understand what the Lord may want to reveal.

According to the word I received, in this hour God is preparing the Church for war. The key words to understand are "prepare," "Church" and "war." Let us first look at the word "prepare."

To prepare means to make ready or get ready, to put together or compound, to formulate, to draft, to draw up, to frame, to ready for action, to gird, to brace, to fortify or to strengthen. God believes strongly in preparation. In fact, the word "prepare" appears in nearly every book of the Old Testament.

We are to be a people prepared to do that which God has called us to do. God will use this time of preparation to release provisions to help us face the war ahead and accelerate His purposes on the earth. Following are six types of preparation that will help build the foundations for future victory:

Preparation That Produces Favor

One of the greatest examples of preparation in the Bible is found in the story of Esther. We can learn many lessons from the book of Esther, including the importance of successful teamwork, the power of unity, the sovereignty of God and how covenant with God brings revelation and favor over our enemies. Esther is also an example of someone who prepared herself in the midst of hostility to take her place for "such a time as this" (Esther 4:14).

Esther, an orphaned Jewish girl who had been adopted by her cousin Mordecai, was hardly fit to become queen of Persia. Nonetheless, when she was taken to the palace to become part of the king's harem, Esther submitted to a prescribed time of personal preparation using costly ointments and perfumes and, undoubtedly, learning protocol before presenting herself to the king as a candidate for becoming queen. Scripture records that Esther gained great favor during her time of preparation and later with the king (see Esther 2:9,15,17). As she allowed the favor of God to rest upon her, she became willing to be used as God's instrument to save an entire people, even if it meant risking her own life.

There are two lessons on preparation to be learned here. The first is to make the most of your situation. Rather than becoming bitter over her situation, she allowed a close bond to form with the man who adopted her. Her relationship with Mordecai became an important factor as she fulfilled her destiny in saving the Jews from slaughter. Unless we, like Esther, allow ourselves to come into the spirit of adoption that the Lord Jesus Christ has offered us, we will never be prepared for what lies ahead. Even if you feel totally abandoned by earthly friends and family, know that the Lord can raise you up and prepare you for that special moment when He is going to use you for the advancement of His kingdom.

The other lesson we can learn is patience in our preparation. Esther 2:12 tells us that 12 months of preparation (away from family and friends) were necessary before a lady could be presented to the king. For six months she was anointed with the oil of myrrh, and for six months she was treated with perfumes and cosmetics meant to enhance her beauty. It is intriguing that Esther should be anointed with myrrh, a bitter resin, before she was anointed with perfumes. As we prepare for moving into what the Lord has for us, we may also find a season when we are faced with bitter, even painful, circumstances. We may find it very difficult to walk through these times not fully understanding their purpose, but these very things prepare us for moving into our destiny.

After Esther had completed her time of preparation, she was then taken to the king for one night. Only if he delighted in her and summoned her by name would she see him again. When Esther went to the king, she won his favor and approval and was exalted to the royal position of queen.

What does this say to us? If we allow the anointing of God to rest upon us, if we allow the beauty of holiness to surround and transform us, we can gain great favor. Also, as Esther submitted to the leadership of Mordecai, if we allow submission to lead us into godly obedience, grace will abound around us and we will be positioned to overthrow the enemies of our future.

Preparation That Produces Confidence

The heart is the center of the physical, mental and spiritual life of men and women. It is vital to the functioning of the body. Biblically, the heart is also synonymous with the rational mind. As a person "thinks in his heart, so is he" (Prov. 23:7). To ponder something in one's heart means to consider it carefully. Among my favorite Scripture passages are Luke 1:66 and 2:19, in which Mary ponders in her heart the words concerning Jesus. She carefully considered the magnitude of that task for which God had chosen her.

The heart is linked not only to the mind but also to the will—human wishes and desires that are functions of our affections and emotions. When the Lord prepares the heart, He is really getting the whole person in line with His purpose. We are commanded to love God with all of our hearts, and we are told that love comes from a pure heart (see Mark 12:30; 1 Tim. 1:5).

Preparing our hearts produces great confidence because we can come before God with a clear conscience:

And by this we know that we are of the truth, and shall assure our hearts before Him. For if our heart condemns us, God is greater than our heart, and knows all things. Beloved, if our heart does not condemn us, we have confidence toward God (1 John 3:19-21).

When our hearts condemn us, it is because we do not have a clear conscience concerning something in our lives and we cannot pray from a position of confidence before the Lord. Paul charges Timothy to "wage the good warfare, having faith and a good conscience" (1 Tim. 1:18-19). Being able to pray and wage war from a position of confidence will make us victorious.

To be ready for war, we must have confidence, but we must also remove idolatry and sin from our lives. The prophet Samuel declared to the people of Israel:

> If you return to the LORD with all your hearts, then put away the foreign gods and the Ashtoreths from among you, and prepare your hearts for the LORD, and serve Him only; and He will deliver you from the hand of the Philistines (1 Sam. 7:3).

If we disconnect our moral and spiritual lives from idolatry and other iniquitous patterns, the enemies who are set against us will have no right to overtake us. We will discuss how to do this in chapter 4.

Preparation That Produces Watchfulness
A good warrior is watchful to determine how his adversary may be lurking to prevent God's will from being done:

> Let your waist be girded and your lamps burning; and you yourselves be like men who wait for their master, when he will return from the wedding, that when he comes and knocks they may open to him immediately. Blessed are those servants whom the master, when he comes, will find

watching. Assuredly, I say to you that he will gird himself and have them sit down to eat, and will come and serve them (Luke 12:35-37).

However, we cannot have the level of watchfulness we need for war if we are keeping one eye on the things of this world. A good warrior is not encumbered by worldliness.

Now is the time to eliminate from our lives all that is not absolutely essential. The Bible says there is "a time to keep, and a time to throw away" (Eccles. 3:6). We are entering a season in which our lives must be lean, ordered and simple. Allow the Lord to deal with your attachments, both physically and emotionally, because we can't be jointly fit if we are attached inappropriately elsewhere. He is telling each of us, "Batten down the hatches. Establish your boundaries. Be careful of borrowing. Pay off what you can. Come and meet with Me, and I will tell you what you need to know!" The Lord is also reorganizing many ministries to get them into fighting trim.

Recently the world experienced great fear and apprehension about the so-called Y2K bug, and many in the Church prepared themselves for an economic and technological disaster. Although nothing substantial materialized on January 1, 2000, I believe that God used this perceived threat to teach the Body of Christ to understand preparation in a new way. Not everyone prepared for world calamity, but the threat of the Y2K bug *did* cause us to look at issues of preparation in a way that many of us have never had to in the past, particularly those of us born after World War II.

Corporate Preparation That Causes Us to Possess Our Inheritance

Probably the best example of corporate preparation comes from the book of Joshua, which begins with the choosing of a new leader to guide the armies of Israel. God's appointed leader, Joshua, went through a preparation process very much like that of Moses in the book of Exodus.

Although there were no burning bushes, the Lord came to Joshua and established his call to lead the people into their inheritance. Joshua then relayed His commands to the people. I believe the Body of Christ has entered a new season in which the Lord is raising up apostolic leadership for the future. This is part of the preparation process.

Notice how Joshua (a type of apostolic leader) gave the order to cross the Jordan: "Prepare provisions for yourselves, for within three days you will cross over this Jordan, to go in to possess the land which the LORD your God is giving you to possess" (Josh. 1:11). Until then, God's people had been provided for each day in the wilderness, and they had been totally reliant on God's sovereignty.

Even though the Lord prepares "a table in the wilderness" (Ps. 78:19), there comes a point when He says it is now time for us to develop, gather provisions and ultimately possess that which He has for us. This is a mentality of personal and corporate responsibility different from what we may have experienced in the past. Our willingness to allow the Lord to knit us together in a new way under apostolic leadership will position us for the battle ahead, just as the children of Israel were positioned for battle once they crossed the Jordan. This will produce in us a new corporate strength that will prepare us for battle and enable us to win the victory.

Preparation That Causes Our Future to Be Unlocked

I believe Isaiah 40 is a pattern for today. This is a transitional chapter in which the Lord speaks of moving His people from judgment to release from captivity:

> Speak comfort to Jerusalem, and cry out to her, that her warfare is ended, that her iniquity is pardoned; for she has received from the LORD's hand double for all her sins (Isa. 40:2).

In preparing for war we must realize there will be a time for our warfare to end and a door to our future to be opened. Many of us look with dismay at the iniquitous patterns of our families, cities and nations, thinking, *How can we hope to ever enter into a glorious future with this awful past?*

There comes a time when the Lord begins to prepare the way into the future—a time when God calls for the departure from the judgments that have caused us to miss the presence of God and to lose touch with our destiny. He begins to speak to us (or someone around us), and that voice begins to cry out, "This is the way to your future!" The voice of one crying in the wilderness calls, "Prepare the way of the LORD; make straight in the desert a highway for our God" (Isa. 40:3). Hear His promise:

> Prepare the way, take the stumbling block out of the way of My people . . . to revive the spirit of the humble, and to revive the heart of the contrite ones (Isa. 57:14).

Isaiah 62:10 says, "Go through, go through the gates! Prepare the way for the people; build up, build up the highway!" This passage goes on to command that we not only remove the stones but also lift up a banner, or standard, so that the people will rally and follow out of captivity into a whole new dimension of victory and freedom.

The Lord is preparing us for war so that we might obtain our future. He is setting new standards for us at the dawn of the third millennium.

Preparation to Build His House

Once our future is unlocked, the Lord prepares us to build, and we gain a new strength and call:

> Even them I will bring to My holy mountain, and make them joyful in My house of prayer. . . . My house shall be called a house of prayer for all nations. . . . I will gather to him others besides those who are gathered to him (Isa. 56:7-8).

Jesus is going to have us accomplish the commission He left us when He ascended to the right hand of the Father (see Matt. 28:19-20).

Our commission is to go forth and make disciples of all *ethnos*, or people groups. The Lord will have His presence established throughout the earth. His perfect will is for His glory to cover all the earth: "For the earth will be filled with the knowledge of the glory of the LORD, as the waters cover the sea" (Hab. 2:14).

Allow the preparation to begin!

Preparing for War

Why such stringent preparation? For war! War is a conflict between two massed enemies, a state of active military operations, an aggressive competition or a struggle to achieve a particular goal. While it is true that the Church has always been involved in spiritual warfare at some level, we have only been in a time of preparation for the future war of the Church—an escalated, no-holds-barred conflict between the kingdom of God and the kingdom of Satan.

This is a season when the Lord is moving to position us and join us together for victory. He also wants to release provisions so that we can endure the turmoil ahead and accelerate His purposes. *In war, one must be prepared!*

> Let your waist be girded and your lamps burning; and you yourselves be like men who wait for their master, when he will return from the wedding, that when he comes and knocks they may open to him immediately. Blessed are those servants whom the master, when he comes, will find watching (Luke 12:35-37).

To be girded means to be ready for action. Those who are found watching will have the opportunity to sit in communion with the Lord (see v. 37). His anointing will ready them to go forth in action.

As we prepare for war there are four important things we must understand:

1. We must know why we are at war.
2. We must know who our enemy is and how he operates against the Church.
3. We must know who *we* are and how God is preparing us for this future war.
4. We must have a strategy for victory.

We will spend much of this book discovering our strategy for victory. The rest of this chapter, however, is devoted to exploring the first three issues that are important to understanding war.

Why Are We at War?

We are at war with an enemy who has set himself against the will of God. We are therefore at war until God's will is done on Earth as it is in heaven. The very heart of seeing God's will accomplished on Earth is to see souls saved and the Great Commission fulfilled. Dr. C. Peter Wagner puts it this way:

> Satan's primary objective is to prevent God from being glorified by keeping lost people from being saved. Jesus came to seek and to save the lost. God sent His Son that whosoever believes on Him should have everlasting life. Whenever a person is saved, the angels in heaven rejoice. Satan hates all of the above. He wants people to go to hell, not to heaven. And the reason this is his primary objective is that each time he succeeds he has won an *eternal victory*.[3]

Remember, war can also be defined as an aggressive competition or a struggle to achieve a particular goal. We are in an aggressive competition with the enemy for the souls of every man, woman and child. Every soul we win is an eternal victory for the kingdom of God. That is the war we face. Of course, we know from Scripture that the Lord will win the war. But as Wagner writes, "This is the first time in human history that we have a viable opportunity of completing the Great Commission of Jesus in our generation."[4]

But the closer we get to winning the war, the more desperate and vicious the forces of Satan become. It is imperative that we understand our enemy as we take up the future war of the Church.

What Are We Warring Against?

The Word of God tells us we are in conflict with five foes:

1. *Satan.* The devil and his demons affect most of us, including Christians. Satan has a hierarchy and a horde under him who are confederated to stop the purposes of God. (See Gen. 3:15; 2 Cor. 2:11; Eph. 6:12; Jas. 4:7; 1 Pet. 5:8; 1 John 3:8; Rev. 12:17.)

2. *Flesh.* The flesh is the old Adamic nature that tries to hang on for dear life instead of submit to the power of the Cross. Galatians 5:24 says we should crucify our flesh each day. The flesh hinders us from obeying God. Unless it is suppressed on a daily basis, we fall back into active sin. The devil loves to keep our soulish nature from being crucified. If he loses ground and our soulish nature becomes submitted to the Spirit of God, he loses the ability to use us as one of his resources here on Earth. (See John 8:44; Rom. 7:23; 1 Cor. 9:25-27; 2 Cor. 12:7; Gal. 5:17; 1 Pet. 2:11.)

3. *Enemies.* Evil spirits will often become attached to, or embedded in, individuals. Then they use these individuals to set themselves against God's covenant plan in another person's life. In the book of Nehemiah, Sanballat and Tobiah were used by the devil to hinder the rebuilding of the walls of Jerusalem. (See Pss. 38:19; 56:2; 59:3.)

4. *World.* The world system is organized contrary to God's will and is being run by Satan, the god of this world.

We, as Christians, are enemies of the world. Though we are not part of this world's system, we still live in it. (See John 16:33; 1 John 5:4-5.)

5. *Death*. Death is our final enemy. Jesus overcame death, and through His Spirit we can also overcome. (See 1 Cor. 15:26; Heb. 2:14,15.)

If we do not war against these things, we will never possess the inheritance God has given us.

We Are Warring for Kingdom Purposes

The Lord is with us! Wars in the Bible always had a religious significance. Since Israel was the firstfruits of God and His inheritance, the priests reminded their armies that Yahweh was with them to fight their battles (see Deut. 20:1-4). Before opening a campaign or engaging an enemy, the priest performed sacrificial rites (see 1 Sam. 7:8-10; 13:9). The warriors were consecrated by the sacrifices (see Jer. 6:4; 22:7; 51:27-28; Joel 3:9; Mic. 3:5).

Isaiah 13:3 declares that the Lord gathers His host and summons His "sanctified ones" to battle. There is a holy sanctification going on in the Body today as He prepares us to stand against the forces that are holding captive our families, churches and cities.

An Order for Victory

For the Israelites, the order of battle was simple. The forces were drawn up, either in a line or in three divisions, with a center and two wings (see Judg. 7:16; 1 Sam. 11:11; 2 Sam. 18:2). There was a rearguard to provide protection on the march and to bring in stragglers (see Num. 10:25; Josh. 6:9). The signals for the charge and the retreat were given by sounding a trumpet. There was also a battle cry to inspire courage and to impart confidence (see Judg. 7:20; Amos 1:14).

The outcome of any battle depended in large part upon the personal courage and endurance of the combatants. But on occasion the decision was left to two individuals fighting man against man, such as the confrontation that took place at the battle of Elah between the giant Goliath and the stripling David (see 1 Sam. 17).

God has an order for victory. However, many forget that the Lord will make room for their gifts. Today, as individuals are attempting to position themselves in the battle line, much usurpation of authority is occurring. An individual who usurps another's proper authority might seem to prosper for a time, but he will find himself struggling in due season. Resist this temptation. Self-evaluation and manipulation of one's own position lead to presumption. They also result in the negation of the Lord's perfect timing and His best plan.

Characteristics a Warrior Must Have

A Kingdom warrior possesses several characteristics that ensure victory:

- We must war with *confidence*. There is no time during this season for self-pity. Insecurity is nothing but pride. The Lord has made you and can keep you! He is forming us into new, sharp threshing instruments! We do not need to control the forming lest we rely upon our own flesh in the day of battle. From prayer we gain confidence.

- We must war with *faith* (see 1 Tim. 1:18-19). We must be a prophetic people who know what the Lord has said and is saying and who war from the power of His voice. Faith comes by hearing and hearing comes by the Word of the Lord.

- We must war with a *good conscience* (see 1 Tim. 1:19). The conscience is the window of the soul. If our conscience is right before God, the enemy is unable to condemn us. This is the source of our strength of spirit.

- We must war with *steadfastness* in the faith (see 1 Cor. 16:13; Heb. 10:23; 1 Pet. 5:9). Steadfastness is a quality different from faith. You do not waver and you keep confessing the will of the Lord until a manifestation occurs.

- We must war with *earnestness* (see Jude 1:3). Earnestness is linked with contending. We must contend for the apostolic truth that was released to the Early Church, and we must contend for its interpretation for this generation.

- We must war with *sobriety* (see 1 Thess. 5:6; 1 Pet. 5:8). Our minds must be clear and not passive.

- We must war with an *endurance* in the midst of hardship (see 2 Tim. 2:3,10). We must persevere and transfer God's riches to others who can carry forth the gospel.

- We must war with *self-denial* (see 1 Cor. 9:25-27). The Cross is our victory. We must let it work in lives to produce the Resurrection power that overcomes the enemy!

A War for Harvest Increase

Finally, there is a mentality of increase and victory that the Lord is working to develop in His people. The Lord is imparting to us a "hundredfold" mentality of victory within us. This mindset will cause us to experience increase and bring the harvest into the storehouse.

I see us as Gideon threshing wheat in the winepress. Gideon was hiding his grain from the Midianites, threshing it inside the winepress rather than out where such work was normally done. We should be outside threshing grain, but the enemy has produced fear in us and has occupied our place in the harvest. However, the Lord is about to visit us. He is then going to have us dethrone the thrones of iniquity in our lives and in the regions where we live. He is going to give us the strength to drive the enemy out of our fields.

Understanding the Antichrist System

It is so important in war to understand who the enemy is and how he operates. In order to do this, we must understand the antichrist system. I am not referring to the personage of the Antichrist but rather to a demonic system that directly attacks the advances of the Body of Christ.

The books of 1 John and 2 John provide a few insights into the antichrist system:

> Little children, it is the last hour; and as you have heard that the Antichrist is coming, even now many antichrists have come, by which we know that it is the last hour (1 John 2:18).

> Who is a liar but he who denies that Jesus is the Christ? He is antichrist who denies the Father and the Son (1 John 2:22).

> Every spirit that does not confess that Jesus Christ has come in the flesh is not of God. And this is the spirit of the Antichrist, which you have heard was coming, and is now already in the world (1 John 4:3).

> For many deceivers have gone out into the world who do not confess Jesus Christ as coming in the flesh. This is a deceiver and an antichrist (2 John 1:7).

Even though the term "antichrist" only appears in these two books, its origins can be traced to the book of Daniel, where the prophet records a vision of the end times. In Daniel 7:25, we see that there is one specific ruler, the Antichrist (capital *A*), who is set against God and His saints. The context of the chapter, however, shows us that there is a collective antichrist (small *a*) system that would one day oppose the Lord and His people. This system would fully persecute the righteous and actually set up a form of worship (see Dan. 8).

There have always been individuals and systems throughout history that can be identified with the antichrist. There have even been empires that can collectively be viewed as antichrist systems. The defining characteristics of an antichrist system are threefold:

1. The system denies the incarnation of Christ and/or His deity.
2. There is usually a strong charisma in the system that sets up the system itself as savior.
3. The system is armed with satanic power that is ordered and organized.

Clear modern-day examples of antichrist systems include Nazism and Communism. But antichrist systems can also be set up apart from government, and they can control entire regions through attitudes and beliefs that are contrary to God's will.

The antichrist system operates in five specific areas of which the Church has remained fairly ignorant. Perhaps these areas have not seemed important in the grand scheme of things, but Satan knows full well that the blessings of God cannot rest on a region that is controlled by any of these. The Church, therefore, is going to have to develop a strategy to gain victory over these things in the days ahead if we are to make progress in winning the war for souls.

1. Anti-Semitism

Whether or not we understand or agree with all the views of Zionists or eschatologists, we cannot read the Bible and *not* see the covenants God made with Israel, using the term "everlasting" on several occasions. These carry over into the New Testament as well. Kevin Connor and Ken Malmin write:

The New Covenant was made by the Lord Jesus Christ immediately prior to His death at Jerusalem. It was made with the twelve apostles, who represented the House of Israel and the House of Judah, after the flesh, but were the foundation of the New Covenant Church, being the twelve apostles of the Lamb. It became the fulfillment of all previous Covenants, fulfilling and abolishing in itself their temporal elements and making possible their everlasting elements.[5]

The apostle Paul reminds us that, as Gentiles, we have come from a wild olive tree and that, through faith in Christ, we have been grafted onto the holy tree (Israel) and have become partakers of its fatness (see Rom. 11:16-24).

The Word is clear that God has not forgotten His chosen people, so neither should we forget them. Not only is Israel referred to throughout the Bible as God's chosen people, but the nation also serves as a prophetic picture of the Body of Christ. As such, Satan hates this people with a passion, and he has worked throughout history to see them destroyed. The spirit behind anti-Semitism is the spirit of antichrist.

Within the past century we have seen how an antichrist system was linked with anti-Semitism through Adolph Hitler and the Holocaust. He was considered by some to be *the* Antichrist—evil personified. Although he was not the Antichrist prophesied by Daniel, those who called him Antichrist were correct in the sense that the system he created was an antichrist system. Why? Because his main target of hate and annihilation was the Jewish people!

God cannot fully bless a region that curses His people (see Gen. 12:3). Therefore, listen for ways that anti-Semitism may be arising in your area. The Church needs to stand and address that spirit so that the Lord can continue to move in your region.

2. Abuse of the Prophetic Gift

Every region has a "prophetic" voice or voices—someone or some message that the people of that region look to for guidance.

In recent years, the Lord has been restoring the prophetic gift to the Church, something that we will discuss further in the next chapter. But if we don't raise up a prophetic people to see that God's voice is heard in a region, Satan will take advantage of our silence and raise up a false prophet who will control entire groups of people. Without a vision, the people perish—without prophetic revelation, the people will miss their opportunity for victory.

Here in the United States, for example, John Dawson has observed:

> America is a paradox. Large and loud, still brimming with promise; an exaggeration of the worst and best of the human condition. This is a nation with a tangled web of righteous and unrighteous roots. . . . Lofty ideals were proclaimed at the time of our independence from Britain, but for most of our history Americans have valued unbridled liberty in the cause of personal success more than responsible servanthood. . . . We are drifting. This is a nation that has both a covenant with God and a pact with the devil.[6]

America has gravitated for decades toward hearing the voice of the enemy—a whispering voice of false prophecy that has led us to blindly follow mammon (money) rather than morality and to assert personal liberty to the detriment of personal responsibility. As a result, we have entered into a post-Christian era because true Christianity does not tolerate such things. The antichrist spirit is responsible for issuing forth a voice to lead people farther from the truth of the gospel. But God has a remnant of prophetic people in this nation who need to rise up against the voice of the antichrist and proclaim the truth.

3. Oppression of Women

Women are an important factor in fulfilling the Great Commission— and for more than serving men and being hospitable. Cindy Jacobs writes:

> Without men and women working side by side, the Church will be ineffective. The complete image of God will only be

manifested in its full expression when men and women stand side by side in the Church. Is there any wonder that the devil fights gender reconciliation at all levels? Satan cannot afford to have Eden restored and man and woman standing together as they did in the Garden. This would bring order to the home and order to the Church.[7]

Jane Hansen adds this insight:

Christ is restoring the house, the dwelling place of the Lord, that He might come to that house and fill it with His glory. His house is not made of brick or stone, but of "living stones" being built into a spiritual house (1 Pet. 2:5). His house consists of men and women, flesh and blood, hearts made one with His. We are His Body, His dwelling place. We are the image bearers on Earth of Almighty God.

The man and woman were the beginning place, the foundation of the House of the Lord—the place where He would dwell and begin to reveal Himself on Earth. Through them, God intended to accomplish something for Himself on Earth that would ultimately speak, not only from generation to generation, but also on into eternity, into the ages to come.

Once again Satan endeavored to rise up against God. . . . He knew it was essential to bring separation, distrust, fear and suspicion between male and female, the image bearers God purposed to use for His unfolding plan on Earth. The strength of the man and woman was their union. Without unity, without oneness, God's plan would fail.[8]

The tendency to suppress women and not allow them to use all their God-given gifts is a trick of the enemy to keep the Church functioning at a level that will never win the war. God calls and anoints people at His discretion, not at ours. It is our job to acknowledge and make room for those who have been given spiritual gifts, regardless of gender. To do any less is to give room to an antichrist spirit whose plan is to render the Church ineffective or, at least, less effective than that for which God has made provision.

4. Ethnic Domination

Wherever one ethnic group is being dominated by another, the antichrist spirit is in operation. Oppression, domination, suppression, enslavement and genocide are evils crafted by the enemy to keep the gospel from making significant inroads. That is why we have seen such an intense focus in the Body of Christ toward racial reconciliation in recent years.

Reconciliation through identificational repentance is causing advancement of the gospel among groups of people that had heretofore been long resistant.

John Dawson, a recognized expert on identificational repentance, writes:

> The greatest wounds in human history, the greatest injustices, have not happened through the acts of some individual perpetrator, rather through the institutions, systems, philosophies, cultures, religions and governments of mankind. . . . We (Christians) are called to live out the biblical practice of identificational repentance, a neglected truth that opens the floodgates of revival and brings healing to the nations.[9]

Why does repentance open the floodgates of revival? Because it allows us to move in a spirit opposite that of oppression and domination, which are energized by an antichrist system. Identificational repentance is a strategy given by God for breaking the back of demonic structures that would keep whole ethnic groups in bondage and blinded to the gospel.

5. Sexual Perversion

Sexual perversion is another key weapon used by the antichrist system to keep people blinded to the gospel. Perversion is, by definition, willful rebellion, wickedness and corruption.

A society that allows sexual perversion to run rampant opens itself to an antichrist system of thinking—as rebellion, wickedness and the corruption of God's truth become a tolerated norm. In fact, those who hold to God's truth may be viewed as lacking tolerance and, therefore, become targeted enemies in the minds of those ensnared in a system of sexuality without boundaries. Perversion soon becomes the standard of what is right—an obvious trend in today's American society.

When we study Baal worship and the Ashtoreths in the Bible, we find that idolatry was often linked with sexual perversion. Male and female prostitutes were part of these religious systems. When people stray and embrace their own devices, they end up perverting, or twisting, God's purposes for their lives.

Homosexual behavior is among the most perverse means of sexual entanglement the enemy uses to ensnare men and women, causing apathy toward the gospel in those who turn a blind eye toward God's ways and call theirs simply an alternative lifestyle. But there are other forms of sexual perversion the enemy uses to permeate both individual and societal attitudes, including incest, fornication, adultery and prostitution. God's hatred for these things is made very clear throughout the Bible. In fact, Israel's great recurring sin was called spiritual harlotry, and this sin caused generations to live apart from God's grace and His intended destiny for them.

We must understand that sexual perversion is more than just someone's private problem. It is a demonic structure that has been set up to invade society at every level to keep God's will from being done on Earth as it is in heaven.

Wake Up or You'll Die!

During the time that my coauthor, Rebecca Sytsema, and I have been writing, we have both encountered vicious attacks meant to kill one or all of our family members. The most dramatic of these attacks occurred in the Sytsemas' home, which they share with her parents, Peter and Doris Wagner.

Rebecca and her husband, Jack, were fast asleep one cold autumn night. At 2:30 that morning their 15-month-old son, Nicholas, woke up screaming—an unusual occurrence. As Rebecca was getting up to see what was wrong, she immediately developed a splitting headache and decided to take some aspirin before tending to her son. As she reached the bathroom, she realized that something was very wrong. She felt weak and faint. She called out for Jack.

Jack got out of bed and ran to the hallway just in time to see Rebecca pass out cold. It was then Jack noticed that Nicholas had stopped crying. Thinking quickly, Jack surmised that there must be some kind of gas leak in the house. He ran into Nicholas's room and grabbed the limp child from his crib. He ran out to the garage, opened the garage door for fresh air and deposited his son in a stroller. Jack then ran back into the house and dragged an unconscious Rebecca out to the garage.

Despite feeling weak himself, he knew the job was not done. Running back into the house, Jack called 911 and frantically explained the situation to the emergency operator. He then realized that Doris was sleeping upstairs and that he needed to get her to safety. (Peter was traveling in Korea at the time.) Jack remembers falling at least once, knocking over several dining room chairs, but he got back up. As he climbed the stairs, the lethal fumes overtook him, causing him to black out and tumble to the bottom.

Jack lay at the bottom of the stairs, thinking, *Oh, this is so nice just lying here. I'll just take a quick nap and then get Mom.* But then reality set in. *Wake up or you'll die!* he told himself. He chose to fight. *God*, he prayed, *if You don't get me up and give me strength, we are all dead!* He then mustered every ounce of physical energy he had left to save Doris. Not realizing that the fall had broken his leg, Jack managed to crawl to the top of the stairs and get to Doris's room. He fell through her bedroom door and, with what little energy he had left, cried, "Get out! There's a gas leak!"

Doris immediately arose and opened her bedroom door to the deck, where she and Jack escaped to safety. Jack and Rebecca later learned that they and Nicholas had all ingested what was considered to be a lethal dose of carbon monoxide (Doris was fine because she had been sleeping with her windows open until a few minutes before Jack came through the door). The doctor commented several times that he was amazed they were alive. They later discovered that the furnace had been leaking enough carbon monoxide to kill a healthy adult in 30 to 45 minutes.

Later that same month, several newly acquired carbon monoxide detectors sounded early one morning and, realizing they had another leak, the family got out quickly. This time a completely separate boiler was the trouble, and it was putting out more than four times the amount of carbon monoxide that the first leak had emitted. Had the Sytsemas not known what to do right away, this leak would have quickly killed them all in a very short time!

The Prophetic Picture

What does this story have to do with the future war of the Church? As I prayed, thanking God for sparing the lives of the Sytsema family, God began to show me how Jack represented the Church in this hour. Once Jack recognized the danger, he leaped into action to fight the enemy. But there came a point when the battle began to overtake him.

Jack had a definite choice: He could lie there feeling groggy and do what felt most comfortable to him—take a quick nap. As he describes it, when he was being overtaken by the carbon monoxide, his thinking was anything but clear. It actually seemed reasonable to him to lie there and gain some strength so that he could continue to fight. But had he chosen to do that, he would surely have died where he slept. Instead, he chose to cry out to God and to fight his invisible enemy, though he was weak and wounded. As a result, he gained a great victory.

We, as the Church, need to realize that although our enemy is invisible, the threat is very real and quite deadly. We can make the choice to ignore the threat and fall asleep. We may feel so overcome by the battle itself that we stop fighting at a crucial juncture. But if we do, we, like Jack, could be killed where we lie. But if we decide to see the enemy for who he is and understand how he can overtake us, if we choose to continue the fight though we grow weary and suffer wounds, we will win a great victory in the future war of the Church.

Furthermore, we need to learn from battles we have fought in the past. The second carbon-monoxide leak in the Sytsema home proved to have a much greater potential for sudden death than the first. But because they had already fought that battle once, they knew exactly what to do when the alarm sounded. They acted quickly and, for the second time in 16 days, saved their lives. We need to keep a constant guard against quick, vicious attacks and listen for the alarms God is sounding. If we allow the Lord to train us for war, we will be prepared and victorious when the attacks come!

Who Is the Church?

As important as it is to know our enemy, it is just as important to know ourselves. So who are we? What *is* the Church? Many people often confuse the Church with the kingdom of God, but they are not the same. The Church exists to see the Kingdom established and operating on Earth. The Church facilitates the Kingdom. The kingdom of God is at war with the kingdom of Satan, and the Church operates as the armed forces of God in that war.

The Greek word *ekklesia* ("church") means those gathered to accomplish something or a group of people who are called out for a purpose. The first time this notion of a people called out appears in the Bible is when the children of Israel come out of Egypt. They were called out in order to move into God's inheritance that He had promised their forefather Abraham. This promise had been passed down to Isaac and then to Jacob. The promise then moved with the sons of Jacob/Israel from the place of fulfillment into a foreign land, the land of Egypt, as had been prophesied in Genesis 15. To bring complete fulfillment of God's purpose, you must be at the right place at the right time. So even though the people of promise had remained in Egypt for 400 years, they had to be called out in God's perfect time so that they could journey to the place of the promise's fulfillment.

What did God do to call out His promise from one place and send it to its place of fulfillment? First of all, we see that He changed governments over the people:

> Now it happened in the process of time that the king of Egypt died. Then the children of Israel groaned because of the bondage, and they cried out; and their cry came up to God because of the bondage. So God heard their groaning, and God remembered His covenant with Abraham, with Isaac, and with Jacob. And God looked upon the children of Israel, and God acknowledged them (Exod. 2:23-25).

Notice the travail that was produced in the hearts of God's children of promise. And as they travailed, He remembered His covenant blessing and promise that were resting upon them.

This calling-out place is also the first time we see God's heart to order His people for war. He chose Moses and Aaron to be their leaders, "the same Aaron and Moses to whom the LORD said, 'Bring out the children of Israel from the land of Egypt according to their armies'" (Exod. 6:26). In other words, the order of the family clans was important for the future of their victories according to the promises He had ordained for them.

God called the children of Israel out of Egypt because He had planned to govern them Himself. He had ways to govern them, and He raised up the order and method of government for His people so that they could accomplish His purposes. In Exodus 18, the Lord spoke to Moses through his father-in-law, Jethro, and gave him the strategy of governing the people through a network of judges and rulers who were responsible for a manageable number of people and who were ultimately answerable to God. Moses set up this God-given system of government that worked well for generations.

But then there came a time when the people wanted to be ruled by a king, and they began to drift from God's pattern of government. Despite warnings from Samuel, they insisted and the Lord gave them a king (see 1 Sam. 8:4-22). Right off the bat Israel got in real trouble with Saul. And then because Saul didn't have the heart to obey God in all his ways, their problems grew worse. Israel would have been better off following God's governmental plan for them.

A New Authority

What can today's Church learn from Israel? God's way has always been the best way to go. He has a way to govern, a sovereign plan that He has clearly spelled out for us.

The first time the word "church" (*ekklesia*) appears in the Word is when Jesus says:

> And I also say to you that you are Peter, and on this rock I will build My church, and the gates of Hades shall not prevail against it. And I will give you the keys of the kingdom of heaven, and whatever you bind on earth will be bound in heaven, and whatever you loose on earth will be loosed in heaven (Matt. 16:18-19).

The context of these verses is a warning to the disciples to beware of the Sadducees and Pharisees.

In those days, the Sadducees and Pharisees held the keys of knowledge of the Scriptures and, therefore, had the authority to teach and discipline the people through their understanding. But they had become corrupt and had lost the ability to gain God's revelation through the Scriptures they knew so well. As a result, they became legalistic and harsh and began to hinder God's work rather than reflecting God to His people. We see Jesus' frustration with them in Luke 11:52 when He says, "Woe to you lawyers! For you have taken away the key of knowledge. You did not enter in yourselves, and those who were entering in you hindered."

When Peter confessed that Jesus was the Christ, the Lord transferred the keys of knowledge and Kingdom authority from those who had them (the Sadducees and Pharisees) to His disciples, and He breathed on them and said, "Now take this all over the earth." That same authority has been delegated to today's Church. *We* are now responsible to draw people into the Kingdom. We have the keys, whether or not we ever use them.

A New Government

As the fledgling Church struggled to gain its footing, God used the apostle Paul to bring order and governmental understanding to His people. God was once again giving a pattern of government by which He would delegate His authority to certain individuals, much as He did with the judges and rulers of the Old Testament.

The pattern for this government is found in Ephesians 4:11-13:

> And He Himself gave some to be apostles, some prophets, some evangelists, and some pastors and teachers, for the equipping of the saints for the work of ministry, for the edifying of the body of Christ, till we all come to the unity of the faith and of the knowledge of the Son of God, to a perfect man, to the measure of the stature of the fullness of Christ.

This pattern is again echoed in 1 Corinthians 12:28: "And God has appointed these in the church: first apostles, second prophets, third teachers."

According to these passages, this pattern was meant to extend beyond the first century, "till we all come to the unity of the faith and of the knowledge of the Son of God, to a perfect man, to the measure of the stature of the fullness of Christ." In the two millennia that have passed since these words were written, the Church has not yet reached these goals. We still need to equip the saints for the work of ministry and to edify the Body—which means we still need apostles and prophets!

God's pattern for government in the Body of Christ is clear: first apostles, second prophets, then teachers, pastors and evangelists. These are what I call the ascension gifts (which will be explained further in the next chapter). Where the biblical order of the ascension gifts is not being established under God's headship, the mind of Christ operating through the Church is hindered.

The Church in Transition

Through the centuries, the Church drifted from this godly pattern of government. Like the Israelites of old, we have often asked for a "king" to lead us, rather than relying on God's first and best for us. But in recent years we have seen God restoring and raising up a godly government within the Church with apostles at the head. God is helping His people to accomplish their purpose by imparting His gracious gifts through the Holy Spirit.

In this world of rapid changes, the Church must also make changes. These transitions need not keep up with the pace of the world but, rather, with the pace God is setting. He is on the move, and the Church must learn to move with Him. He is calling His Church to arise and shine, for her light has come!

In 1 Chronicles 12:32, we see that the children of Issachar had an understanding of the times, so they knew what Israel should do. This was a time of transition from the house of King Saul to the house of King David. The children of Issachar had to understand the times so that Israel could make the transition correctly in order to bring forth God's purposes for that hour.

The Church as a whole is undergoing a major transition in our day. Like the children of Issachar, we must understand the times in which we live so that we transition correctly. Scholars and watchers of church trends agree that God is fashioning a new wineskin for His Church that will cause us to arise and take a stand against the kingdom of darkness.

Graham Cooke writes:

There is a new prototype of church emerging that will clash with the world and institutional Christianity. A prototype is the first in a series. The Church will rediscover her radical edge, but not by playing with the world's toys and using them differently. Real radical behavior in church is grounded in the supernatural. It proceeds from the mouth of God; it emanates from simple obedience to His ways; it emerges out of Holy Spirit boldness to follow the plans of God with fervent faith. It is to be willing to look foolish in order to confound the world.

We all will be pioneers in this next move of God. His plans for our churches will mean profound changes to the structure, vision, personality and effectiveness of our meetings, missions, training and discipleship forums. We will see a radical change in leadership style and methodology.

When building a prototype church, all our mistakes are public. One thing we should note here: Real pioneers do not criticize other pioneers because they know how hard it can be to build something new. Settlers usually make the most vicious of critics. They haven't done it themselves and have no intention of taking what they perceive to be insane risks. Their credo is that it is better to snipe from the sidelines and then borrow the new thing once it has been proved out. Some even argue that it is their "refining" comments that have played a valuable part in maturing the original concept.[10]

New Wine

The transition taking place in the Body of Christ is really a changing of wineskins (see Mark 2:22). The new wine God is longing to pour into His Body is the power, understanding and wisdom we will need to face the future war of the Church. Changing the wineskin—in this case a changing of government in the Body—is a crucial part of our preparation for the war.

In his book *The Complete Wineskin*, Harold R. Eberly writes:

Whenever the Holy Spirit fills people with "new wine," the structure or organization in which they function must change. Old wineskins rip. New wineskins must be used to hold the additional life and power of God. . . . The time for God to move is at hand. Therefore, we should expect our present wineskins to rip.

There can be no mighty spiritual awakening in our day without a great shaking of our Church organizations, leaders and structures. If you are looking for the Second Coming of Jesus, or if you are praying to God to move upon your church, your city, your local schools, your family or your own heart, then the first thing you must look for is a new wineskin.[11]

The new wine only comes when it's time for God to give the Church revelation for how to be victorious in the next season. To do that God has to restructure our wineskin in order to lay the foundations we need for future victory. Let's take a look now at what this new wineskin will look like in the days ahead.

God's Unfolding Revelation: Aligning with God's Heavenly Government

By being properly aligned in God's plan of order, we establish ourselves on the Rock, but we also become a stumbling rock of offense to the world. Governments are clashing around the world—our foundation must be firm. Proper alignment with God's heavenly government causes us to become steadfast and sure in our lives. Here are several important things I hear the Spirit of God saying that will help us to pray effectively.

We are entering into a transition of power. This is a day when the apostolic-prophetic mantle of the Church is being fully restored for the next season of demonstration of power throughout the world. We are about to see a new wave of the baptism or release of the Holy Spirit in the Church. In the past 10 years, we have tried to become "normal and acceptable." In doing so, we have lost a measure of power. We cannot see transformation in our cities without a sweeping move of the Spirit of God.

I believe Joshua 5 is a key biblical pattern for us. After 40 years of waiting, God had a group of leaders with a desire in their hearts to enter into their ultimate promised inheritance. When the priests' feet stepped into the Jordan River with the Ark of the Covenant, a supernatural miracle occurred—the same miracle that God had worked 40 years before at the Red Sea. This miracle shook up the enemies holding the promised inheritance captive. We read in Joshua 5:1 that their hearts melted and "there was no spirit in them any longer."

After crossing the Jordan on dry land, the children of Israel didn't immediately sweep across the land and overcome their enemies. Instead, the Lord asked them to do an unusual thing: He commanded them to sharpen flint knives for circumcision (see Josh. 5:2). Before the children of Israel claimed their inheritance, they submitted themselves to bear the sign of the covenant. In a similar way, I see us becoming very vulnerable, submissive and humble. As our hearts are circumcised, God's promised power will arise within us.

We will see a restoration of the war mantle of the Body of Christ as the apostolic-prophetic mantle of the Church is being restored. Why did the Lord command circumcision for the children of Israel? He commanded circumcision to restore covenant with the children of Israel and to restore the faith of the warriors. The warriors of the past season had fallen into unbelief and had passed their faithlessness on to the next generation. The Lord not only wanted to demonstrate His power but also wanted to cut away the unbelief the people had carried with them out of Egypt.

I see a shaking of systems. Watch for conflict to begin in the political, economic and religious structures. God will prepare us for this warfare by restoring our war mantle. He will call us to fast individually, corporately and territorially. These will be supernatural fasts, as in the biblical pattern we find in Daniel 10. After fasting for 21 days, Daniel found out that his prayers enabled God's messenger to overthrow a principality that was holding back revelation for the future. As you fast, expect God to show you how to establish yourself in the new arising around you. Know that Jezebel, a controlling system, will be plotting to prevent the restoration of God's purposes in the earth. This spirit will try to hold old laws and legalism in place and redirect God's supply for His kingdom purposes.

We must understand Amos 9, which is key to our future. We are seeing a great move of God to restore the Tabernacle of David in the
earth (see Amos 9:11). We find this occurring in each historical season. It was prophesied by Amos. It happened in the earliest days of
the Church (recorded in Acts). Now, we will see it happen again
during this new millennium.

The Tabernacle of David represents fervent prayer and praise as
it was practiced under David's oversight (see 1 Chron. 16:1,4).
Prayer and praise in every region is key in the Church's future, but
the verse in Amos 9 that speaks to me most this year is verse 13:
"The plowman shall overtake the reaper." This means that great
blessings are coming quickly. The more we allow God to build His
plan on the earth, the greater the cycle of blessings that will begin
in our homes, churches and regions. Prophetic seeds that have been
sown and declared in your region should be plowed up this year.
They should be declared and planted again. I see teams of plowmen
being connected together. Many of us have received revelation but
tried to plow alone. However, if we connect and plow together, the
harvest of God in a region will be gathered.

We must beware ungodly handshakes occurring in the earth. In days
ahead, political and religious spirits will align just as they did in
Jesus' day. The goal of these structures will be to persecute the
Church and wear us down so that we do not operate in God's authority or demonstrate His power. However, the Lord will have a strong
people who do exploits. His rule will be the overcoming government
in the earth realm.

The Church Will Increase in Mercy to the Jews

Civil governments will be judged based on how we stay aligned with
God's covenant land of Israel. God's mercy has been evident in his
dealing with the Gentiles, but we are approaching a time in which
God is attempting to restore His covenant plan into Israel. It is
time for the spirit of stupor that we find in Romans 11 to be broken from the Jews' eyes and for them to be provoked to jealousy by
the power of salvation that is displayed by the Church. There are
great doors of opportunity in key Jewish areas that are going to

open to the Church. Watch for this to occur in places such as New York City, Miami, West Palm Beach, Los Angeles, Detroit, Houston, Baltimore and Philadelphia. The world will rise up and begin to persecute the Church as it begins to display mercy to the Jews in a region. This persecution is an indicator that walls of ethnicity are being broken down. All ethnic groups in regions where the Church shows mercy to Jews will have unprecedented opportunities for grace.

Ron Cantor, a member of Tikkun International, Inc., recently wrote an article titled "The Most Hated People on Earth" in which he states:

Who are the most hated people on earth? The Christians? The Jews? White Anglo-Saxon men? The truth is that the most hated people on the face of the earth are *the Messianic Jews*. We are hated by just about every group out there, from the [Klu Klux] Klan to Iran. Why? Just think about it:

- We are Jews, the most hated group in history.
- We are Believers in Yeshua, and who isn't against true Bible believers?
- The non-Messianic Jewish Community is poisoned against us.
- Much of the Christian Community sees us as Judaizers (Gal. 3), trying to bring believers under the Law (which we aren't).

So one can imagine why a Messianic Jew might be happier blending into the larger Christian world than boldly identifying himself as a Jewish believer. Some Messianics go the other way, distancing themselves from the Church world—sometimes even denying Yeshua in the end—because of pressures from both Jewish and Christian communities.[12]

Antichrist and anti-Semitism hold hands to work against God's covenant plan and people. Almost daily in the news we hear threats and hatred for God's covenant land of Israel and those connected or grafted onto the root. There is a growing threat that says, "We must do away with all the Jews and the infidel Christians." This is used as a curse to attempt to defeat God's plan to redeem mankind by sending our Messiah, the Lord Jesus Christ. Militant Islam can be justified only if Israel is fully destroyed. The Antichrist can only reign if God's covenant root does not remain.

In an article titled "Anti-Semitic Acts Across Europe Rose Significantly in 2006," *Haaretz* correspondent Amiram Barkat reports the following:

> The number of anti-Semitic incidents rose significantly in Europe last year, according to a joint study released Sunday by the Jewish Agency's Forum for the Coordination of the Struggle Against Anti-Semitism, the Foreign Ministry and the Prime Minister's Office. Figures for anti-Semitic acts in Germany, Austria and the Scandinavian countries increased dramatically in 2006, the study said.
>
> The study indicated that 360 incidents were registered in France in 2006 (compared to 300 in 2005), 312 in Britain (compared to 321), some 300 in Russia (250), 83 in Austria (50) and 53 in Scandinavia (35). The study shows an increase of 60 percent in anti-Semitic incidents in the Berlin area, though figures were not provided for Germany as a whole.
>
> The Lebanon war produced a wave of criticism against Israel, it said, and comparisons of its actions to those of Nazi Germany. Venezuelan President Hugo Chavez said in August that the Israeli offensive in Lebanon "is reminiscent of the Fascist nature of Hitler."
>
> Likewise, a caricature in a Norwegian newspaper showed Prime Minister Ehud Olmert as the sadistic SS officer portrayed in the film *Schindler's List*. Studies were released in various European Union countries throughout the year testifying to the breadth and severity of the phenomenon.

A report released by the British parliament indicated that Islamist and radical leftist sources were responsible for the heightened anti-Semitism in the United Kingdom. A German study pointed to the widespread use of anti-Semitic slurs in schools, particularly by Muslim students. A study conducted in Ukraine revealed that a third of the country's residents had negative opinions of Jews. The authors of the document stressed the difficulties in determining whether an incident can indeed be defined as anti-Semitic, but said the paper reflects a broad trend of growing anti-Semitism in the countries polled.[13]

Recently, noted film star and director Mel Gibson had a drunken encounter with legal authorities. When the police arrested him, he cursed Jews and declared that they were "responsible for all the wars of the world." This anti-Semitic outburst was peculiar, because Gibson directed *The Passion of the Christ*, the highest-grossing film in history. This movie touched many and was perhaps the most accurate depiction shown on screen of Jesus Christ's crucifixion. Gibson later said, "I did have a chip on my shoulder about a lot of things that happened [in filming and releasing the movie] that I felt were unjust. Stuff comes out in a distorted manner when you're drunk. Those were the ravings of an inebriated, angry person." When he realized what an impact his tirade had made, he said, "My God, I don't want to be that monster." He has since apologized and pleaded forgiveness for the incident.[14]

Iranian president Mahmoud Ahmadinejad has even said in a statement that he does not believe the Nazi Holocaust actually took place. He seems to want to "discredit the historical event that laid the groundwork for the creation of (the present day nation of) Israel. Then his dream of destroying the Jewish state seems like a perfectly reasonable correction of a previous mistake."[15] What statements like this do is activate extremist thinking around the world.

There is a deep root planted in people throughout the world that is anti-God and anti-His people. We must ask God to deliver us of hidden hatred toward and misunderstanding about His covenant land and plan.

CHAPTER THREE

The Third Day Church Arising

Arise, shine; for your light has come!
And the glory of the LORD is risen upon you.
ISAIAH 60:1

He will win whose army is animated by the same spirit throughout all its ranks.
SUN TZU, *THE ART OF WAR*

During the past few years, the Church has celebrated the two-thousandth anniversary of Jesus coming to Earth to redeem us. If a thousand years is as a day to the Lord (see Ps. 90:4; 2 Pet. 3:8), then we might say that we have just completed a "two-day" period in history. We have now entered into the third day.

The third day has great meaning throughout Scripture.

After three days of preparation for His people, the Lord appeared in thunder and glory at Mount Sinai (see Exod. 19:16-17).

On the third day, God made the shadow go backward for Hezekiah (see 2 Kings 20:5-11).

In the eighth century, the prophet Hosea wrote:

Come, and let us return to the LORD; for He has torn, but He will heal us; He has stricken, but He will bind us up. After two days He will revive us; on the third day He will raise us up, that we may live in His sight (Hos. 6:1-2).

Here God was promising through His prophet that He would never abandon His people but instead raise them up once again after their "death" at the hands of Assyria and Babylon.

Of course, the New Testament tells of an even greater third day when Jesus Christ rose from the dead.

The third day is a day of Resurrection power! As the Church transitions from the "second day" to the "third day," we can expect to see not only revival but also Resurrection power that will overthrow the demonic forces that have kept us from seeing God's will done on Earth. The new wineskin to receive this power is now being formed by the Holy Spirit, even as He is preparing the wine to be poured in. God is transforming the Church, preparing us to receive revelation for future victory. The Church is arising and the Kingdom is coming.

To arise means to get up from a prostrate position, come up out of oppression, to awaken or ascend. The Church is arising with favor and strength for a latter-day advancement against the wicked forces that are holding the harvest captive. We must begin to see ourselves as the Third Day Church, emerging with the power to fulfill the mandate of the Great Commission. What can we expect to see as the Third Day Church arises?

This will be a season when we will awaken to our latter-day blessings (see Hos. 6:1-3). The Lord will break discouragement, disillusionment and disinterest from our ranks. He will give us new strength to labor in our cities with a victorious mindset, and we will see His glory come. We are entering into a building phase like we have never experienced in the Kingdom. Pray and watch the church of your area change.

The people of God will arise with new, refreshed and obedient hearts. "On the *third day* there was a wedding in Cana" (John 2:1, emphasis added). So begins the story of Jesus turning water into wine—the first miracle He performed. This was the beginning of a new day in the life of the world, the beginning of His glory being manifested on the earth.

The old wine of one season is now coming to an end, and a new level of obedience is arising in the people of God. The Lord is going to speak unexpected things to each of us. Don't be so rigid in your hearing that the Lord can't reveal the new to you. Whatever He tells you to do in this season, do it (see John 2:5)! You will then see a manifestation of His glory in your life and in the Church.

We will bring forth seed after our own kind (see Gen. 1:12). This is a season when our fruit will be seen. We must be purified, because what we sow we will reap. We must ask the Lord to draw His best from us. The enemy is going to resist, attempting to keep our gifts from coming forth. Yet now is the time for us to be released into a new anointing. Resist the enemy and he will flee (see Jas. 4:7).

Our testings will produce a release of vision and provision. If we are willing to lay the vision the Lord has given us on His altar and receive His purifying fire, new provision will arise in the days ahead, just as God provided the ram for Abraham's sacrifice.

God tested Abraham, telling him, "Take now your only son Isaac, whom you love, and offer him as a sacrifice" (see Gen. 22:2). So Abraham took his son and set out for the place God had indicated. "Then on the *third day* Abraham lifted his eyes and saw the place afar off" (Gen. 22:4, emphasis added). Abraham took his son and laid him on the altar; but the Angel of the Lord stayed his hand, and God provided a ram to be sacrificed in his stead. Then Abraham called the place "The-LORD-Will-Provide" (Gen. 22:14).

We will change our garments, receive new boldness and come before our King with requests of deliverance. "Now it happened on the *third day* that Esther put on her royal robes and stood in the inner court of the king's palace" (Esther 5:1, emphasis added). Be willing to intercede for the deliverance of those around you. Be willing to overturn the decrees that the enemy has set against God's people in your area, just as Esther did. Receive a new favor and confidence.

I have the following prayer for you:

> *May the Lord bring a new release and liberty to your life. May*
> *new favor rest upon you. May the oppressions of your past*
> *season break. May the breaches from broken relationships be*
> *mended. May the losses of the past season be returned to you in*
> *this season. Proclaim and declare restoration over your life,*
> *your church and your area. See the promises that lie ahead*
> *of you. May your latter be greater than your former.*
> *Arise and enter into your Third Day. Amen.*

On Earth as It Is in Heaven

> And war broke out in heaven: Michael and his angels fought
> with the dragon; and the dragon and his angels fought,
> but they did not prevail (Rev. 12:7-8).

The power of the Third Day Church will be like nothing we have
known before. As we pray the Lord's Prayer, we ask that God's will
be done on Earth as it is in heaven. God is giving the Third Day
Church an understanding of the warfare it takes to see His will
accomplished here on Earth.

Let's take a look at heaven and Earth and how God is bridging
the gap between the two.

The Third Heaven

As we think about heaven, we are most likely pondering the "third
heaven" (2 Cor. 12:2). This is the place where God the Father is seated on His throne and Jesus is seated next to Him. Jesus intimately
knows what is on the Father's heart, and we know that from this
place at the right hand of God Jesus makes intercession for us
(see Rom. 8:34).

Ephesians 1 and 2 are beautiful passages on our inheritance
in the Lord and how we are positioned to sit together in heavenly
places with Jesus (see Eph. 2:6). This is the place where there is no
obstruction to God's will being fully carried out. This is the place
where we receive our marching orders.

When Jesus ascended to this place, He gave gifts to the human
race. We find these gifts listed in Ephesians 4:11 with "some to be
apostles, some prophets, some evangelists, and some pastors and
teachers." He gave these gifts to equip the saints for the work of the
ministry and for the building up of the Body of Christ. He gave these
gifts to produce unity of faith in the knowledge of Himself, and He
continues to release revelation so that we will not be tossed to and fro
by the craftiness and trickery of the enemy. He is also releasing revelation that will cause us to "grow up" into His headship. All of this is
occurring from Jesus' place in the Throne Room in the third heaven.

The First Heaven

We live in our physical bodies here in the earthly realm—a place that we can see, touch and feel. This universe in which we live, which includes the sun, the moon and the galaxies of stars and planets, may be called the first heaven. Through Christ's death and resurrection, we here on Earth have access to communicate beyond this universe and into the realm of the third heaven where God is seated. That is what we call prayer.

Psalm 24 says, "The earth is the Lord's and the fullness thereof." So He also rules the earthly realm. When Jesus went to the cross and then overcame the grave, He broke the headship of Satan in this realm. He then set a structure in place on Earth with a gifted government and army (the Church) to enforce His headship.

The Second Heaven

So if we live on Earth but have access to heavenly places through prayer, why is God's will not always done on Earth as it is in heaven? The answer lies in the second heaven where Satan, the "prince of the power of the air" (Eph. 2:2), and his demons contest God's reign and His angels. Satan is the prince of this world (see John 12:31; 14:30; 16:11).

The word "world" is *cosmos* in the Greek. In Matthew 4:8 we find, "The devil took Him up on an exceedingly high mountain, and showed Him all the kingdoms of the world and their glory." The kingdoms of this world have been arranged in such a way that they have an enticing glory about them; this cosmos region has the ability to entrap. The prince of this world is also known as the god of this age:

> The god of this age has blinded the minds of unbelievers, so that they cannot see the light of the gospel of the glory of Christ, who is the image of God (2 Cor. 4:4).

The enemy attempts to block heaven's will from being done on Earth through a demonic hierarchy that is positioned between us and the third heaven (see Eph. 2:2). This hierarchy establishes a ruler as the strongman. The strongman rules and reigns over a kingdom of dark spirits. We find a listing of this hierarchy—principalities, powers, rulers of darkness of this age and spiritual hosts of wickedness in the heavenly places—in Ephesians 6:12.

This hierarchy gains legal right to block heaven's will on Earth through our own rebellion against God and our complicity with the devil's agenda. Satan gains access to us and to entire territories through individual and corporate sin. In such an individualistic society, it may be difficult for us to grasp that we, as a society, are held responsible in the eyes of God for corporate sin. Just as in our own lives and in the generations of our family, sin can also be an opening for Satan to establish strongholds that directly oppose God's plan for a territory. The following are a few examples of corporate sin that can give Satan legal right in a region or in our lives.

Idolatry

Idolatry is that place where we have physically or spiritually bowed down and exalted something—whether it be a carved image or the likeness of anything—higher than God (see Exod. 20:3-4). Many places in the world today are being held captive by the enemy because of idolatry. As a result, Satan has the legal right to blind the eyes of unbelievers from the glorious gospel of Jesus Christ.

Bloodshed

The first recorded murder was that of Cain's killing his brother, Abel. God said to Cain, "What have you done? The voice of your brother's blood cries out to Me from the ground" (Gen. 4:10). From this we see that bloodshed affects the very land on which the violence occurred. As the blood of violence penetrates the ground, the prince of the power of the air gains rights to the land. Curses on physical land often gain a foothold through violence and bloodshed.

Immorality

The classic biblical example of how immorality can affect entire territories is that of the cities of Sodom and

Gomorrah. Immorality and perversity had so overtaken those cities that God could not find even 10 righteous men within their walls. Any redemptive plan that God had for those cities was wiped out as everyone, including the children, was destroyed. This issue is one that we in America must take seriously. Immorality has become a vague term, even a non-issue for those in power. Many in our society have come to believe that anyone can do whatever is right in his or her own sight (see Judg. 17:6; 21:25). Satan has gained enough strength within our borders that we have entered into a post-Christian era.

Covenant Breaking

During the reign of King David, a great famine came on the land. When David inquired of the Lord concerning this famine, God said to him, "It is because of Saul and his bloodthirsty house, because he killed the Gibeonites" (2 Sam. 21:1). The Gibeonites were a group of people who had entered into covenant with Israel in the days of Joshua. This covenant guaranteed their safety. Yet Saul broke covenant with the Gibeonites by murdering many of them and planning the massacre of the rest.

As a result, famine came on the land as God removed His blessing and Satan was allowed access. The famine did not strike immediately but rather came when a new king had come to power. This should be a wake-up call for the United States where more than 350 treaties with Native Americans have been broken.

In John Dawson's booklet *What Christians Should Know About Reconciliation*, he writes:

> If the people of your nation have broken cov-enants with God and other nations and violated relationships with one another, the path to reconciliation could begin with your act of confession. The greatest wounds in human history, the greatest injustices,

have not happened through the acts of some individual perpetrator. Rather they have happened through the institutions, systems, philosophies, cultures, religions and governments of humankind. Because of this, we are tempted to absolve ourselves of all individual responsibility. However, God looks for individuals to "stand in the gap" just as He spoke through Ezekiel: "And I searched for a man among them who should build up the wall and stand in the gap before Me for the land, that I should not destroy it; but I found no one" (Ezek. 22:30, *NASB*).

Let us take this more personally. How many marriages have been destroyed because there was no one who would stand before the Lord for them? How many race riots have erupted because there was no one to stand in the breach for them? How many churches have perished because no one would identify with the breach so as to stand in it before the Lord for that congregation? We might think, *Well the Lord could do this for Himself*, but it is fundamental to His plan that everything He will do here He will do with us—He is always looking for a man or woman to work through, even in His ministry of intercession.

Unless someone identifies themselves with corporate entities such as the nation of our citizenship or the subculture of our ancestors, the act of honest confession will never take place. This leaves us in a world of injury and offense in which no corporate sin is ever acknowledged, reconciliation never begins, and old hatreds deepen.[1]

Breaking Through the Second Heaven

The only entity on Earth with the power to break strongholds of Satan and break through his domain in the second heaven is the Church. While we have always had the tools, within the past few decades we have come to a greater understanding of the spiritual warfare that is necessary to destroy the strategies and structures the enemy has in place in the second heaven.

God is establishing a new authority in His Church to break through to the third heaven, gain the heart of God and carry that revelation back to Earth where we can accomplish His will. As we do, we will change the very atmosphere around us—God's will being done on Earth as it is in heaven. This is what we pray for every time we pray the Lord's Prayer!

However, many of us try to avoid the second heaven. Revelation 12:7 says, "And war broke out in heaven: Michael and his angels fought with the dragon; and the dragon and his angels fought." Dick Eastman writes about the casting down of Satan that results from the great battle between the hosts of heaven and the hordes of hell, as depicted in this passage:

> In this battle, heaven's warriors force Satan and his demons forever from the heavenly realm. But we must note that victory is not achieved solely by the angels, but also by believers' use of spiritual weapons. The angels fight, but God's saints provide the "firepower." This is clearly shown by v. 11, "They overcame him by the blood of the Lamb and by the word of their testimony." The angels did not overcome the Accuser alone; the saints were in partnership through prayer-warfare; the angels were God's means for administering the victory, which prayer enforced. Notice the mention of Michael, the archangel (v. 7, one of four places where he is mentioned in Scripture). In each mention, spiritual warfare is clearly implied. This is true in Daniel 10 where Michael's involvement in battle to victory is the direct result of Daniel's fasting and prayer.[2]

From the "To" to the "New"

With the dawning of the third day, the Church is moving from the old wineskin to a new wineskin. This "from-to" transition is very important for us to understand. The "from"—the Church government we have known during the past several decades—will not be able to overthrow the antichrist kingdom we have described. Therefore, the government of the Church must now make a transition and increase in authority, strength and wisdom.

The "to" is the transition that we are currently in, but this transition must come to an end. *The Church must now war to come out of the "to" and into the "New"!* The New is not a different message of the gospel of the Lord Jesus Christ but rather a new structure for presenting that gospel to a lost and dying world. We must be transformed into a vibrant, fire-filled army that marches forward.

Even now the Lord is preparing us for advancement. I love the words of Isaiah 41:14-16:

> "Fear not, you worm Jacob, you men of Israel! I will help you," says the LORD and your Redeemer, the Holy One of Israel. "Behold, I will make you into a new threshing sledge with sharp teeth; you shall thresh the mountains and beat them small, and make the hills like chaff. You shall winnow them, the wind shall carry them away, and the whirlwind shall scatter them; you shall rejoice in the LORD, and glory in the Holy One of Israel."

He knows that we must become new instruments in His hand, threshing sledges that can pulverize the mountains of discouragement and resistance set against us as we advance to build His Church.

The Lord is blowing His Spirit on His Church to make it a new, sharp threshing instrument. His purpose is to prepare a structure and a government that can relate to His mind and purposes. He says, "I need a leadership to demonstrate My purposes on Earth anew. I need an army that will come forth to break up the enemy's strategies and display My will on Earth. I need government that takes what has been scattered and gathers it together to advance My kingdom."

Several issues arise with our moving forward into the "New." The word "transition" means we will be going from one place to another, crossing over into a new sphere of authority. In transition you must stay focused on where you are going or what you are birthing. Although you have not yet settled in the new place or received the new thing, there has been a conception of vision in your heart. The new place is where the change will manifest.

Here are three specific areas to keep in mind during transition:

1. *Move from strength to strength.* Psalm 84:5,7 is a great passage for today: "Blessed is the man whose strength is in You, whose heart is set on pilgrimage. They go from strength to strength."

2. *Move from faith to faith.* Paul says he is not ashamed of the gospel, for it is the power of God to those who believe. In it "the righteousness of God is revealed from faith to faith" (Rom. 1:17).

3. *Move from glory to glory.* Paul talks about the veil of the law being lifted and the Spirit of God releasing new liberty. He says we all are being transformed into His image "from glory to glory" (2 Cor. 3:18). The enemy never wants us to complete the "from-to"! He wants to hold us in last season's strength, faith and glory. Satan knows that if he succeeds in doing this, we will never see our Lord's plan for the coming season made manifest. He also knows that he can keep an entire generation from advancing forward into the riches and blessings of a covenant God.

We are on our way to a new day with new methods for victory. So, where is the Church headed in this new third-day season? What is the New into which we are coming?

A New Order

Many in the Body of Christ are referring to the direction the Church is taking as the New Apostolic Reformation, a term coined by

C. Peter Wagner. In his book *Churchquake!*, he has this to say about where the Church is headed in this hour:

> The New Apostolic Reformation is an extraordinary work of God at the close of the twentieth century, which is, to a significant extent, changing the shape of Protestant Christianity around the world. For almost 500 years Christian churches have largely functioned within traditional denominational structures of one kind or another. Particularly in the 1990s, but with roots going back for almost a century, new forms and operational procedures began to emerge in such areas as local church government, interchurch relationships, financing, evangelism, missions, prayer, leadership selection and training, the role of supernatural power, worship, and other important aspects of church life. Some of these changes are being seen within denominations themselves, but for the most part they are taking the form of loosely structured apostolic networks. In virtually every region of the world, these new apostolic churches constitute the fastest growing segment of Christianity.[3]

These churches are bringing with them a whole new order—a new way of doing church. Wagner describes the transition to this new order this way:

> We are seeing a transition from bureaucratic authority to personal authority, from legal structure to relational structure, from control to coordination and from rational leadership to charismatic leadership. This all manifests itself on two levels: the local level and the translocal level.
>
> On the local church level, the new apostolic pastors are the *leaders* of the church. In traditional Christianity, the pastors are regarded as *employees* of the church.
>
> On the translocal level, one of the most surprising developments for those of us who are traditionalists is the

growing affirmation of contemporary apostolic ministries. We are seeing . . . reaffirmation, not only of the New Testament *gift* of apostle, but also of the *office* of apostle.[4]

What this means is that the Church of the future is going to look very different from the way it has in the past.

The shift in governmental order and authority we are seeing today is even greater than the shift that the Church experienced in the days of Martin Luther and John Calvin. Old denominational structures will not be able to contain the new wine God is bringing to the Church.

This does not mean that denominations will die out. But it does mean that if they cannot become flexible enough in their structure to move with the shifts God is bringing, then they will become old wineskins—brittle and stiff—and will eventually become useless and lose the inheritance of God that was imparted to them in the past season.

No matter what our church backgrounds, we must seek God's heart in this hour and allow Him to set the new order that must be in place before the Church can come into her full inheritance.

A New Authority

Once we understand the new order that God is bringing, we will then see a new authority begin to arise in the Church. This authority will enable us to overthrow the enemies that have resisted us in past seasons. God will reveal new strategies of warfare that we have not considered before, and He will give us a new place of authority in the territories where He has positioned us.

Our new authority will be linked with favor—the world will begin to see the Church in a whole new way. One of my favorite Bible passages is Matthew 8:5-13, in which Jesus heals the centurion's servant. A Gentile leader, concerned about his paralyzed servant, presents his case to Jesus as He arrives in Capernaum. Jesus is touched by his devotion and says, "I will come and heal him" (v. 7).

But the centurion tells Jesus it is not necessary for Him to come, because he understands Jesus' authority. He declares that if the Lord will only say the word, his servant will be healed. Jesus marvels and says to those around Him, "Assuredly, I say to you, I have not found such great faith, not even in Israel!" (v. 10).

This is an important passage for us to understand in this time of preparation and war. This kind of faith and understanding of authority is needed not only to enter the Kindgom but also to see the Kingdom advance.

A New Anointing

As the Lord brings His Church into new favor, He will clothe us in a whole new garment—a garment that will carry with it a new anointing for ministry that we have never seen before. Whereas we have been a candle of light to the world, we will now begin to blaze like a forest fire!

The word "anointing" means to smear with oil. It is the same word that is linked with the Messiah, the "anointed one." This is a time of smearing, in which we will receive from the Holy Spirit the anointing that breaks the yoke of the enemy.

A specific anointing we will have is for healing and miracles. The Bible links the apostolic anointing with signs and wonders in several places:

> Then fear came upon every soul, and many wonders and signs were done through the apostles (Acts 2:43).

> And through the hands of the apostles many signs and wonders were done among the people (Acts 5:12).

> Truly the signs of an apostle were accomplished among you with all perseverance, in signs and wonders and mighty deeds (2 Cor. 12:12).

God is going to release an anointing that will flow through the authority structure of the Church. From this authority the anointing will have power to overthrow the dark kingdoms of this Earth that are now holding back the harvest.

As the Third Day Church enters into an apostolic anointing, we are going to see great miracles that will produce evangelism! Although we have seen some signs and wonders recently, God is going to dramatically increase displays of His mighty power so that the world will know He is God!

New Connections

The Third Day Church is not going to comprise a number of denominations operating with complete disregard for (or at least ignorance of) what the rest of the Body of Christ is doing. God is establishing a whole new system of networks that will help bring the Church to a place of unity.

Unity in the Body does not mean coming into agreement with one another about what we are going to believe with regard to secondary issues. We may continue to hold differing beliefs on baptism, Communion, liturgies or philosophies of ministry. There's nothing wrong with that.

The kind of unity we're talking about occurs on three levels.

1. *Common Life*

We are required as believers to have unity of common life. That means that because we are all connected with Christ, we are required to have a common love for each other and be willing to demonstrate that love if required. That love has to permeate sectarian structures, transcend race, overcome prejudices and supercede gender barriers.

2. *Unity of Knowledge*

We must have unity of knowledge, although this is a little more difficult because we do not all come out of the same paradigm structures. The Body of Christ usually does fine cooperating on social projects in the city, because these are built around common life and a love for our society. However, when we try to organize a prayer meeting where we all are praying from different levels of knowledge, we have many more problems. Let us not try to force unity without first praying that the availability be there for a certain call and mission of God.

3. *Unity of Vision*

Vision is linked with revelation. Revelation comes from the throne room. When we gain this revelation, we can unlock the field that the Lord has assigned to us, as well as all of its resources. The enemy hates unity of vision.

The unity we are to come into does not mean that we are all going to become the same "flavor." It does mean, however, that we are going to come into agreement over God's covenant plan for a territory, seeing where each of us fits into that plan.

Bob Beckett, a pastor in Hemet, California, describes how this looks in his community:

> In the past few years the pastors of Hemet have enjoyed unity and mutual support as we have learned to view one another as brothers and sisters rather than competitors. As we have come together, God has shown us an amazing thing: Every church in our community has a unique strength that adds to the richness of the Christian community in Hemet.
>
> God has given us just what we need. Some churches have great expository preaching, while others have exceptional Sunday school programs. Some excel in evangelism, while others focus on social needs. Some minister to the retired community, while others reach gang members. Some feature exciting contemporary worship, while others have beautiful pipe organs and majestic choirs.
>
> Each church has its own strengths and contributes uniquely to the work of God in our valley. Together, we have discovered, we form a beautiful picture of the Bride of Christ in our community.[5]

Third Day Church members will be connected to one another in ways that we would have viewed with suspicion in the past.

When change occurs, relationships are redefined. You find you have new mentors and new peers. Don't be afraid to be connected with the rest of the Body. Independence will not benefit you as we move forward into the Third Day.

The Third Day Church Arising!

The ascension gifts—apostles, prophets, teachers, pastors and evangelists—have been in existence since the foundation of the Church. Whether or not we have recognized it, the apostolic gifting has functioned in some way throughout the centuries. Jesus breathed on His disciples and made them apostles (see John 20:22). He established the apostolic gifting so that His purposes would be maintained on Earth from generation to generation. However, we have not yet seen the apostolic ascension gift come into its fullness.

What does the apostolic gift look like in this new season of the Third Day Church? Here are six key functions of the modern-day apostle.

1. Governing

As we have seen, a new governmental structure is coming into place for the Third Day Church. Rather than the government of the Church relying exclusively on committees and boards, God is now raising up apostles throughout the Earth who will bring order to that government.

As God brings the gift of apostle into proper order, a great governmental revolution will take place in local churches everywhere. We are already beginning to see this happen. For an excellent look at how apostolic forms of government are shaping up throughout the world, I strongly recommend C. Peter Wagner's book *The New Apostolic Churches*, in which he and 18 other recognized apostolic leaders tell how God is now setting new governmental structures in place.

In Dr. Wagner's book *Apostles and Prophets*, he specifically discusses one important aspect of the apostolic role. During the past several years, the Lord has been restoring to His Church the office of the prophet. The prophetic is becoming much more widely accepted as a reality for today, and it is the prophets who have heralded the next move of God in restoring the full government of the Church back to an apostolic structure.

When the offices of apostle and prophet are fully restored, God will then renew the office of evangelist and we will see the greatest harvest ever to come into the Church. Why? Because through the restoration of the Ephesians 4 ascension gifts, the government will be in place that can maintain the awesome harvest that God is bringing into the storehouse!

Wagner writes, "Apostles and prophets can change the world if they are properly hitched together to each other and if they are able to pull together."[6] Wagner uses the analogy of a horse pull at a livestock show. At one competition, he watched the winning team pull 5,000 pounds, while the runner-up pulled 4,000 pounds. But when the two teams were hitched together, they pulled 13,000 pounds!

> What does this say about apostles and prophets? Apostles can do certain good things on their own. Prophets can do certain good things on their own. But hitched together, they can change the world![7]

2. Warring

The Third Day Church is changing what goes on not only within church walls but also outside church walls. Through prayer and spiritual warfare, we have been learning principles for taking whole communities and territories for God. This is part of changing the spiritual atmosphere over our cities and nation.

Through the resurgence of the prophetic and apostolic, we are destroying the demonic structures in the second heaven that have been holding both the Church and the unsaved world captive. God is teaching us methods and strategies that will rip the blinders off the eyes of whole territories of people. This new warring anointing will cause us to reap a great and bountiful harvest of souls!

3. Transgenerational Anointing

The "double portion" anointing is a principle of God meant for succeeding generations; it is part of our inheritance (see 2 Kings 2:9; Isa. 61:7). Proverbs 13:22 says, "A good man leaves an inheritance to his children's children." A godly provision of inheritance is not just physical but also spiritual. Each generation should be partaking of a double portion of what was passed to the generation before. That simply cannot happen without godly parenting.

In the past few years, a tremendous resurgence of awareness of the importance of fatherhood has taken place in the Church and in society. Promise Keepers has been God's chosen instrument of the hour for bringing many men into their proper places as fathers, both natural and spiritual.

Fatherhood is an earmark of the New Apostolic Movement where those in leadership do not see themselves as denominational leaders but rather as fathers of the house. They take the role of spiritual fatherhood seriously, and they are determined to raise up the next generation to accomplish even greater things in the kingdom of God.

Spiritual mothering also plays a key role in imparting godly principles to the next generation. I had a very wise mother and godly grandmother who guided me through many tough situations, even though my father had left the ways of God. Without their influence, I might not have found God's destiny for my life. Today, I have the pleasure of working with Peter and Doris Wagner, whose influence, administration and leadership have caused the Church to advance more in recent decades than we can begin to comprehend. I can think of no better example of apostolic authority than this father and mother of the faith.

In the Third Day Church, God is going to use the fatherhood and motherhood anointings to secure the inheritance for, and impart double-portion anointing to, the next generation. We are going to learn strategies for bringing our prodigals back home, and furthermore, our hearts will be prepared to receive the prodigals back into the Church.

4. Building

The Third Day Church is a building church!

> Now set your heart and your soul to seek the LORD your
> God. Therefore arise and build the sanctuary of the LORD
> God, to bring the ark of the covenant of the LORD and the
> holy articles of God into the house that is to be built for
> the name of the LORD (1 Chron. 22:19).

God is telling us to arise and build that which He has for us in
this hour. It is a season of building both spiritually and physically.
The Church must have a building mindset in order to build new
forms and structures as future storehouses, to expand that which
exists and to rebuild those places that have fallen into desolation.
Those who have apostolic authority are building in this hour.

A major part of the building anointing will go toward church
planting. The Third Day Church is busy planting networks of
churches that will draw in the latter-day harvest. The storehouse is
being prepared!

5. Sending

The Third Day Church is a mission-minded Church with a call
and an anointing to send missionaries throughout the world to
penetrate its dark, unreached places. Missions has not just been
business as usual these past years, but rather it has become a
whole new adventure through prayer and spiritual warfare.

Get ready! There is a call to the Church to go into places
where we have never gone before. We will be given new strategies
to go into inner cities and tear down structures of violence. We
will also have new wisdom to rebuild the family unit that has fall-
en into dysfunction.

There are those who have never considered themselves to be missionaries but who have affected the nations through diligent prayer.
AD2000 and Beyond and other such organizations have taught the
Church about the need for prayer targeting the 10/40 Window, and
we are now just beginning to learn about the 40/70 Window.

And for the first time in history we have been able to quantify the goal of the Great Commission. We know, for example, how many unreached people groups we have left to reach. We have been learning how to send in the spiritual warriors *before* sending in the laborers to gather the harvest that results from our warfare.

6. Finishing

The Third Day Church is a Great Commission Church! I believe the Third Day Church has the physical ability and the spiritual power to see the Great Commission fulfilled. Wagner puts it this way: "We are the first generation since Jesus' death at Calvary that has the measurable potential of fulfilling Jesus' Great Commission. [There is] light at the end of the Great Commission tunnel!"[8]

Here are seven things we need in order to become a finishing Church:

1. A heart for change
2. A new intercessory call
3. A passion for God
4. Zeal for the lost
5. Strength to travail for the harvest
6. A new level of faith that produces miracles
7. A new level of interactive authority

As we move toward finishing the Great Commission, we will not only unlock our own inheritance but also the inheritance of those who have not been reached, which is, after all, the very heart of God!

As the Third Day Church arises, we must have the weapons necessary to defeat our enemy in the future war of the Church!

Transforming Cities

As we begin to understand God's call on the Third Day Church (particularly as it relates to the apostolic structure), it is imperative that we understand that God has given us boundaries within which we are able to operate effectively: "We, however, will not boast beyond measure, but within the limits of the sphere which God appointed us" (2 Cor. 10:13).

When God gives apostolic authority within the Church, He establishes spheres of influence that allow us to see our cities and territories transformed. God is establishing apostles and He is giving them spheres, or covenant boundaries, for which they are responsible. If you want to see your city transformed, the Church in your region must understand God's use of apostles for this purpose:

> If the apostles of the city are not recognized and empowered to lead as God has anointed them to do, the divine government of the city will not be in its proper place. This can retard the transformation process, and it can cause the nagging frustration that has been characteristic of so many of our cities in recent years. Here is a theological thought on what is happening in such a case. God may desire to move in miraculous ways to transform a city, but He may not be willing to release the process until the apostles are in place. Why? Because without the proper foundation, revival can be short lived.[9]

God longs for our cities to be fruitful and to reap a great harvest for His kingdom. In order for that to happen, the proper foundation must be in place. We must recognize the divine government of the city that God is setting in place.

We must also recognize how Satan schemes to keep that government from coming into order. We have seen how corporate sin can give Satan legal access to a territory that God is longing to transform. Let's take a look now at how to dethrone the thrones of iniquity that can keep the Third Day Church from arising in your city.

God's Unfolding Revelation:
Transformation into the "New"

In *Changing Church*, C. Peter Wagner writes, "The most radical characteristic of the New Apostolic Reformation is the widespread
recognition that the office of apostle was not just a phenomenon
of the first couple of centuries of Church history, but that it is also
functioning in the Body of Christ today."[10]

God is better defining spiritual gifts in the Body of Christ. As
"first, apostles" and "second, prophets" align (see 1 Cor. 12:28), the
teaching dimension of the Church will go to a new level. Present
truth for this age will be understood. The pastoral leadership role
will change drastically. Many apostles and prophets who have
been held captive by the title of pastor and who have been expected to accomplish all of the duties associated with that title will
be released.

Wagner uses the terms "New Apostolic Reformation" and
"Second Apostolic Age" to describe this historical season in which
intercessors, prophets and apostles have aligned in an accelerated
manner during the last 10 years. Wagner then goes on to say:

> Even though the New Apostolic Reformation is a relative-
> ly recent development, it is not an insignificant part of
> world Christianity. David B. Barrett, one of the most
> accomplished statisticians of the Christian church, has
> divided world Christianity into six "megablocs." Roman
> Catholics compose the largest megabloc, but of the five
> non-Catholic megablocs, the one embracing the New Apo-
> stolic Reformation (Barrett uses the terms "Independent,"
> "Post-denominational" and "Neo-Apostolic") is the largest.
> It is larger, for example, than Anglicans, Orthodox, Prote-
> stants and Marginals (Mormons, Jehovah's Witnesses and
> so on.)
>
> Not only do the new apostolic churches compose the
> world's largest non-Catholic megabloc, but the number of
> churches also are currently growing much faster than that

of all the other five megablocs combined. In his massive research report *World Christian Trends, AD 30 – AD 2200*, David B. Barrett found that the churches of what I call the Second Apostolic Age have increased in number by 323 percent between 1970 and 2000, compared to a 65-percent increase of all other churches over the same 30 years.[11]

We are living in a season in which new wine is being poured from heaven. God's people are coming into a new understanding and wisdom of how to operate in this age against the demonic forces that attempt to stop the kingdom of God from advancing. "Wine" represents revelation, while "wineskin" is linked with developed structures. The strongest opposition to a new wineskin is usually the most recent old wineskin—that is, the second-newest structure. As Wagner states:

> The most radical change brought about by the new wineskin is this: The amount of spiritual authority delegated by the Holy Spirit to individuals. The two operative words in this statement are "authority" and "individuals." In the old wineskin, authority invariably resided in groups. That is why terms such as "deacon boards," "sessions," "vestries,' "consistories," "congregational meetings," "presbyteries," "synods," "district councils," "general assemblies," "mission boards," "plurality of elders," "cabinets," "study commissions," "general councils," "executive committee" and the like have become common currency among denominational churches. The underlying message is that individuals should not be entrusted with the kind of decision-making that might affect a whole church body.[12]

Bringing Forth New Wine

Over the last 15 years, we have heard the word "transformation" used in relation to changes in the Church and, consequently, to shifts in society. Transformation comes when we think differently. Our minds must be renewed so that we can break out of the present blueprint of societal structure that the enemy is using to limit our sphere and demonstration of authority. We become new when we think differently. We must break old cycles in our thinking processes. This is how repentance works. We change our minds.

We are changing! Leaders continue to transition from denominational structures to the New Apostolic Reformation. The state of our nation is in constant change, and we can also see the God of the Nations restructuring and realigning the nations, forming new power centers worldwide. The greatest desire expressed by the Body of Christ must be for God's new plan and structure in the Church to come forth. The time is *now* to press into the *new*.

The Vine Is Vital

In the New Testament, Jesus often used the vineyard as an analogy for the kingdom of God (see Matt. 20:1-16). Those who hope to enter the Kingdom must be like the son who at first refused to work in his father's vineyard but later repented and went to work (see Matt. 21:28-32).

One of the best descriptions for entering into the *new* of God's kingdom comes from Matthew 9:17: "Nor do they put new wine into old wineskins, or else the wineskins break, the wine is spilled, and the wineskins are ruined. But they put new wine into new wineskins, and both are preserved." In this passage, the Lord was addressing some of John the Baptist's disciples, who were questioning the methods He was using to train up His disciples. Jesus then makes an analogy of putting a patch of new cloth on an old garment or putting new wine into an old wineskin. He was saying to John's disciples, "Don't limit Me to just what John did, but expect Me to move in a new way." Through this analogy, He was revealing His intention to preserve the old wine and wineskins even as He created new wine and wineskins.

Wine is a beverage made primarily from fermented grapes. Grapes grew throughout ancient Palestine. In New Testament times, enough dew fell at night to support thriving vineyards even in areas with limited rainfall. People produced wine by pressing the grapes in large stone vats that had a small drain at one end. The juice was collected in troughs, poured into large jars and allowed to ferment in cool rock cisterns. After fermentation, the wine was kept in skin flasks and often diluted with water. Scripture condemns drunkenness and overindulgence, but wine was a part of the typical ancient meal and was also used as a medicine and disinfectant.

You can't have wine without a vine! Any plant with a flexible stem that creeps along a surface or climbs a natural or artificial support is known as a vine. The word "vine" in the Bible almost always refers to a grapevine or vineyard. Scripture traces the origin of viticulture to the time of Noah (see Gen. 9:20-21). Along with olive and fig trees, the grapevine is used throughout the Old Testament to symbolize the fertility of the land (see Deut. 6:11; Josh. 24:13; 1 Sam. 8:14; 2 Kings 5:26; Jer. 5:17; 40:10; Hos. 2:12). The planting and cultivation of a vineyard required constant and intensive care. The most detailed description of the work involved is found in Isaiah 5:1-6.

In John 15, Jesus said that He is the vine and we are the branches. *He is the source of our life and fruitfulness when we cultivate our relationship with Him.*

Pruning Is an Important Process

To understand the pruning process, we need to understand how vines grow. Vines, for the most part, were allowed to run on the ground, though occasionally they might climb a nearby tree (see Ps. 80:8-10; Ezek. 15:2; 19:11). Perhaps it was this latter occurrence that made it possible for a man to "sit under" his vine (1 Kings 4:25). It was not until the Roman period that artificial trellises were introduced. After the grapes had set on the branches, the vines were pruned (see Lev. 25:4; Isa. 18:5; John 15:1-2). This process produced stronger branches and a greater fruit yield. The pruned branches were useless except to be used as fuel (see Ezek. 15:2-8).

The vine is often used as a symbol for Israel in Scripture. Israel is said to have been brought out of Egypt and planted as a vine on the land but then forsaken (see Ps. 80:8-13; Isa. 5:1-7). Israel was "like grapes in the wilderness" when God found them (Hos. 9:10), and the remnant who survived the exile were compared to a cluster of grapes (see Isa. 65:8). Israel was planted as a "choice vine" but became a "wild vine" (see Jer. 2:21; Hos. 10:1). Just as the dead wood of a vine is good for nothing but fuel, so too the inhabitants of Jerusalem would be consumed (see Ezek. 15:1-8; 19:10-14).

We need to allow God to complete the pruning process so that a greater joy can come forth in our lives. An abundance of the vine symbolizes the glorious age to come, when the Treader of the grapes will overtake the one who sows the seed (see Amos 9:13-15; Gen. 49:10-12). Joy produces strength. Let all the dead wood be cut off of you. Let the sorrow and failures of the past season be removed so that you become a sweet new drink in the hands of the Lord.

What Is New Wine?

Before the invention of refrigeration, it was not possible to keep wine many months past the harvest before fermentation began. Sour wine, perhaps vinegar mixed with oil, was a common drink of day laborers (see Ruth 2:14; Luke 23:36). "New" or "sweet" wine was likely wine from the first drippings of juice before the grapes had been trodden. Some interpreters argue that new wine was unfermented, but some texts in which it is mentioned allude to its intoxicating effects (see Hos. 4:11; Acts 2:13).

I define new wine this way: *New wine is the anointing of God to release the abundance of God's life, joy and blessing in the lives of His people.* A good picture of the new wine anointing is found in Acts 2. When the Spirit of God fell on the apostles, He released the life of God on them. They were so overwhelmed by the overflowing joy of His presence that many observers assumed they were drunk. The crowd thought they were filled with new wine, but in fact they were filled with *new wine*! In the same way, God wants *us* to be filled with new wine—to walk in fullness of joy with a vibrant spirit that is full of life!

The abundance of vines and vineyards were seen as expressions of God's favor. In the Bible, the fullness of God's blessing is described as "grain, new wine and oil" (Jer. 31:12). Psalm 104:15

tells us that *wine* makes the heart glad, *oil* makes our face shine and bread (*grain*) gives us strength. This full blessing is God's desire for each one of us. He wants our hearts to be *gladdened* by overflowing, abundant life here in the earth realm. He wants us to *shine* with His glory and fulfill our destiny in the earth. He wants us to have *strength* to stand against the enemy.

God wants us to have the fullness of His blessing in every season, but there are seasons when He focuses on a particular portion of His blessing. *We are in a season when the Spirit of God wants to release a fresh supply of new wine to His Church.*

The Winepress of the *New*

The first step in winemaking is the stomping. New wine cannot be released until grapes are stomped! The yeast that produces fermentation grows on the outside of the grape skin, while the grape juice is on the inside. If the skin remains unbroken, the process of fermentation cannot begin and the grape will eventually shrivel up and turn into a raisin. When the grapes are stomped, the skin is broken. The yeast mixes with the juice and new wine comes forth.

This is a picture of how God deals with our flesh. When God gives us a vision, our flesh grabs it and tries to make it happen in fleshly energy. But the flesh cannot please God, so He puts our desires and ambitions into the winepress and stomps them until our flesh lets go.

This process is called "death of a vision." It is a process every character in the Bible went through to come into a place of God's blessing. For instance, God promised Abraham a son but then waited 25 years until Abraham recognized his own inability to make it happen. God anointed David to be king but then allowed him to be hunted by Saul until he entrusted his future entirely to God. God raised up Moses to set Israel free but then sent him out to the backside of the desert until he died to his own abilities.

God always works through life, death and resurrection. He will allow your vision to be stomped. He will wait for it to die and then resurrect it in supernatural power. If you are in a season in which it seems that all your hopes and dreams are being stomped to death, I have good news: Resurrection is coming! *God is preparing to release His new wine in you!*

If you are in the winepress, it's important to allow the stomping to have its full effect. If you resist the stomping, the new wine cannot flow. If you refuse to die to your own desires and ambitions, what comes out is not the new wine but the *old whine*! You will see your hopes and ambitions frustrated, and you will start to murmur and complain, "I don't see why this is happening! God, this isn't what You promised!" Old whine is full of frustration, bitterness and anger! It will never bring the results God wants. If God has you in the winepress, He is looking for a *shift*! He wants you to shift from ambition to submission, from trying to trusting, from your old plans and mindsets to a walk of faith, and from "I can make it happen" to "God, You will do it!"

Out of that shifting flows the new wine of the Spirit. If you are in the winepress, it's important that you stop reaching back to the old and familiar. Die to your ability to make it happen. Declare God's word by faith. Trust God completely to do all that He has promised!

Watching Over the Vineyard

Stone walls or hedges were usually built around the vineyard to protect the grapes from animals and thieves (see Song of Sol. 2:15; Jer. 49:9). Watchtowers were also built to provide further protection. The hewing out of a winepress or vat completed the vineyard installation (see Isa. 5:2). During the harvesting season, the owner of the vineyard might live in a booth to stay close to his valuable crop (see Isa. 1:8).

A 21-Day Prayer Focus for the *New*

The following 21-day prayer focus can be used to break old cycles in your life that resist change and to help you develop a new way of thinking.

Day 1: *Read Isaiah 28:23-29 and Isaiah 41.* There is a bruising and a breaking that you must go through. Don't resist the stomping. Unless the skin is broken, you will end up as a raisin. So many in the old wineskin have resisted being broken. Declare that all the seeds within you will awaken and come forth. Enter into your personal harvest. Ask the Lord to make you into a new, sharp threshing instrument.

Day 2: *Read James 4.* Submit your gifts and stand under the authority God is giving you. Bloom where God has planted you. Draw near to God and be faithful!

Day 3: *Read Hebrews 4 and 12.* Don't live in the past; that leads only to regret and bitterness. If you have repented, God's grace will cover past sins and failings. Allow your past to be pruned away. Instead of being a bitter drink offering, you will become a sweet drink offering to the Lord.

Day 4: *Read Jeremiah 29.* Don't live in the future, but know that you have a good future. God has a future for you, but joy and fulfillment are found in Him *now!*

Day 5: *Read John 14, 15 and 16.* Allow the pruning process to bring forth the New in you. Seek your joy in Him now. There is a place of overwhelming life and joy in Him. Press in to Him! Draw closer to Him! As you do, the new wine will begin to flow!

Day 6: *Read Matthew 6.* Be anxious for nothing. List the top five priorities in your life. Seek Him first and His kingdom and His righteousness and everything else will fall in place.

Day 7: *Read Psalm 4.* Allow the Lord to set you apart for the future. Let new joy and gladness arise. Declare that you will sleep in peace and feel safe in the presence of God.

Day 8: *Read Deuteronomy 33:26-29.* New wine brings the fullness of God's security and provision. Pray that you will be open to receive these good gifts.

Day 9: *Read Joel 2 and 3.* New wine is a sign of God's presence dwelling with His people and the land being restored. Declare the restoration of all God has for you and rejoice.

Day 10: *Read Jeremiah 31.* The new is for you. New wine is part of the bounty of the Lord. Make your praises heard and shout for joy!

Day 11: *Read Song of Solomon 2, 3 and 4.* Ask the Lord to reveal to you the little foxes that try to crush the vine that will bring forth the new wine. Get a vision of your future identity. Ask the Lord to send a new wind to blow on your garden.

Day 12: *Read Proverbs 3:1-10.* Ask the Lord how to give the first fruits of your increase so that your vats will run over with new wine. Understand and experience God's blessing.

Day 13: *Read Song of Solomon 8 and Psalm 16.* Ask the Lord to come into your vineyard. Let Him prophetically reveal to you the fruit you will bring forth in the future. Enter into your promised inheritance.

Day 14: *Read Matthew 16.* Ask the Lord for revelation, for the building plan for your future, and for keys. Just as Peter connected with the Father in heaven, connect with the Father in a way that unlocks the kingdom of God within you.

Day 15: *Read Hosea 2:14-23.* Unlock your door of hope. Know that there is hope in your valley of Achor. Ask God for mercy and for that new door of hope to open up.

Renew your covenant with God. New wine occurs when heaven and Earth agree.

Day 16: *Read Revelation 14:14-20.* Declare that the harvest in the nations will come into the winepress.

Day 17: *Read Psalm 119:81-88.* Declare that any premature aging or stiffness will begin to break from you and that you will become a new wineskin.

Day 18: *Read Ezekiel 37.* Declare that all that has been scattered will come back together in a new structure.

Day 19: *Read Ephesians 4.* Pray for the government of God in your region. For new wine to come forth, the government of God must be established in its fullness.

Day 20: *Read John 2.* Let the Lord change your water into new wine. He will replace the pots of religious ritualism with new wine. Ask the Lord to remove the spirit of religion from you. Let His glory begin to shine.

Day 21: *Read Matthew 9 and 14.* Be willing to let go of any old method that is operating in your life, business or church. In this passage, the lady who had an issue of blood for 12 years pressed through and touched Jesus, who was on His way to awaken the 12-year-old daughter of Jairus. Declare that now is the time to press into the New, even in your weakness. Declare that what needs to wake up will wake up now. There is a time when the old season must end. Allow the old to end and the new to begin.

It's time for new wine. It's time for the new wineskin. Both are coming forth. Enter in!

CHAPTER FOUR

Dethroning Thrones of Iniquity

The art of war is simple enough. Find out where your enemy is.
Get at him as soon as you can. Strike at him as hard as you can
and as often as you can, and keep moving on.
ULYSSES S. GRANT (1822-1885)

The Son of God goes forth to war,
A kingly crown to gain;
His blood-red banner streams afar;
Who follows in His train?
REGINALD HEBER (1783-1826)

How can an understanding of our God-ordained territorial boundaries and spheres of authority and influence make a difference in our efforts to transform our cities? Our spiritual authority in the place where we live is inexorably linked with God's covenant purpose for that area. We have much more authority to wage effective spiritual warfare in the place where God has planted us than we do anywhere else.

Our Covenant Place

Did you ever stop to consider that God created your city for a specific purpose meant to advance His kingdom? It's true! God has a destiny for the cities in which we live. Furthermore, God positions us within specific territories for the purpose of seeing that destiny fulfilled. The Bible says that God has set the boundaries of our dwelling (see Acts 17:26). That's why God moves us around sometimes. The strength of His covenant in a territory requires that He send a certain person with a certain spiritual gift to that certain place in order to fulfill His purpose.

Psalm 24:1 reminds us, "The earth is the LORD's, and all its fullness, the world and those who dwell therein." God positions people throughout the earth to bring forth the fullness of His purpose. That purpose is stated in Habakkuk 2:14, which says, "For the earth will be filled with the knowledge of the glory of the LORD, as the waters cover the sea." In order for His glory to cover the earth, we as His people need to be sure that we are living in the place that God has established and ordained for us.

In his excellent book *Commitment to Conquer,* Bob Beckett puts it this way:

> Ask yourself two questions: Who put you where you are, and why are you there? There can only be two answers to these questions: obedience or rebellion. You are in a place either because God put you there or because you put yourself there. . . . If you are where you are out of rebellion, I have a word for you: Move as fast as you can! Find out where God wants you and get there. . . . If you know God has placed you where you are, even if it seems like Babylon, I have a word for you: Stay there as long as God asks.[1]

If you know you are in a place because God put you there, you are positioned where you are because you are part of God's covenant plan—a plan not only for your own life but also for the territory in which you live.

It's not just the preacher on Sunday morning who effects God's covenant plan for your territory. Nor is it just the dedicated intercessor who prays over your region for hours on end. True, through their actions covenant is maintained and the lamp of intercession does not go out. But what God is trying to do is set spiritual fire to your territory, and for that to happen, all His people in the region must understand their covenant place.

Satan's Plan

What does knowing our covenant place have to do with the future war of the Church? Our positioning is important, not only so that we may see God's destiny for our city come to pass but also that we may thwart the plans of the enemy for the place where we live. We must be aware that just as God has a plan for our cities, so too does Satan. In the same way that Satan goes about wreaking destruction and misery in the lives of individuals, he also targets our cities.

Satan's objective is to block the plans of God by gaining legal access to a region and establishing his control over it. As we mentioned in the last chapter, Satan gains access to an area in the same way he gains access to an individual's life or a family line: through sin. He does this by encouraging individual or family sin to escalate into corporate sin. When corporate sin enters into our assigned boundaries, we need to be aware of how that sin can build a throne of iniquity and how we, being positioned in God's army, have the authority to dismantle it.

Iniquity Builds a Throne

Corporate sin—for example, idolatry, bloodshed, immorality and covenant breaking—creates a break in God's purpose, or order, for a region. Once this break begins to occur, Satan will take advantage to gain an upper hand and begin to establish his influence in that area. From that place of influence, Satan can build a throne upon which he is seated in a territory. Revelation 2:13 says, "I know your works, and where you dwell, where Satan's throne is."

Satan's assigned hierarchy rules from a throne built on the corporate iniquity of a region, and his throne is linked with the worship in that area. Remember, Satan wanted to exalt himself to become like God so that he would be worshiped. Satan continues to exalt himself, attempting to draw all people to his counterfeit light. Satan knows that men and women were created as vessels of worship and, whether they realize it or not, they will worship something. The simple fact is that either they are worshiping the true and living God or they are worshiping Satan and his demonic forces, whether overtly or through their sin (whether sins of omission or commission). It is this corporate sin that builds the foundation of the throne on which Satan is seated, and it is from that throne that demonic forces work to perpetuate the sin and establish the throne of iniquity to an even greater extent.

Satan's System of Worship

All iniquity on Earth is actually working from a satanic system of worship meant to usurp God's authority and keep lost souls in darkness to the truth of the gospel. Just as godly worship is made through sacrifice—for example, the sacrifice of Jesus that reconciled our relationship to God and our own sacrifice of praise (see Heb. 13:15)—Satan's system of worship is also based on sacrifice.

A good example of this can be found in 2 Kings 3, in which Moab rises up against Israel in rebellion. Israel attacked the Moabites and was winning the battle, not only driving the Moabites back but also taking Moabite cities along the way. However, the Moabite king, seeing that he was being soundly defeated in battle, took his oldest son, who was to inherit the throne, and killed him, offering him as a burnt sacrifice along the wall (see v. 27). This hideous act of sacrifice caused Israel to retreat.

Sacrifice has great spiritual power. That is why fasting, for example, can be such an effective weapon of warfare. By definition "sacrifice" means "the surrender or destruction of something valued for the sake of something having a higher or more pressing claim."[2] Sin, in our own lives as well as corporately, surrenders the covenant promises of God's blessing for the more pressing claim of whatever the sin promises.

Who ultimately benefits from the sacrifice of sin? Satan and the forces of hell. Just as our sacrificial giving unlocks resources to advance God's covenant plan, sacrifices to Satan release demonic hordes into an area. It is through this sacrifice of sin that Satan sets up a system of worship. In fact, Revelation tells us, there is a synagogue of Satan:

I know your works, tribulation, and poverty (but you are rich); and I know the blasphemy of those who say they are Jews and are not, but are a synagogue of Satan (Rev. 2:9).

Satan uses ongoing problems within a community, such as murder, violence, pornography or gangs, to strengthen his throne of iniquity within the community. If your community is plagued by these and other corporate sins, you must realize that Satan has a throne of iniquity firmly in place that is being maintained through these sins.

Satan's Confederation

Another way that Satan maintains his system of worship in an area is through a local confederation of people. Even though we are not warring against flesh and blood, the demonic forces in an area are usually working through a group of people who have aligned themselves with Satan through idolatrous worship, forming a churchlike entity—a fellowship devoted to Satan. Such confederations can take on many forms, including covens of witches, churches of Satan, Wicca groups and pagan worship.

Demonic forces use these people to help perpetuate the darkness over an entire area. We see a clear example of this in Acts 16, in which Paul casts a demon of divination out of a slave girl. Paul's actions did not merely set one girl free of demonic torment but also allowed the gospel to flow into a territory once held captive by the spirit that inhabited her. In his commentary on the book of Acts, C. Peter Wagner explains how the spirit of divination in this girl was actually a powerful Python spirit which was a strongman of Satan in the area.[3]

These are times when the Body of Christ must mature so that we can properly discern what is in our territory, how Satan maintains his thrones of iniquity and who he is using to do it.

According to one recent survey, witchcraft is the No. 1 interest of teen-age girls. TV shows such as *Sabrina the Teenage Witch* and *Charmed* and movies such as *Practical Magic* and

The Craft have made the once-forbidden occult both fashion-
able and fun across the United States and overseas.

Not that it is limited to girls. Justin Melanson . . . has
been a Wiccan for nine years. Raised Roman Catholic, he
turned to witchcraft because, he says, "As a child I was continually questioning, and no one would give me the right
answers. All I would get was, 'Because the Bible says.'"

Witchcraft is viewed as an acceptable religion in the
United States today. That was obvious this summer when
it was disclosed that the Pentagon allows Wiccans to worship openly on military bases.[4]

We must not fool ourselves into thinking that witchcraft is powerless or that it is not a real threat to the gospel. The romanticism
that the entertainment industry brings to witchcraft can easily lull
us into thinking little or nothing of it.

There is in our society a hunger for the supernatural. The
younger generations in particular are looking for something more.
They know that a supernatural realm exists. I believe the Body of
Christ, however, is afraid of the supernatural. We forget that the Holy
Spirit who lives inside of us is a supernatural Spirit. If we are unwilling to mentor and train the Body of Christ in this next generation to
operate in the supernatural, they will be drawn toward any and every
device or belief system that promises to satisfy this longing.

Recently, a denominational magazine published an article
about the controversy surrounding the Harry Potter series of books.
As you probably know, these stories are about a boy who attends the
Hogwarts School of Witchcraft and Wizardry, and many in the
Christian community are concerned that the books cause the use
of dark powers to seem good, or at least harmless. The article states:

[Some Christians] seek to ban [these books]; some think
burning them in bonfires would be even better. In the case
of *Harry Potter*, some Christians even believe the books to
be the leading edge of a conspiracy to make witches and
warlocks out of our kids.[5]

The author of the article calls such beliefs "mindlessness" and concludes that the problem is not the harmful effects of the books themselves, but rather, that more parents need to send their children to Christian schools to prepare our youth to be ambassadors to the world. While the author of this article does admit that books like these and shows like *Buffy the Vampire Slayer* may have some effect on the psyche and soul, he somehow feels that attendance at a Christian school will negate any potential problems.

Satan and his powers of deception that lure young people into his grip are beyond the thinking of this author. Undoubtedly, many young graduates of Christian schools have either dabbled or become fully engulfed in witchcraft because many of these schools do not teach the spiritual warfare skills necessary to overcome Satan's influences. Christian schools may provide an excellent education; however, they are not preparing our young people to live a supernaturally empowered life unless the schools are imparting and training kids in the manifestations of the Holy Spirit.

Do not be deceived! There is real power in witchcraft that is neither beautiful nor fun. God's views on witchcraft are clearly spelled out in Deuteronomy 18:10-12:

> There shall not be found among you anyone . . . who practices witchcraft, or a soothsayer, or one who interprets omens, or a sorcerer, or one who conjures spells, or a medium, or a spiritist, or one who calls up the dead. For all who do these things are an abomination to the LORD, and because of these abominations the LORD your God drives them out from before you.

As we raise up the next generation, we need to recognize Satan's devices that he would use against them. We must not bury our heads in the sand because of our own fear of the supernatural. Not only should we guard our children from being drawn into Satan's snare, but we also need to train our children in the release of the anointing, the discerning of evil spirits and how to receive divine revelation from the throne room of God. I do not want my children (I have several) to be afraid of the supernatural.

The prophet Daniel was trained to understand the supernatural. When the magicians and diviners could not interpret the king's dream, Daniel knew that he could enter into a higher dimension of divine revelation. His life was spared in a hostile land because he knew how to receive divine revelation (see Dan. 1:17-20). The Lord wants us to prepare our children to receive divine revelation in the days ahead.

Satan's confederation, through which he maintains his system of worship, is not just limited to witchcraft or covens but can manifest itself through many forms of occultic practices, including satanism, psychic hotlines, spiritism, paganism, goddess worship, voodoo, fortune-telling, palmistry, demon worship, the use of spirit guides, and other New Age practices. The enemy's confederation also extends to those who practice any form of false religion—including Mormonism, Islam, Jehovah's Witnesses, Hinduism, Eastern religions, Native religions, Christian Science, and Bahai—and to those embroiled in secret societies such as Freemasonry, Shriners, Oddfellows and the Elks.

Even though many involved in these practices would deny that they are being driven by a satanic confederation, the fact is that through their practice of what the Bible clearly identifies as evil, these people are contributing to the throne of iniquity upon which Satan is seated in their area.

The Power Behind the Confederation

The Church needs to recognize those who are involved in a satanic confederation. These people do exist and they are operating at some level in your city, perpetuating a throne of iniquity from which Satan enjoys a great deal of freedom.

However, we also must recognize that the true power is not found in these lost souls for whom Christ died, but rather, is with a demonic hierarchy that uses these deceived people to achieve their own agendas. Ephesians 6:12 reminds us, "We do not wrestle against flesh and blood, but against principalities, against powers, against the rulers of the darkness of this age, against spiritual hosts of wickedness in the heavenly places."

This hierarchy is like a dark black band formed in the second heaven and connects this structure of powers and principalities with the individuals in Satan's confederation. These poor souls in Satan's service are puppets used by powers and principalities to maintain Satan's rule in a given region.

When we cast a demon out of an individual, Satan's hierarchy begins to crumble, just as when Paul cast the spirit of divination out of the slave girl. In this hour the Lord is telling us that we must get active; He wants to see this whole structure crumble so that the captives underneath can be liberated. We must stare down demon forces and declare, "You must let go! No longer will this demon have the right to rule over me, my family or my city."

Dethroning Thrones of Iniquity

How do we do this? How do we rebuke this level of demonic forces? This is where we get back to boundaries and to our proper covenant place. As we have seen, when God gives the Church in a city the right order of government and gifting, when the Church begins to come into proper order, we then have the authority to dethrone the thrones of iniquity that rule in our cities.

Many times in Scripture, people mixed the worship of God and idols. God is not one to tolerate divided loyalties. Therefore, He said to Israel, "I will destroy your high places. Then your altars shall be desolate" (Ezek. 6:3-4; see also Num. 33:52). The Lord showed the Israelites that they would need to drive out from within their boundaries any form of worship that did not lead them to Him. If they did not, this divided form of worship would deplete their faith and cause them to lose their spiritual and physical blessings.

In times of restoration under the Old Covenant, God commanded those in governmental authority to tear down high places. Those who did so prospered; those who did not were judged. Under the New Covenant, the Lord has given us access through His Spirit to dismantle the things in the heavens that are holding back His inheritance for a territory. We are to war with the powers and principalities that are withholding blessings. The Lord will clothe us in authority and release to us power that will cause His glory to be seen all over the earth.

The Greatest King

God is always raising up people on Earth to overthrow satanic systems of worship. He has given us examples of such people and their strategies throughout the Bible. Consider King Josiah:

> Now before him there was no king like him, who turned to the LORD with all his heart, with all his soul, and with all his might, according to all the Law of Moses; nor after him did any arise like him (2 Kings 23:25).

Josiah is declared by the Word of God to be the greatest king in all of Judah's history! Why? Because Josiah dethroned the thrones of iniquity of his day. He overthrew the satanic system of worship in order that God might once again be worshiped in the land.

In 2 Kings 22-23, we see there are eight things Josiah did to restore God's order:

1. *Josiah acknowledged the problem.* When Josiah began to have repairs made to the Temple, the high priest Hilkiah revealed that he had found a book of Law, which was brought and read to Josiah. In hearing the Law read, Josiah realized his forefathers had not followed God's law.

2. *Josiah humbled himself and repented.* Even though the Bible does not record that he had personally been involved in disobedience to the Lord, Josiah humbled himself and repented before the Lord for the actions of his forefathers. Today we would call this identificational repentance.

3. *Josiah inquired of the Lord.* He then had the high priest inquire of the Lord on his behalf and on behalf of the people of Judah concerning the Law. Inquiring of the Lord was a strategy of war that David used in his day and still has great power for those today who have an ear to hear what the Spirit is saying to us (see Rev. 2:29).

4. *Josiah received the word of God's prophet.* The prophetess Huldah then gave Josiah a word from the Lord. Her prophetic utterance told of how the Lord had been provoked to anger because the people had forsaken Him and burned incense to other gods. During the past several years, the Lord has been restoring the gift of prophecy to the Body of Christ. Paul tells us to desire the gift of prophecy (see 1 Cor. 14:1). Amos 3:7 says, "Surely the Lord GOD does nothing, unless He reveals His secret to His servants the prophets." Josiah understood, as we must today, that prophecy will help us to understand a problem and point us in the direction the Lord is requiring of us.

5. *Josiah made declarations about the law of God.* As we will see in the next chapter, lawlessness causes spiritual chaos. When Josiah came to the throne, spiritual chaos and idolatry had taken over the land. After hearing from the book of the Law and hearing the voice of the prophet, Josiah then gathered all the people, both great and small, and had the Law read aloud. Not only was Josiah reviving the Law for the people, but he was also declaring God's covenant to the heavens.

6. *Josiah made a territorial commitment before God.* "Then the king stood by a pillar and made a covenant before the LORD, to follow the LORD and to keep His commandments and His testimonies and His statutes, with all his heart and all his soul, to perform the words of this

covenant that were written in this book. And all the people took a stand for the covenant" (2 Kings 23:3). Josiah knew his boundaries. He knew where his kingly authority extended and where it ended. And within those boundaries he promised before God to perform the words of His covenant. All the people within that territory took a stand with Josiah.

7. *Josiah tore down the high places.* Josiah then did many physical acts within his sphere of influence to see the throne of iniquity overturned. He burned the articles made for Baal and Asherah (see 2 Kings 23:4). He removed the idolatrous priests who had been burning incense to Baal and the sun and the moon and the stars (see v. 5). He burned the idol of Asherah that had been placed in the Temple (see v. 6). He tore down the houses where the Temple prostitutes had been located (see v. 7). He destroyed the pagan altars placed on the rooftops (see v. 12). He confronted high-ranking demonic spirits such as Ashtoreth, Chemosh and Milcom (see v. 13). He wiped out idolatrous high places and executed the priests who would not repent (see vv. 19-20). He also punished anyone who had consulted with mediums or spiritists (see v. 24).[6]

8. *Josiah restored true worship.* Josiah then commanded that all the people keep the Passover, which had not been held since the days of the judges (see v. 22). As we will see later, once the throne of iniquity is overturned, the throne of God needs to be established over an area in order to see it transformed and God's covenant established in the land.

In our book *Ridding Your Home of Spiritual Darkness*, we show how to dethrone iniquity in your own home. This is a unique book that I highly recommend. In it we talk about how Christians are often completely unaware of how the enemy has gained access to their homes through what they own:

> Objects that we may possess, although not wrong in themselves, often represent a demonic stronghold in our lives. . . . Take, for example, lust. Perhaps there is something in your home from a past romantic relationship (maybe a gift or some old love letters or hidden photos) and one or both of you is now married to another person. A demonic stronghold of lust or of inappropriate love could easily attach itself to that item. Destroying whatever it is will help you overcome the enemy's grip in that area of your life.[7]

Understanding how to dethrone iniquity in our own lives in order to restore God's order will help us to understand how we, like Josiah, can overthrow iniquity in our city.

Elijah and Jezebel

Another great example of dethroning a throne of iniquity is the story of Elijah and Jezebel. The familiar story is found in 1 Kings, where we find Elijah contending with the queen, Jezebel, leading to a great power encounter that ended when all the prophets of the Baal system of worship were killed. This is a classic story of how Satan's throne was overthrown.

Eventually, Jezebel was dethroned when she was killed and her flesh eaten by dogs (see 2 Kings 9). But this was not the end of Jezebel's influence in the region.

Athaliah Rises

Every generation is responsible for dethroning thrones of iniquity. Even if a throne has been overturned, it may try to reestablish itself in the next generation. Such was the case with Jezebel's daughter Athaliah.

The Lord promised David there would always be someone from his line sitting on the throne (see Ps. 89:3-4). There would never be anyone on the throne of David who was not from the house and the line of Judah. That was a promise. But there came a time in history when the devil thought he had won and had positioned someone else on that throne.

In 2 Kings 11:1 we read that Athaliah rose up and destroyed all the royal heirs (because her own son had been killed). Jezebel's throne was not completely done away with when she died, but rather, that system reared up in all of its strength, and Jezebel's daughter killed everyone who was in line for the throne who would keep God's covenant plan moving forward. The enemy will always look for ways of destroying God's covenant plan, and that was the case here. Athaliah tried to do away with everything that could cause God's covenant plan to manifest within her area. Instead of submitting to apostolic authority (represented by David and his line), she put herself into that place of authority and tried to remove everything that could bring her any competition.

The Seed Is in Hiding

The Lord, however, always keeps His covenant promises. The Bible goes on to tell us that Athaliah's daughter took Joash, one of the king's sons, and hid him from Athaliah so that he was not murdered. In other words, God hid the one who had legal right to reign so that God's covenant plan might move ahead and His promise to David would be kept. Joash was hidden in the house of the Lord for six years, while Athaliah reigned over the land (see 2 Kings 11:2-3).

But there came a time seven years later when the priesthood rose up and took authority over Athaliah by showing Joash to the people and saying, "Look who has been hiding out in the house of the Lord." The priesthood got into proper alignment with the Lord's plan in order to achieve spiritual victory and to overthrow that which was illegally reigning in their area.

In days ahead, that which has been hidden for several years in our cities is suddenly going to come alive; and that which is currently ruling and reigning in the land is going to have to submit to it. Here in America we tend to think that because of our disobedience to Him as a nation, God's only recourse with us is judgment. But I believe that the Lord has been keeping His seed in hiding, waiting for the right time to release His people. There are churches that have been waiting for God's timing. There are intercessors who have kept themselves hidden, waiting to be released into their area. There are hidden apostles (and that's what Joash's story represents) who have been trained and are just waiting for the Lord to release them and position them for the future fulfillment of His will in this nation.

We mustn't despair. God has a plan and a proper time to bring His seed out of hiding!

The Priesthood Comes into Position

After bringing Joash out of hiding, the priesthood then came into the proper position necessary to take back the authority that Athaliah had usurped and to protect Joash from harm:

> Then he commanded them, saying, "This is what you shall do: One-third of you who come on duty on the Sabbath shall be keeping watch over the king's house, one-third shall be at the gate of Sur, and one-third at the gate behind the escorts. You shall keep the watch of the house, lest it be broken down. The two contingents of you who go off duty on the Sabbath shall keep the watch of the house of the LORD for the king. But you shall surround the king on all sides, every man with his weapons in his hand; and whoever comes within range, let him be put to death. You are to be with the king as he goes out and as he comes in" (2 Kings 11:5-8).

As we seek to dethrone thrones of iniquity in our areas, we must also come into the proper position. Two important keys to learn from the actions of the priesthood in this story are (1) establish the watchman anointing in your territory and (2) set up a strategy in your area and start praying for the Lord's government to arise. Begin protecting what is going on spiritually in the house of the Lord. Establish the prayer ministry that will begin to watch after that which God is about to birth.

This is a time of birthing in the Body of Christ, but God is not going to bring His seed out of hiding if we don't establish the watch that will keep it protected. The Lord is getting ready to move, but He won't move until we get established. Once we do, then He will come in.

This passage also tells us, "You shall keep the watch of the house, lest it be broken down." In other words, if we do not keep watch over the house, the enemy is going to overrun it. That's why the Lord is calling us to a new dimension of prayer ministry at this time—not just so that we can say we have a prayer ministry in our church but instead to establish a watch. Then, when the time comes for the Lord to overthrow the enemy's plan in your area, the watch will already be established, prayer will be operating, and the enemy will not only be overthrown, but he will also have no further right to break down that which God is establishing.

Athaliah Is Dethroned

When Athaliah heard the commotion in the Temple, she went to investigate. She ended up walking right into a service alive with rejoicing, faith and praise to God. The priests were all in their positions on the wall, sounding trumpets. Athaliah accused them, shouting, "Treason!" and started declaring illegal authority over them. But because the priests were positioned correctly, she had no chance.

> And Jehoiada the priest commanded the captains of the hundreds, the officers of the army, and said to them, "Take her outside under guard, and slay with the sword whoever follows her." For the priest had said, "Do not let her be killed in the house of the LORD." So they seized her; and she went by way of the horses' entrance into the king's house, and there she was killed. Then Jehoiada made a covenant between the LORD, the king, and the people, that they should be the LORD's people, and also between the king and the people (2 Kings 11:15-17).

That's the type of priesthood we need—one that says, "Get that demonic spirit out of here and take care of it!"

God is doing a work with us. He is saying, "Get positioned. Get in order, because I'm ready to bring change. I'm tired of what's been ruling in your city. Get in your place, start worshiping, establish the watch of the Lord, and get the prayer room going, because it's time for change. And that which has been ruling illegally in your area, I'm about to dethrone it. So I say to you, come into a new order. Come into a new anointing, because I've been planning an overthrow of the enemy for many years now, and I've been waiting for My Body to come into right order. And if you will come into right order, that which has been holding Me back from moving, I will begin to overthrow it!"

There is a perfect time to dethrone the throne of iniquity, whether it be in your life, your church, your city, your state or your nation. The Lord is calling the Body of Christ in this hour to come into a new order, for He is about to bring out of His treasury and out of hiding that which He has been planning to display to this earth. He is getting ready to move. God is saying, "Come into a new place of strength. Come out of that old place of fear. Get aligned with Me for My house is about to change. I'm going to bring the enemy in, right into your faith, and I am going to dethrone the enemy in days ahead. I say, get in line, for change is coming. And I'm sending you forth so that change will occur from city to city to city in Jesus' name!"

The Ancient of Days

Once we have dethroned that which is usurping God's authority in an area, we must then establish God's throne. In the book of Daniel, we find a revelation of God's everlasting reigning power:

> I watched till thrones were put [set] in place, and the Ancient of Days was seated . . . and behold, One like the Son of Man . . . came to the Ancient of Days, and they brought Him near before Him. Then to Him was given

dominion and glory and a kingdom, that all peoples, nations, and languages should serve Him. His dominion is an everlasting dominion, which shall not pass away, and His kingdom the one which shall not be destroyed (Dan. 7:9,13-14, *NKJV*).

This name of God, Ancient of Days, is a phrase that describes the everlasting God, the Father of Years, the One who rules over time. The name implies dignity, endurance, judgment and wisdom. His number of years are undiscoverable (see Job 36:26).

The Ancient of Days has promised that the earth will be full of His purposes and that He will be long-suffering until all have heard. The heart of God is to form covenant with all peoples on the face of the earth and to establish a house of prayer for all (see Isa. 56:5-8), including those in your city. That is why we must learn how to prophesy to that which has been scattered through these thrones of iniquity.

Just as Ezekiel did, we must speak to the dry bones and command them to be brought back to life (see Ezek. 37). This kind of prophetic declaration will not only reestablish God's covenant purpose for a territory, but it will also bring those within the territory to give up hope deferred (see Prov. 13:12) and instead rebuild that which the enemy has destroyed.

Wisdom for Present-Day Victory

The Ancient of Days releases ancient wisdom for present-day victory! The following Scripture has revolutionized my prayer life:

We speak wisdom among those who are mature, yet not the wisdom of this age, nor of the rulers of this age, who are coming to nothing. But we speak the wisdom of God in a mystery, the hidden wisdom which God ordained before the ages for our glory, which none of the rulers of this age knew; for had they known, they would not have crucified the Lord of glory. But as it is written: "Eye has not seen, nor ear heard . . . the things which God has prepared for those who love Him." But God has revealed them to us through His Spirit (1 Cor. 2:6-10).

God gives us several keys for victory when we pray:

- God has wisdom greater than any worldly wisdom we see.
- Powers and principalities do not have access to this wisdom.
- The authority of demonic forces is limited.
- There is wisdom that has been hidden since the beginning of time for His glory.
- Through the redemptive cross of Jesus Christ, you have access to this wisdom.
- God is prepared to release this wisdom to us as we get to know Him intimately through prayer.
- This wisdom will overthrow high places and release captives.
- Wisdom dismantles demonic structures and dethrones thrones of iniquity.

When the Lord showed this to me, I knew any demonic force holding a territory captive could not withstand the wisdom that God will release to His people. I knew that if the Spirit of the Lord burdened me to pray for a city, I had authority to gain the keys for their release.

This day the Lord is extending a fresh call of prayer to His people. He is going to show us our city as it really is and say to us, "Overcome every obstacle that is keeping these people from coming to know Me! Open the door for My house to be built within them so that they may experience My love throughout eternity. Through prayer, gain wisdom that will dethrone the thrones of iniquity where they have been established. Then establish My throne that many may worship Me and gain life everlasting!"

This is how entire cities will experience conversion. This is how we will overthrow thrones of iniquity and see God's covenant plan for whole territories flourish in days ahead.

Establishing God's Throne— Thy Kingdom Come

In Luke 11 we find the model prayer given to us by Jesus, a cry for the kingdom of God to come. The Lord's Prayer in *The Amplified Bible* begins, "Our Father Who is in heaven, hallowed be Your name, Your kingdom come. Your will be done [held holy and revered] on earth as it is in heaven" (Luke 11:2). God wants to build His kingdom in our hearts, our families, our churches and cities, our states and nations. He longs for His kingdom rule to reside in the earthly realm. Therefore, we must have a Kingdom mentality for the throne and rule of God to be victorious in days ahead.

The kingdom of God is already here, but it is not yet here in its fullness. In a sense it is already, but also it is not yet. It is here today, yet it is still to come in the future. Therefore, in order to see God's kingdom come in its fullness, we must learn how to pray and position ourselves for the future. Let's now look at how, through our prayers, we can outwit the devil in order to advance God's kingdom toward the promise of fullness.

God's Unfolding Revelation: Overthrowing Strongholds

Since this book was written, we have been through an incredible season. The United States and various allies went to war with Iraq. Within days, the ruling dictator, Saddam Hussein, fled his government headquarters as a fugitive. His towering statue in Baghdad— very much like the statue of Nebuchadnezzar (see Dan. 3)—was pulled down. But victory is not complete until God's rule is established.

In every territory or nation, there are ruling thrones of iniquity. There are leaders throughout the world who are empowered by demonic forces from the kingdom of Satan to work havoc in the earth realm. The absence of the presence of God always indicates that a curse is working. We must be a people that are wiling to establish the presence of God in our spheres of authority and the territories we live in.

In 2003 and 2004, Dutch Sheets and I visited every state in our nation. As we relate in our book *Releasing the Prophetic Destiny of a Nation*, the best example of overthrowing a stronghold occurred in Texas during our 50 State Tour. This meeting was a powerful model of how a spiritual breakthrough uncovers hidden structures that are ruling in the earth realm.

A Model for Overcoming Strongholds

When Dutch began to preach on the evening of December 9, declaring the redemptive gift of Texas and connecting it to the purposes of the entire nation, a prophetic anointing began to fill the room. It was as if I *knew* God's heart and mind and why we were there. I actually felt I was being lifted into the heavenlies to stand before the Lord. I grabbed hold of Alice and said, "I am going up before God." In this spiritual place, I heard Him say, *"I am going to tell you why you are here. Do not think—just go and decree what I tell you."*

I then began to prophesy, "Watch the bridges that begin to fall. For even now there are some that are sitting on pillars that will not stand in days ahead. These will become signs to you. Bridges will be coming down so that I can reroute what I need to do at this time. There is strength in this state to turn the battle at the gate. Allow your strength to rise up . . . the heavens are opening tonight and the revelation is beginning to pour out."

At the meeting, Dutch had shared about our time in Detroit during the 50 State Tour. At that time (April 3-5, 2005), the coalition troops were stalled in going through the gate into Babylon. God gave us a revelation about how the key had been turned over and how He had even caused the voice of that region to be lost. I felt as if we had made a break. As we broke through and repented and the key people came forward, it allowed us to enter in and bring confusion and declare a dropping of the stronghold. However, since that time we had seemed to lose ground in that nation.

I then shared what the Lord was saying to me: *"Just as you were there then, I have you here now. What has fallen into confusion where ambushes have come, I say to you that I am raising up a people here tonight who can put a stop to the ambushes. In this place tonight, you have been given the power to stop what has been scattered and call things back into place. Start with yourself and declare that scattering will flee. Where the enemy has tried to bring scattering even into the leadership of this state, decree it stopped tonight. Now declare over this nation that the power of scattering that would create plans to go this way and that way and another way are now being stopped in Jesus' name. And declare that President Bush will have a clear mind tonight."*

The Lord then showed me a nest of snake eggs. He said, *"There are four snake eggs that are lying in wait, and from this state I am giving you the power tonight to crush those snake eggs. In this state tonight, you will be able to decree to Babylon that the strongman that has not been found will now be found in the next seven days."*

Then Pastor Dutch said, "Expose him. We declare exposure. We declare the eggs are being crushed under our feet in Jesus' name. Under our feet, under our feet, under our feet. Break it! We say witchcraft is broken that hides him in Jesus' name."

Members of the local pastoral leadership and the national military agreed with the prophetic decree. Pastor Darrell Feemster declared that the Fourth Infantry Division from San Antonio would be blessed to bring down the spirit of Babylon and to raise up a Christian nation in Iraq. Greg Jackson, a representative of the military, proclaimed, "As a witness to the prophetic word in this house, as a representative of the Armed Forces in the state of Texas, I declare in the name of the Lord, it shall be!"

A roar went up from the crowd. That roar entered the atmosphere and, I believe, traveled by the Spirit of God all the way to Iraq. The roar of God is a prophetic release that creates a covering of God's authority in the earth realm. Amos 3:7-8 says, "Surely the Lord God does nothing, unless He reveals His secret to His servants the prophets. A lion has roared! Who will not fear? The Lord God has spoken! Who can but prophesy?"

Troops from the Fourth Infantry went in and found Saddam Hussein three days later! Even though many were praying around the world, I believe it takes corporate gatherings at times to express God's purpose in the earth. I could see why God had wanted this revelation decreed in San Antonio, Texas.[8]

40-Day Prayer Focus: A Faith Release to
Overthrow Thrones of Iniquity

Warfare is intensifying throughout the earth. In the midst of warfare, God is saying two things to His people: "*Come up!* Ascend under the shadow of My wing and war from the abiding place that I have prepared for you!" and "*Stand still,* cease and desist from striving, and worship Me!"

With war and rumors of war flying around the world, it is important that as God's people we remind ourselves that we can have peace in the midst of the war. The war is a supernatural spiritual war, not just a war against flesh and blood. We must also remind ourselves that the war is a worship war. Who will be worshiped? We declare that our God is worthy to be worshiped. During these next 40 days, it is critical that we worship the Lord and declare that the enemy of God's covenant will be bound.

Dutch Sheets quotes the following five verses together, which I believe summarize the Lord's call to us at this time to "go up, ascend and war from a heavenly perspective":

> Blessed be the God and Father of our Lord Jesus Christ, who has blessed us with every spiritual blessing in the heavenly places in Christ . . . which He worked in Christ when He raised Him from the dead and seated Him at His right hand in the heavenly places, and raised us up together, and made us sit together in the heavenly places in Christ Jesus . . . to the intent that now the manifold wisdom of God might be made known by the church to the principalities and powers in the heavenly places . . . For we do not wrestle against flesh and blood, but against principalities, against powers, against the rulers of the darkness of this age, against spiritual hosts of wickedness in the heavenly places (Eph. 1:3,20; 2:6; 3:10; 6:12).

Now is the time to come to an understanding and to overthrow the thrones of iniquity that are ruling and influencing the earth. God is calling His Church into a new and intimate place where the anointing will break the yoke and overturn the structures holding many captive. God is stirring up His people's faith. He is releasing a gift of faith to break the power of generational iniquitous patterns that have stopped families from experiencing the blessings of God. He is empowering people with faith to see His glory spread throughout cities, regions and states.

The only entity on Earth that has power to break strongholds of the enemy's domain is the Church. The Church must now war to come out of its status quo and into a new structure that presents the gospel to a lost and dying world. Just as the structure was new in the first century, it is being reformed to meet the needs of the world in the twenty-first century. We must change into a vibrant, fire-filled army that marches forward. This call to advance will bring the Body of Christ into a vibrant worshiping force. This is a time to enthrone Christ as king so that other thrones will be toppled.

Satan's objective is to block the plan of God by establishing his legal right to control an area. Satan gains access into an area the same way he gains access into an individual's life or family line: through sin. He is seeking to escalate individual or family sin into corporate sin. When corporate sin enters into our assigned boundaries, we need to be aware of how that sin can build a throne of iniquity and how we, positioned in God's Army, have the authority to dismantle it. Sin creates a break in God's purpose or order. When these breaks occur, Satan takes advantage and begins to establish his influence in an area. From that place of influence, Satan can actually build a throne on which he is seated in a territory. Revelation 2:13 says, "I know your works, and where you dwell, where Satan's throne is."

In exalting himself, Satan is attempting to draw all people to his counterfeit light. He knows that all people are created as vessels of worship and that, whether or not they realize it, they will worship something. They will either worship the true and living God or they will worship Satan and his demonic forces, either overtly or through sin (whether they be of omission or commission). It is this "worship" of corporate sin that builds the throne on which Satan is seated; and it is from that throne that demonic forces work to perpetuate the sin and establish the throne of iniquity to an even greater extent.

It's time to go up into the gaps (see Ezek. 13:5) and block Satan's opportunity. In Luke 11, we find the model for our prayers, a cry for the kingdom of God to come. The Lord's prayer in the *Amplified Bible* begins, "Our Father Who is in heaven, hallowed be Your name, Your kingdom come. Your will be done [held holy and revered] on earth as it is in heaven" (v. 2). We must invite God to build His kingdom in our hearts, families, churches, cities, states and nations. He longs for His kingdom rule to reside in the earth realm. It is already here, but not in its fullness. In a sense, it *is already* and it is *not yet*. It is here today, yet still to come in the future.

In order to see God's kingdom come in its fullness, we must understand how to pray and position ourselves for the future. Get ready for a great shaking! Thrones of iniquity are going to fall. We are about to see a tremendous shift in worship throughout the world as God's throne is re-established and the Church rises into a new glory.

How to Pray

To conclude this update, the following is a 40-day prayer focus that will assist you in whatever area you are praying to see a ruling throne displaced.

> **Day 1:** *Read Acts 17:26.* The Bible says that God has set the boundaries of our dwellings and predetermined our times. Be very aware of the times you are living and walking in. Praise God for your boundaries. Or if you feel misplaced, ask Him to shift you supernaturally into the place you belong.

> **Day 2:** *Read Psalm 24.* Psalm 24:1 reminds us, "The earth is the LORD'S, and all its fullness, the world and those who dwell therein." God positions people throughout the earth to bring forth the fullness of His purpose. Declare that you will see the full purpose of God in your life and submit

yourself fully to Him anew and afresh. Declare that you will position yourself to receive that purpose. Ask the Lord for a revelation of His glory.

Day 3: *Read Habakkuk 2:14.* In order for His glory to cover the earth, we as His people need to live in the place that God has established and ordained for us. Ask the Lord to confirm our boundaries.

Day 4: *Read Revelation 2:13.* Ask the Lord to reveal any throne of iniquity that Satan has built in your life, family or city.

Day 5: *Read Psalm 94.* Satan's objective is to block the plan of God by establishing his legal right to control an area. Satan gains access into an area the same way he gains access into an individual's life or family line—through sin. When corporate sin enters into our assigned boundaries, Satan has an opportunity to build his throne. Ask the Lord to reveal how you can dismantle his throne within your boundaries.

Day 6: *Read Psalm 16.* Ask the Lord for supernatural help to possess your inheritance, the portion He has given you.

Day 7: *Read Genesis 12.* Understand the power of covenant. As born-again believers, we are grafted into God's covenant with Abraham. Covenant involves promise, commitment, faithfulness and loyalty even unto death. The war in the earth realm is over God's covenant blessings, and He will war through His people to maintain His covenant in the earth. The blood of Jesus says to the enemy, "Hands off! This is not your territory!" Declare the same.

Day 8: *Read Psalm 89,* especially verses 15-23. God made a covenant that David and his seed would sit on the throne and reign forever and ever. As heirs of Christ, we share in this covenant promise.

Day 9: *Read Psalm 110 and Ephesians 1:22.* Through Christ and His reign, all of His enemies are put under His feet. Your enemies become His enemies because of His covenant relationship with us.

Day 10: *Read Hebrews 11.* Look at the heroes of faith. Meditate on what they had to overcome. Meditate on what they had to confront. God is calling you to be a hero like them.

Day 11: *Read Matthew 8:5-10.* The centurion was a man who understood authority and the power of the word. Make a list of the authorities that you are aligned with in your life. When we are properly aligned, the Word of God has great power to overthrow our enemies.

Day 12: *Read Matthew 15:22-28.* This Canaanite woman knew that even the crumbs of bread that had fallen from the Master's table could liberate her daughter. It's not the amount of your faith, but the quality of it.

Day 13: *Read Matthew 17:14-21.* Fast for a day and allow your faith to arise. Then address that one issue that seems to be too strong for you to overthrow.

Day 14: *Read Matthew 12:22-30.* Ask the Lord to reveal to you how the strongman has robbed you. Think of three strongmen: One in your family, one in your city and one set against our nation. Declare that those strongmen be bound.

Day 15: *Read 1 Kings 17-18.* Ask the Lord to give you the prophetic decree that will change the atmosphere of the heavens around you. Be willing to birth the will of God in heaven by travailing and persevering until you see God's plan moving into the earth realm.

Day 16: *Read 1 Corinthians 13 and Galatians 5*. Faith works by love. Ask God to increase your love for Him so that your faith will increase.

Day 17: *Read Ezekiel 28:11-19*. Ask the Lord to allow you to see the invisible behind the visible. Ask the Lord for understanding about the enemy's characteristics so that you can discern how he might be working in your life to deceive you.

Day 18: *Read Isaiah 14:3-21*. Notice Lucifer's desire to ascend, and his fall. Focus on verses 16 and 17 so that you keep proper perspective on the Lord's majesty and the reality of the enemy's smallness when compared to God's greatness.

Day 19: *Read Genesis 4*. Notice the war of worship. Renew the sacrifice of God in your life. Declare that you will bring to Him the best that He requires.

Day 20: *Read Jeremiah 33:11*. All iniquity on Earth works from a satanic system of worship meant to usurp God's authority and keep lost souls in darkness and blinded to the truth of the gospel. Just as godly worship is made through sacrifice (that is, the sacrifice of Jesus that reconciled our relationship to God, and then our sacrifice of praise in response), Satan's system of worship is based on sacrifice.

Day 21: *Read 2 Kings 3:24-27*. Have eyes to see the enemy's sacrifices around you. Here we find where Moab rose up against Israel in rebellion. The Moabite king, seeing that he was being soundly defeated in battle, took his oldest son who was to inherit the throne and killed him, offering him "as a burnt sacrifice along the wall" (v. 27).

Day 22: *Read Hebrews 13:15.* Let worship arise within you. Enthrone the Lord as King. Ask Him to forgive you for not worshiping on a daily basis. Ask Him to help you come into a new dimension of worship.

Day 23: *Read 2 Kings 22:3-20.* We are in a "Josiah season" in the Body of Christ. When Josiah began to make repairs to the Temple, the high priest Hilkiah found a Book of Law, which was then brought and read to Josiah. After hearing the reading of the Law, Josiah realized that there were problems in the land because his forefathers had not followed God's law. Ask the Holy Spirit to identity any area where you are not following God's law.

Day 24: *Read 2 Kings 22:11.* Even though the Bible does not record that Josiah was personally involved in disobedience to the Lord, he humbled himself and repented for the actions of his forefathers. Today, we would call this "identificational repentance." Like Josiah, humble yourself and repent for personal and corporate actions contrary to God's plan.

Day 25: *Read 2 Kings 22:12-13.* Josiah had the high priest inquire of the Lord on his behalf and on behalf of the people of Judah. Inquiring of the Lord was a strategy of war that David used in his day, and it has great power for those today who have an ear to hear what the Spirit is saying to us (see Rev. 2:29). Ask the Lord to open your ears and inquire of Him anew and afresh.

Day 26: *Read 2 Kings 22:14-20.* Josiah received the word of God's prophet. Over the past several years, the Lord has been restoring the gift of prophecy to the Body of Christ.

Paul tells us to desire prophecy (see 1 Cor. 14:11), and Amos 3:7 says, "Surely the Lord GOD does nothing, unless He reveals His secret to His servants the prophets." Josiah understood, as we must today, that prophecy will help us understand the problem and point us toward the next step the Lord requires of us. Thank God for prophecy and commit to receiving revelation through this gift.

Day 27: *Read 2 Kings 23:1-2.* When Josiah came to the throne, spiritual chaos and idolatry had taken over the land. After hearing the Book of the Law read and hearing the voice of the prophet, Josiah gathered all the people and had the Book of the Law (also called the Book of the Covenant) read aloud. Josiah was not only reviving the Law to the people but was also declaring God's covenant into the atmosphere. Declare that God's law will be heard in your city, state and region.

Day 28: *Read 2 Kings 23:3.* Josiah made a territorial commitment before God. He knew his boundaries. He knew where his kingly authority extended and where it ended. It was within those boundaries that he promised before God to perform the words of His covenant, and all the people within that territory took a stand with Josiah. Commit to stand for the plans and purposes of God in your home and city.

Day 29: *Read 2 Kings 23:4-25.* Josiah tore down the high places and did many physical acts within his sphere of influence to see the throne of iniquity overturned. Declare that false thrones and forms of worship in your region will be overturned.

Day 30: *Read 2 Kings 23:22.* Josiah restored true worship. Josiah commanded that all the people keep the Passover, which had not been held since the days of the judges nor in all the days of the kings that ruled before him. Once the throne of iniquity is overturned, the throne of God must be established over an area in order to see it transformed and God's covenant established in the land. Declare that the throne of God is established anew and afresh in your region.

Day 31: *Read Daniel 7.* The enemy works through law and time. Ask the Lord to break any legal structure that might be working against you. Confess any sin of presumption or insecurity that has made you get out of God's timing.

Day 32: *Read Deuteronomy 18:10-12.* Confess any occult in your bloodline as sin. Occult forces align with false religions, including Freemasonry. Declare yourself righteous through Christ (see 2 Cor. 5:17).

Day 33: *Read Ephesians 4–6.* Be sure that you are standing on God's right foundation. Evaluate your relationships. Declare them to be reconciled and in God's order. Now stand against the hierarchy of the enemy that is set against your prosperity.

Day 34: *Read James 4.* Ask the Lord to give you insight about why you might be in war, and then follow God's plan of victory: Submit. Resist. Draw near.

Day 35: *Read Luke 19.* Make sure you are being a steward of what God is giving you. Ask Him for stewardship strategies. Look for His perfect time for visitation in your life. Ask Him to give you an understanding of visitation. He has a *kairos* time for you to walk in. Ask Him to place you in your perfect opportune time.

Day 36: *Read 2 Chronicles 20.* This passage seems to be a pattern for today. Notice the confederation of demonic forces that would love to overtake God's covenant plan. Many thrones are built through a confederation of Satan's forces. Follow the pattern of success in 2 Chronicles 20.

Day 37: *Read Ezekiel 3 and 33.* Declare that the Lord will establish the watchman anointing anew and afresh in you and your territory.

Day 38: *Read 2 Kings 9–11.* Declare that every inheritance of Jezebel that has influenced you or your region will be overturned. Notice that Jezebel was taken down and then Athaliah began to reign, but Athaliah was also dethroned.

Day 39: *Read Daniel 7:9-14.* Daniel had a revelation of God's everlasting reigning power. The name of God, "Ancient of Days," is a phrase that describes the Everlasting God, One advanced in days or knowledge, the Father of Years and One who forwards time or rules over it. The Ancient of Days has a covenant with the earth. In this covenant, the earth will be full of His purposes and He will be long-suffering until all have heard. The heart of God is to form covenant with all peoples on the face of the earth and establish a house of prayer for each one (see Isa. 56:5-8), including those in your city. Ask the Lord to reveal Himself to you and your region as the Ancient of Days.

Day 40: *Read 1 Corinthians 2:6-10.* This Scripture has revolutionized my prayer life. The Ancient of Days releases ancient wisdom for present-day victory. God has given us two keys of prayer wisdom. First, God's wisdom is greater than any worldly wisdom. Second, powers and principalities do not have access to this wisdom—the authority of demonic forces is limited. Receive "new" wisdom from the Ancient of Days.

The Lord is extending a fresh call of prayer to His people for our cities and regions. He is saying, "Overcome every obstacle that is keeping these people from coming to know Me. Open the door for My House to be built within them so that they may experience My love throughout eternity. Through prayer, gain wisdom that will dethrone the thrones of iniquity where they have been established. Then establish My throne that many may worship Me and gain life everlasting!" This is how entire cities will experience conversion. This is how we will overthrow thrones of iniquity and see God's covenant plan for whole territories flourish in days ahead.

CHAPTER FIVE

Urgent, Fervent Prayer: How to Outwit the Devil

Set off on the path of prayer with confidence, then swiftly and speedily will you reach the place of peace, which is your stronghold against the place of fear.
EVAGRIUS OF PONTUS (C. 305-400)

So let us arm ourselves with devout prayers and set off showing signs of genuine humility and barefooted to combat Goliath.
DOMINIC (1170-1221)

The Lord is calling to His people in this hour, "Through prayer, gain wisdom that will dethrone the thrones of iniquity where they have been established. Then establish My Throne that many may worship Me and gain life everlasting!" He has big plans for us to secure His inheritance among the nations.

All the nations of the world are intended to come under Christ's rule and domain: "Ask of Me, and I will give You the nations for Your inheritance, and the ends of the earth for Your possession" (Ps. 2:8). God gives a command in this verse. He says to His Son, "Ask." We find Jesus asking in John 17. He prays for His corporate Body on Earth to come into unity, receive His heart and act in the authority that He releases to them.

This agreement between heaven and Earth will cause us, as His Church, to see the nations become our inheritance and the ends of the earth made our possession for the gospel. And I believe that in this new millennium there is a new call of prayer upon the Church that will result in the Lord's glory covering the earth.

In the Old Testament, Joshua and the people of Israel were commanded by God to dethrone and annihilate all the "-Ites" that stood in the way of what God had given them through the covenant of Abraham. But one of the -Ites, the Jebusites, would not be taken:

> As for the Jebusites, the inhabitants of Jerusalem, the children of Judah could not drive them out; but the Jebusites dwell with the children of Judah at Jerusalem to this day (Josh. 15:63).

The Jebusites represented a stronghold from the curse of Canaan that was not overthrown until several generations later by David. Before David received his full kingship, his first assignment from God was to overthrow this people and the throne of iniquity that had gained strength since the time of Ham's son (see 2 Sam. 5:1-7).

God never forgets a demon structure that has established itself on Earth, and He will seek until He finds a generation that will overthrow that stronghold. If we are to be a generation that reaches our full destiny for the kingdom of God, we must come into a place of prayer and communion with Him that will give us the keys and the strategy to overthrow the -Ites that are keeping our inheritance from us.

We must understand and employ the strategies God provides for us to outwit our enemies, and much of that strategy and wisdom will come through prayer. As we enter into the future war, we will not only need all we have learned in the past; we will also need to allow the Lord to raise us to new levels of prayer, where we will have authority and power beyond what we have ever experienced.

Prayers, They Are a-Changin'

Within many churches there has been a marked shift in the role of prayer, even during worship services. This shift has laid a groundwork for how prayer will be viewed and used to overcome the enemy in the future.

C. Peter Wagner has researched and written extensively on the differing roles of prayer in traditional churches (represented in my vision from the Lord as the existing Church structure) and new

apostolic churches (represented by the Church of the future).
Wagner writes:

> Since I have spent many years as a member of traditional
> churches and many years as a member of new apostolic
> churches, it is fairly easy for me to highlight the differ-
> ences. Here are some:
>
> - In traditional churches prayer is *incidental*, while
>   in apostolic churches it is *central*. Some take
>   prayer so seriously that they have added a pastor
>   of prayer to the church staff.
> - In traditional churches prayer is *routine*, while in
>   apostolic churches it is *spontaneous*. True, there
>   are times in virtually all services where prayer is
>   routinely expected; but in apostolic churches we
>   also hear "Let's stop and pray," followed by
>   unprogrammed prayer action, more frequently
>   than in traditional churches.
> - In traditional churches prayer is *occasional*,
>   while in apostolic churches it is *frequent*. During
>   worship, for example, the worship leader may
>   break out in leading the congregation in prayer
>   several times in one service.
> - In traditional churches prayer is *passive*, while in
>   apostolic churches it is *aggressive*. Answers to
>   prayer are expected; they are not surprises.
> - In traditional churches prayer is *quiet*, while in
>   apostolic churches it is *loud*. During prayer there
>   is much more vocal audience participation and
>   the noise level is notable. At times the entire con-
>   gregation will engage in "concert prayer" when
>   everyone is praying out loud at the same time.
> - In traditional churches prayer is *reverent*, while
>   in apostolic churches it is *expressive*. People pray
>   with their eyes open at times, they kneel, they

fall on the floor, they lift their arms up and down, and they walk around.

- In traditional churches prayer is *cerebral*, while in apostolic churches it is *emotional*. There is much more passion in apostolic praying. Some churches keep boxes of Kleenex under the seats because it is expected that certain ones will start weeping during prayer. After a prayer time, many will release their emotion by applauding or even shouting.[1]

Throughout the 1990s the Lord has been changing how many of us view prayer, both in our churches and in our personal prayer times. The reason is simply that as we draw closer to the end times and we see spiritual warfare intensify, we need to pray in such a way that we may receive revelation for the battle—and to live in such a way that we may withstand the enemy. God is leading us into new levels of strategic praying so that the enemy does not overtake us and will not defeat us in days ahead.

Our Covenant Position with God

I have made a covenant with My chosen, I have sworn to My servant David: "Your seed I will establish forever, and build up your throne to all generations" (Ps. 89:3-4).

The basis for strategic prayer that outwits the enemy comes from an understanding of our position with God. We, as Christians, are in a covenant relationship with God. Everything we have and everything we are flow from that covenant relationship.

In our book *Possessing Your Inheritance*, we go into great detail as to how our covenant relationship with God positions us personally with the Lord so that we can understand His plan for our lives and actively participate in taking hold of that which He has for us. Here, however, we want to focus on how our covenant with the Lord gives us access to the throne room and how that access produces the communion we need to outwit the devil.

God had such a covenant with David, son of Jesse:

I have found My servant David;
With My holy oil I have anointed him,
With whom My hand shall be established;
Also My arm shall strengthen him.
The enemy shall not outwit him,
Nor the son of wickedness afflict him.
I will beat down his foes before his face,
And plague those who hate him (Ps. 89:20-23).

And with the Lord as his strength and his shield (see Ps. 28:7), David won many victories over his enemies. While we can learn principles of covenant and victory from virtually every verse of Psalm 89, a psalm written by David, we have chosen here to highlight just a few principles from the verses above that show how our covenant with God positions us to overcome the schemes of our enemy.

There Is a New Anointing

Psalm 89:20 says, "I have found My servant David; with My holy oil I have anointed him." To anoint means to consecrate, or make sacred, or to formally choose for a sacred task. Anointing carries with it the authority necessary to accomplish the task at hand. Our covenant with God positions us to receive the anointing and authority we need to outwit the enemy.

There Is a New Strength

Psalm 89:21 says, "With whom My hand shall be established; also My arm shall strengthen him." Strength means to have power, vigor, might, energy and fervency. But another definition of strength is to have power by reason of influence, authority or resources. Our covenant with God positions us for strength over the enemy by the very influence, authority and resources He makes available to us.

Having strength also means having power to withstand an attack. Isaiah 52:1 says, "Awake, awake! Put on your strength, O Zion; put on your beautiful garments." Strength is something that we actually have to put on. We need to review the condition of our armor and repair every place that has been weakened through apathy or a spirit of slumber, which can rob us of strength. We need to order our prayers and allow our steps to be ordered of the Lord. In doing so, we will gain the strength necessary for the war that lies ahead. This exercise is also an important part of receiving the new anointing God has for us.

We Will Not Be Outwitted by the Enemy

"The enemy shall not outwit him, nor the son of wickedness afflict him" (Ps. 89:22, *NKJV*). The *New International Version* reads, "No enemy will subject him to tribute; no wicked man will oppress him." Because of our covenant position with God, we stand clean and blameless before Him through the blood of Jesus. Therefore, we are not indebted to the enemy, and we need not be outwitted or afflicted by him.

Instead, we have the power to thwart the devil's attempts to steal from us. He is, in fact, in debt to us, and because of our covenant position, we have a right to demand back through strategic prayer what Satan has stolen.

God Will Take a Stand on Our Behalf

Psalm 89:23 says, "I will beat down his foes before his face, and plague those who hate him." Because we are in covenant with the Lord, He displays Himself to overthrow the power of the enemy on our behalf:

> So shall they fear the name of the LORD from the west, and His glory from the rising of the sun; when the enemy comes in like a flood, the Spirit of the LORD will lift up a standard against him (Isa. 59:19).

In Old Testament times, a standard was a token of protection and fidelity. According to the *New Unger's Bible Dictionary*, God's lifting or setting up of a standard implies a peculiar presence, protection and aid in leading and directing His people in the execution of His righteous will and gives them comfort and peace in His service.[2] Our covenant with the Lord positions us under His powerful standard.

Using these four principles derived from God's covenant promises to David, we too can outwit the devil through our own covenant relationship with Him. By appropriating the strategic prayer available to us because of our access to God through covenant, the revelation that is needed is available so that we can advance victoriously every step of the way. This alone should motivate you to pursue a strong, active prayer life and a prayer ministry.

Four Types of Prayer for Outwitting the Devil

Not all prayer is the same. A prayer of supplication, for example, accomplishes something much different from a prayer of thanksgiving and praise. Let's look at four different types of prayer the Lord has given us to outwit the devil in the days ahead as we seek to fulfill the Great Commission. While each of these types of prayer can be valuable for our personal lives, we will present these in the context of working toward great breakthroughs for entire cities and territories and advancing the gospel throughout the earth.

1. Prayer of Agony, or Travail

> Be in pain, and labor to bring forth, O daughter of Zion, like a woman in birth pangs. For now you shall go forth from the city, you shall dwell in the field, and to Babylon you shall go. There you shall be delivered; there the LORD will redeem you from the hand of your enemies (Mic. 4:10).

One of the most poignant biblical examples of agonizing before God is the story of Hannah. As the story opens, Israel was in moral decay as a nation. The priesthood had fallen into total disarray.

Nevertheless, as required by the Law, a man named Elkanah took his entire family to Shiloh to offer sacrifices and worship the Lord.

Hannah, one of Elkanah's two wives, was barren. The destiny of her creation had not been fulfilled, and this lack of fulfillment had led her into grief and affliction of spirit, which the Bible calls "bitterness of soul" (1 Sam. 1:10). At the tabernacle of the Lord, Hannah wept in anguish and made this vow:

> O LORD of hosts, if You will indeed look on the affliction of Your maidservant and remember me, and not forget Your maidservant, but will give Your maidservant a male child, then I will give him to the LORD all the days of his life, and no razor shall come upon his head (v. 11).

Hannah agonized before the Lord to give her a child. The priest Eli was seated nearby and saw her lips move but did not hear her words. He thought she was drunk and rebuked her. But Hannah opened her heart and honestly expressed her grief to Eli, who answered, "Go in peace, and the God of Israel grant your petition which you have asked of Him" (v. 17). Hannah soon conceived and gave birth to the prophet Samuel.

Hannah was a woman of great faith and destiny whose agonizing provides a great pattern for us to follow:

1. She prayed to the Lord.
2. She wept in anguish (travailed).
3. She lifted her affliction to Lord.
4. She said, "Remember me"; in other words, "Remember why I was created."
5. She pleaded, "Fulfill my request and You can have my firstfruits offering."
6. She told the priest her problem and expressed her emotion.
7. She asked for favor to come upon her.
8. She got up in victory.
9. She birthed a new thing in Israel.

Hannah then fulfilled her vow to the Lord by giving her child to the priest, an act that would change the course of Israel. Samuel began to prophesy as a young man and the nation began to shift, although not everything went well. While Eli was still priest, Israel was defeated in war with the Philistines. As a result, they lost the Ark of the Covenant, which represented God's presence among them. This defeat, however, set the nation of Israel on a course that would restore the presence of God in the land, and David would return the Ark to its resting place in Jerusalem years later.

Travailing Produces Birth

Travailing may be defined as a painfully difficult or burdensome work, particularly the anguish or suffering associated with the labor of childbirth. You may be wondering, *What does that have to do with prayer?*

When Hannah approached the Lord, she was in anguish over her circumstances. Her plea to God came from the very depths of her being. Her agony before the Lord did not arise simply from an emotional response to an unmet need or desire in her life; rather, it rose up out of her spirit because the destiny for which she had been created had gone unfulfilled. At the time Hannah did not know she had been chosen to give birth to a great prophet and judge of Israel. But somewhere in her spirit she knew that she could not settle for barrenness. She knew that was not God's portion for her life.

Before Hannah gave physical birth to Samuel, she travailed for and birthed something spiritually that overcame the curse of barrenness—not only in her own body but, ultimately, for the nation of Israel. When we travail in prayer, we allow the Holy Spirit to birth something through us.

Cindy Jacobs says, "There are times when we are called by God to pray strong prayer and help to birth the will of God into [an] area":

Usually there is a sense of wonder after the prayer, and a sense that God has done something through it. . . . Here are four points to help you recognize the work of the Holy Spirit:

1. Travail is given by God and is not something we can make happen. Travail is often a deep groaning inside, which may be audible or which cannot be uttered, as described in Romans 8:26.

2. Travail sometimes comes as a result of praying in an area that others have prayed about before you. God then chooses you to be one of the last pray-ers before the matter is accomplished. You are the one who gives birth to the answer.

3. Those with the gift of intercession will often pray more travailing prayers than those [without the gift].

4. The travail may be short or extended. Some prayers will be accomplished quickly, and some will be like labor pangs at different times until the birth of the answer comes.[3]

How Travailing Prayer Works

There is tremendous power in travailing prayer because it births the will of God on Earth. This type of prayer always outflanks the devil, who is so strongly opposed by the new thing God is producing as a result of travail. Therefore, we need to have an understanding of what God is wanting to birth through us. We, like Hannah, need to be in tune with what God is ready to bring forth in this hour. That can only be done through intimacy with God and a willingness to allow Him to use us in travail.

Once we identify the burden God wants us to pray about, we begin to agonize and feel a sense of urgency like that of a mother in labor. The burden becomes our own baby, as God's heart for seeing that thing brought forth begins to press down on our spirits. With this burden comes an oppression, but it's not the oppression of the devil. If your assignment, for instance, is a travail to break oppression over a certain family on God's heart, you may actually begin to feel the oppression they are under. War until the oppression breaks—until, as in natural childbirth, the opening in the second heaven (see chapter 3) is large enough that God's will can come forth on the earth.

Some Cautions

Because travailing is such an intense and often misunderstood form of prayer, we offer some cautions.

Timing. We cannot simply enter into travailing prayer by choice any more than a woman can choose to enter into labor before her time. It is something the Holy Spirit chooses to do in His time and through whom He chooses, as long as we are open to allowing Him to work travail through us. If we try to birth something before its season, like a baby born prematurely, it is much more susceptible to destruction and death than that which is born in due season.

Becoming overwhelmed. Cindy Jacobs offers a helpful word on this subject:

> Many times travail can be so strong that it seems to overwhelm the intercessor. Those around need to intercede for the one in travail if this happens in a group situation. We need to help bear the burden in prayer. . . . We also need to bind the enemy from entering into the travail. One word of caution. The Holy Spirit will rule over our emotions in a time of travail. We must be sure that we don't let our emotions run wild. Intercessors need to walk in the fruit of self-control.[4]

Bearing a false burden. If someone enters travail but does not have God's burden, they will accomplish nothing. Isaiah 26:18 says, "We have been with child, we have been in pain; we have, as it were, brought forth wind; we have not accomplished any deliverance in the earth, nor have the inhabitants of the world fallen." Many well-meaning Christians travail with the wind because they do not understand God's heart in a matter and move forward in presumption. They either do not know or have not taken the time with God to identify with what He is doing. Instead, they go straight into intercession and get lost in it somewhere.

Not completing the assignment. "This day is a day of trouble, and rebuke, and blasphemy; for the children have come to birth, but there is no strength to bring them forth" (2 Kings 19:3). There are instances in which the timing is right and the burden is right, but we have no strength to bring forth the new thing. We must not grow weary in Spirit, but rather, we must allow God to give us the strength we need to complete our travailing prayer.

2. Prayer of Confrontation

To confront someone or something means to face them in hostility or defiance, or to come with opposition. Unlike the prayer of travail, which brings forth new birth, the prayer of confrontation directly addresses a structure that has been set in place in opposition to God's will.

The prayer of confrontation has become known in missiological terms as a power encounter. C. Peter Wagner defines a power encounter as "a visible, practical demonstration that Jesus Christ is more powerful than the spirits, powers or false gods worshiped or feared by the members of a given people group."[5]

This type of prayer not only outwits the devil but also humiliates him and his forces in the process. God allows us to enter into this type of encounter to show His power over the territorial spirit(s) to which a particular group of people has been in bondage. As God displays that His power is greater than that of a given demonic structure, that structure begins to crumble and those who were held captive are then free to follow Christ.

Moses' Great Confrontation

A wonderful biblical model for this type of prayer was Moses' confrontation with Pharaoh. As Moses declared God's will to Pharaoh in the earthly realm, he was also confronting in the spiritual realm the gods of Egypt—false deities (territorial spirits) linked with the oppression and captivity of God's covenant people. Through the plagues and destruction unleashed upon the nation of Egypt as a result of Moses' confrontation, God's plan was fulfilled, the power of oppression was broken, and His people were released.

Let's take a look at how each demonstration of God's power through Moses was actually a power encounter with a specific Egyptian god.

The Rod Becomes a Serpent (Exodus 7:8-12)

Two main Egyptian gods were linked with serpents. Apep was the Egyptian snake god, the personification of darkness and evil. Edjo, the serpent goddess of the Delta, was the protectress of Lower Egypt and was symbolized on the royal diadem (crown) as protection for the king. When Aaron's rod became a serpent and swallowed the magicians' serpents, there was an undeniable display of whose power was stronger.

The Nile Turns to Blood (Exodus 7:14-25)

In this first plague, God demonstrated His power over Khnum, the ram god who was the supposed protector of the source of the Nile, and over Hapy, god of the Nile in inundation. Although the court magicians were able to imitate the phenomenon, they were unable to stop the effects of the plague. So the fish died and the water became putrid and undrinkable.

The Plague of Frogs (Exodus 8:1-15)

The second plague was directed against Heqet, the goddess of creation, birth and the germination of corn. Heqet was depicted as a frog, which was considered a sacred animal in Egypt. Once again, the magicians were able to imitate the plague but were unable to remove it. So Pharaoh had to summon Moses and Aaron to put a stop to it.

The Plague of Lice (Exodus 8:16-19)

This third plague came against Geb, the Egyptian earth god that was believed to play a role in fertility and vegetation.

Geb was also supposed to imprison the souls of the dead, and his laughter was said to cause earthquakes. The magicians were unable to reproduce the sign of the lice and conceded to Pharaoh, "This is the finger of God" (v. 19).

The Plague of Flies (Exodus 8:20-24)

"If you will not let My people go, behold, I will send swarms of flies on you and your servants, on your people and into your houses. The houses of the Egyptians shall be full of swarms of flies, and also the ground on which they stand" (v. 21). This plague was set against Dua, the Egyptian god of toiletry. This fourth plague made clear that God was the author of the plagues and had authority in the land over the gods the Egyptians served.

The Cattle Die (Exodus 9:1-7)

Hathor, the Egyptian cow goddess, was next in line for humiliation at the hands of God's wrath. She was the suckler of the king and the goddess of love, fertility and women. She was also said to cleanse the land of unbelievers. This plague was a judgment from God and a direct insult to the religious hierarchy, as calves, cows and bulls were all worshiped and considered sacred by the Egyptians.

The Plague of Boils (Exodus 9:8-12)

The sixth plague came against Imhotep, venerated as the god of learning and medicine. The magicians appeared to try to protect the Pharaoh, probably through Imhotep's power, but were instead attacked themselves.

The Plague of Hail and Fire (Exodus 9:12-35)

The seventh plague challenged Horus the Elder, the powerful falconlike deity and originally the sky god, who was identified with the king during his lifetime. This was the first plague that apparently caused human death—

enough so that Pharaoh even admitted he had sinned and begged for the plague to be stopped (see Exod. 9:27-28).

The Plague of Locusts (Exodus 10:12-15)
The eighth plague targeted Shu, god of the air, the atmosphere and dry winds. It was through an east wind that lasted for a day and a night that the Lord ushered in swarms of locusts that "covered the face of the whole earth, so that the land was darkened; and they ate every herb of the land and all the fruit of the trees which the hail had left. So there remained nothing green on the trees or on the plants of the field throughout all the land of Egypt" (v. 15).

The Plague of Darkness (Exodus 10:21-23)
The ninth plague demonstrated God's power over the light of the sun and one of Egypt's chief deities, the sun god Ra. Ra was thought to be the father of the gods, head of the great ennead (a group of the nine most powerful deities) and supreme judge. This plague dealt a heavy blow to the evil powers and principalities of the spirit world.

The Slaying of the First Born (Exodus 12:29-33)
The tenth and most devastating plague was directed against a family of three deities. The first was Isis, the most important of all Egyptian goddesses, who assumed all the attributes and functions of virtually every other important goddess at some point in Egyptian history. Her primary functions were motherhood, marital devotion, healing the sick and the working of magic spells and charms. The second deity was Osiris, the god of the dead and the ruler, protector and judge of the deceased. The third deity was the son of Isis and Osiris, Horus the Child, a suckling child represented as a young boy sucking his finger. This final plague so overwhelmed the Pharaoh and so thoroughly defeated the gods of Egypt that the Israelites were finally set free.[6]

God's power has not diminished in the years since Moses! Power encounters through the prayer of confrontation that see people groups released from demonic structures are going to become more and more common as we enter the future war of the Church. We need to enter into an expectant mindset that believes God will display His power greatly over the earth and over demonic structures in order to see great throngs loosed from Satan's grip. And from that mindset, we must pray with unwavering faith prayers of confrontation according to His will.

3. Inquiring of the Lord: Releasing Strategic Revelation

Inquiring of the Lord is a prayer in which the desires of your heart are expressed to the Lord with an expectation that He will answer with revelation and overcoming strategy. Many in the Bible prayed this type of prayer, and in answer, God showed them how to overthrow their enemies and secure victory.

David often prayed the prayer of inquiry. Time and again we see him inquiring of the Lord and receiving the strategic revelation he needed to overcome the enemy at hand. Here are three examples of instances in which David inquired of the Lord, received strategic revelation and acted on that revelation. In each case, the revelation he received led to victory.

1. *1 Samuel 23:1-5*

Then they told David, saying, "Look, the Philistines are fighting against Keilah, and they are robbing the threshing floors." Therefore David inquired of the LORD, saying, "Shall I go and attack these Philistines?" And the LORD said to David, "Go and attack the Philistines, and save Keilah." But David's men said to him, "Look, we are afraid here in Judah. How much more then if we go to Keilah against the armies of the Philistines?" Then David inquired of the LORD once again. And the LORD answered him and said, "Arise, go down to Keilah. For I will deliver the Philistines into your hand."

And David and his men went to Keilah and fought with the Philistines, struck them with a mighty blow, and took away their livestock. So David saved the inhabitants of Keilah.

2. *1 Samuel 30:8,17-19*
So David inquired of the LORD, saying, "Shall I pursue this troop? Shall I overtake them?" And He answered him, "Pursue, for you shall surely overtake them and without fail recover all." Then David attacked them from twilight until the evening of the next day. Not a man of them escaped, except four hundred young men who rode on camels and fled. So David recovered all that the Amalekites had carried away, and David rescued his two wives. And nothing of theirs was lacking, either small or great, sons or daughters, spoil or anything which they had taken from them; David recovered all.

3. *2 Samuel 5:19-25*
So David inquired of the LORD, saying, "Shall I go up against the Philistines? Will You deliver them into my hand?" And the LORD said to David, "Go up, for I will doubtless deliver the Philistines into your hand." So David went to Baal Perazim, and David defeated them there; and he said, "The LORD has broken through my enemies before me, like a breakthrough of water." Therefore he called the name of that place Baal Perazim. And they left their images there, and David and his men carried them away. Then the Philistines went up once again and deployed themselves in the Valley of Rephaim. Therefore David inquired of the LORD, and He said, "You shall not go up; circle around behind them, and come upon them in front of the mulberry trees. And it shall be, when you hear the sound of marching in the tops of the mulberry trees, then you shall advance quickly. For then the LORD will go out before you to strike the camp of the Philistines." And David did so, as the LORD commanded him; and he drove back the Philistines from Geba as far as Gezer.

David enjoyed remarkable success over his enemies because of his access to God through covenant and because he inquired of the Lord and heard from Him. Others in the Old Testament who did not have such access to God had to use various articles to hear Him. For instance, the Urim and the Thummim were gems, or stones, carried by the high priest that were cast, like dice, to determine God's will in certain matters to help the priest in making important decisions.

But we do not have to rely on devices. We, like David, have the right to enter into the throne room of God and inquire of Him. Furthermore, because of our position with Him, we should expect to hear the answers that will provide us with strategic revelation to overcome the enemy! Here are four steps to help you in praying the prayer of inquiry to gain your revelation for victory:

1. *Receive a new anointing.* Earlier in the chapter we discussed a new anointing, but it bears repeating here: The Lord is bringing a new anointing to His people. That anointing will cause prophetic words that have been dormant to be activated in the atmosphere. The anointing breaks the yoke. Go with a receptive heart to where the anointing is moving.

2. *Open your eyes and you will see the path of victory.* If you come into a new place of intimacy and communion with God, your eyes will be opened to see new strategies that break the enemy's power. Don't be afraid to get your knees dirty. Crawl through that narrow place and surprise your enemy.

3. *Don't allow the enemy's backlash to throw you off course.* Many of God's people begin to know victory but then fall short. When the enemy sees a believer moving in a new anointing, he raises up new forces to come against the believer. When you sense this backlash, or retaliation, dampening your victory, don't let fear engulf you.

Stop and pray. Just as David did, ask the Lord if you are to war or to wait. If you hear Him say, "War!" then do it!

4. *Don't drop your shield until you see your enemy completely pushed back.* Even after victory occurs, stay alert to the enemy's movements. Anytime you discern the enemy's presence, inquire of the Lord. Creativity is needed to utterly defeat the enemy. Where you went one way and had a strategy yesterday, today there will be a new path to take, much like we saw in the passage above from 2 Samuel 5. God is faithful morning by morning. Receive your direction from the Lord and see the enemy (who has encroached on your territory) totally removed.

4. Breakthrough Prayer

To break means to cause to come apart by force; to separate in pieces by shattering; to burst and force one's way through, resulting in splitting a barrier; to interrupt or bring about suspension of an operation. There are times when God calls us to use prayer to break the power of the enemy over an area of our lives or over a city or territory.

The enemy will often attempt to ensnare us in a vicious cycle through adverse circumstances. Satan will attempt to weaken our faith, disillusion us and keep us going around Mount Sinai until we are so weary that we may forget there *is* a Promised Land. We can see a similar sense of desperation come over a territory that Satan has held captive for a period of time.

We must use the power of breakthrough prayer to smash the vicious cycle of unbelief and declare a breaking of the enemy's scheme. This type of prayer is important to understand and employ for the future war of the Church.

Earthquake in Turkey

There is no doubt that God still displays His mighty power on Earth today, just as He did in the days of Moses. At the end of the twentieth century, this fact was reinforced to many of us through events that took place in Turkey.

In 1998, I joined Peter and Doris Wagner of Global Harvest Ministries in spearheading a mission project called Operation Queen's Palace. The primary focus of this project was to pray that the demonic entity known as the Queen of Heaven would let loose her grip over the region. The central focus of our prayer was the city of Ephesus.

Why did we focus on Ephesus? First of all, one of the greatest revivals in Church history occurred in Ephesus (see Acts 19:10,17-20). In what is now the nation of Turkey, the Early Church was prominent and thriving. Today, that once-thriving body of believers is now a church of approximately 1,200 among a population of 65 million! When we began to look at the region's history, we knew that the Lord would show us both patterns of how the Church came to thrive there as well as patterns of how the Church had since declined so dramatically.

So in 1998 we began an organized thrust to pray for this region of the world, a thrust that was to culminate with Celebration Ephesus in October 1999. In preparation for Celebration Ephesus, we sent 16 prayer teams throughout Europe and Turkey to pray breakthrough prayers for the area. Our last team was still in Istanbul when one of the greatest earthquakes ever recorded hit the region on August 17, 1999, killing thousands. The eyes of the world turned toward Turkey, and hearts were filled with compassion.

Almost immediately the love of God was poured out on the people of that nation! The Turkish people saw the love of Christ manifested through His people responding to their need and bringing relief. A TV reporter in Turkey quoted the proverb "A Turk has no friend but another Turk." He then stated, "But with the outpouring of foreign aid, that proverb is no longer true!"

Perhaps because of this tragic event and the love of Christ that was experienced in this nation as a result, thousands upon thousands will turn and come to know the Lord's saving grace.

Why?

Why did disaster strike after we prayed for breakthrough in Turkey? Could it be that prayer can actually effect such a dramatic change in the spiritual atmosphere over a region that it visibly and unalterably affects the natural environment on a similar level? Admittedly, many of our team members were perplexed by these events in the region where they had concentrated their prayers so heavily.

I believe informed intercession is like an arrow, penetrating a region and creating change so that the gospel can advance. Matthew 28:2 says, "And behold, there was a great earthquake; for an angel of the Lord descended from heaven, and came and rolled back the stone." When Jesus faced off against the power of hell that was stopping the world's redemption, creation could not remain the same. Even though He was entombed, death had been defeated and no structure on Earth could withstand the change that the Lord had released in the heavenly realm.

When there is such a spiritual breakthrough that angelic forces come down from the heavens and visit the earth in any region, creation responds to this visitation and the natural order is rearranged. This often produces the change necessary for the gospel to advance throughout a region. At the end of Matthew 28, such a great shaking occurred, and we find the Lord commissioning us to go throughout the world and exercise His authority to all nations until the end of the age. We will continue to see similar events as we take His gospel to all the world.

Advance of the Gospel in Central America and Japan

Two great modern examples of spiritual breakthrough occurred in Central America and Japan. Wagner has written about the tremendous Church growth that has taken place in the countries of Guatemala and Nicaragua:

> Studies have shown that the accelerated rate of growth in both those countries can be traced back to their respective earthquakes. The earthquakes created instant needs, the evangelicals were sensitive enough and sufficiently able to

locate the resources to help meet those needs. The result? Large numbers of people became receptive to the gospel as a result. Again, change has helped to ripen the harvest.[7]

Wagner goes on to tell the story of Japan:

> Japanese Christians speak nostalgically of the "seven wonderful years." They refer to the seven years immediately following World War II when the American military was occupying the country. The Japanese had considered their emperor a god, and the war was a holy war for them. Then they lost, and the emperor admitted that he was no god at all. A spiritual vacuum was created which allowed Japanese Christianity to experience its greatest growth in modern times.[8]

Not Afraid to Pray!

Don't be afraid to confront those things in your area that would hinder spiritual breakthrough and deliverance. God is now burdening His people for prayer throughout the earth. We feel His urgency within to liberate those who are held captive. Do not be afraid to pray! Although there may be dramatic and unforeseen results, such as the earthquake in Turkey, God's ultimate purpose will be accomplished.

Any time we pray and the earth responds with shaking, flooding, fires or drought, we need to be ready to respond with Christ's love and an expression of His fullness to the affected region. If nothing else, the Turkish earthquake has changed the way the people there perceive Christianity.

Pray boldly for change to come. Such prayer can alter the course of the world.

The Emerging Apostolic Prayer Movement

I have been privileged to work with many ministries to mobilize thousands of intercessors in strategic prayer for harvest. We have also known the joy of sharing in the visions of others for citywide

and national spiritual breakthrough. We have watched from front-
row seats the unfolding of God's plan for developing a praying
Church. What an honor!

With the rise of the New Apostolic Reformation and the
restoration of the apostle, the Church is experiencing a new level of
authority. Captives are being released in dynamic ways, and we are
seeing the crumbling of traditional spiritual strongholds. Apostolic
authority, combined with the valuable role of the prophet, is allowing us to mobilize intercession with incredible results.

Recently I had a dream. In the dream there was a huge balcony
that overlooked a valley beyond description in its depth and width.
On the balcony were key leaders. Each leader was summoned to
stand at a certain point in time and to call forth across the valley in
a loud voice. By the command of the leader's voice, those individuals who were like the leader came from the sides of the valley into a
formation. This happened over and over in the dream until the valley was filled.

The valley was a most amazing sight to behold with people of
every race and color forming row after row as far as the eye could
see. Then, as if by supernatural command, all the leaders on the
balcony arose. When this occurred, the whole valley burst into celebration, and each knew how to follow his or her leader into the
place they would be commanded to go. As each leader departed
the balcony, those who were connected to that person followed
after that leader into their next assignment. As I awakened, incredible joy swelled up in my heart, and I felt excitement as well as a
tinge of fear of the unknown.

Immediately the Spirit of God began to reveal to me what
He was communicating through this dream. He showed me the
vast army He was gathering from around the world. He also
showed me that the troops understood leadership and their
leaders' voices, and that the leaders were fully submitted to the
common purpose of advancement. He also revealed that these
leaders all knew their proper timing, purpose and direction, so
that those whom they had responsibility for would not be in
confusion when the time came to move forward. God showed

me the *kairos* moment He had designated for His army to march.

Suddenly, I had a name for that which I saw through the revelation of the dream: the Emerging Apostolic Global Prayer Movement. To emerge means to come out and come forth into view. It also means to rise from obscurity or to reappear after being eclipsed, to leave the sphere of the obscuring object. To emerge means to come into sight from a hidden place, as a train emerging from a tunnel. The global prayer movement is now like a powerful locomotive moving at high speed, and it is about to emerge in a new dimension of power!

In a recent article, Wagner described 10 major prayer innovations of the '90s. He noted that the change in the course of prayer in the Church has changed the course of the world. Innovations such as identificational repentance, strategic-level spiritual warfare, on-site praying and spiritual mapping stamped an indelible mark on the progress of the prayer movement. The progress made through these prayer innovations has become the basis for how we now conduct effective spiritual warfare.[9]

When the first decade of this new millennium draws to a close, what prayer innovations will mark the decade? The essentials will almost certainly include the rise of apostles, prophets and strategic prophetic intercession. The core value for the success of this next series of innovations will be relationships.

Below are four changes we can expect to see as the prayer movement continues to emerge:

1. *Intercessors will receive an increasingly intense burden of God to pray for harvest.* God always begins by communicating His heart to those who will stand in the gap and pave the way for His glory to come to Earth.

2. *Prophetic revelation will be released, revealing strategies for reviving the harvest fields that have long been held in desolation.* The Lord said in Matthew 16:18-19 that He would give us the keys to the Kingdom, and upon this revelation, He would build His Church.

3. *Apostolic leadership with a heart for harvest and an under-standing of the times will begin to arise throughout the earth.* At every major turning point in the Church, the Lord has called forth leaders who understand the times and His methods for advancing the Kingdom.

4. *Supernatural connection and communication between apos-tolic and prophetic leadership will begin to occur.* Apostles and prophets worked together throughout biblical his-tory to usher in key moves of the Spirit of God. A new connection between these two governmental gifts is now releasing vision and setting an order for harvest.

Another phenomenon we can expect to see is prophetic inter-cessors (who know how to break through the powers of darkness) connecting with the apostolic leadership that God is raising up. I was in Singapore recently when the following phrase came into my heart: *Strategic prophetic intercession must be properly aligned with apos-tolic government for spiritual breakthrough and harvest to occur.*

We must pray that communication among intercessors becomes very effective and that it connects properly with apostolic leadership and vision. This is different from what occurred in the last decade of prayer. Intercessors paved the way for where we are now, but they had not connected with apostolic vision. When apostles and intercessors connect, we are going to see a whole new level of urgent, fervent prayer that will truly outwit the devil!

God's Unfolding Revelation: Apostolic Prayer Watchmen

The prayer movement in America and worldwide continues to grow. The movement of God is probably stronger now than ever before in the history of the Church. One reason for this is because of communication—we are better connected now than ever before. Many ministries have devoted entire departments to strategic prayer. Each U.S. state has a major prayer movement.

The Church is changing from a movement that prays to an apostolic, prophetic army decreeing change in the earth. At the beginning of 2006, I wrote the following:

> There is a need for key apostolic/prophetic authorities in territories to be connected with the prayer movement. We must know who we are serving with and how to communicate in days ahead very quickly and efficiently. *The Prayer Movement is shifting rapidly.* Over the last 15 years, we have seen the Lord use His intercessors to pave the way for the maturing apostolic movement—now the prayer movement will unlock the apostolic movement in a new way. This will cause the kingdom of God to advance, demonic powers and territorial structures of the enemy to be bound, worship gatherings to change the atmosphere of entire states and harvest storehouses to be developed.

Peter Wagner has given a charge to the prayer movement to advance into apostolic decreeing. Prayer and intercession is what creates the wine that changes the wineskin. Cindy Jacobs, a leader in the prayer movement, prophesied the following in 2006:

> It is time to shift the prayer movement. We must become apostolic in our expression. We must find the intercessors and the prophets and align them with the apostles in each state. If each leader of the present movement will shift, their state will shift. If this shift does not occur, the Lord said, "My kingdom will not be established from state to state and a nation will suffer greatly."

Cindy also admonished us to receive a new anointing that would be a powerful new expression of the old and to move from a network of intercessors to an apostolic network that would change the course of this nation. In response to this word from the Lord, the U.S. Global Apostolic Prayer Network has been developed in all 50 states.

Other nations, such as Mexico, are now beginning to request we help them mobilize their prayer movements. The Body must go to the next level. I see the watch of the Lord as a key for us to make this shift.[10] The prayer movement must continually change. We will move from praying intercessors to apostolic, decreeing watchmen. Apostles will watch for strategies to unlock harvest fields. Prophets will become decreeing intercessors. Intercessors will become bolder and bolder as they enter into the Throne Room. God is raising up harvest watchmen!

CHAPTER SIX

The Transference of Wealth

For all we have and are,
For all our children's fate,
Stand up and take the war.
The Hun is at the gate!
RUDYARD KIPLING (1865-1936)

Some nations increase, others diminish, and in a short space the genera-
tions of living creatures are changed.
LUCRETIUS (99-55 B.C.)

Once we are praying strategically and with power and our prayers are properly linked from the head (Jesus) to vision-driven apostolic leadership on Earth, we will begin to see a tremendous increase in the harvest. God is pouring out upon His people a mind for increasing His kingdom. We, therefore, need to allow Him to give us this mind and desire for building.

When Nehemiah set about rebuilding the wall of Jerusalem, he said the people had a mind to work (see Neh. 4:6). The people had a mind to build the thing that God wanted built. We need to have this same mindset. If our minds are not connected to the mind of Christ, if we do not desire to build His house on Earth, that which He wants to accomplish in our generation will not come to fruition.

Building with a Mind for Increase

If we are to tap into God's mind for building, we must have a biblical understanding of increase. When we look at the concept of increase in the Word of God, we see that it is often linked with government. Isaiah 9:7 says, "Of the increase of His government and peace there will be no end."

Increase is a harvest principle. The Hebrew word for "building," *banah*, signifies the adding of sons and daughters so that the plan of God can be passed from one generation to another.

Increase rises through faith and follows effort and deeds linked with faith. Increase also comes through connecting with one another. When we are linked together, when we eschew independence, we gain strength in multiplied corporate measure.

Increase is also a reward for obedience. There is joy in obedience (see Col. 1:9-11), and the joy of the Lord causes our strength to increase (see Neh. 8:10). With such strength we are capable of building according to God's strategic plan for the future.

In the book of Matthew, we find Jesus' plan for building His Church. In Matthew 16:13, He asks His disciples what the people are saying about Him. They tell Him that some think of Him as a powerful prophet, while others think He is Elijah returned. Jesus asks, "But who do you say that I am?" (v. 15). Peter replies, "You are the Christ, the Son of the living God" (v. 16). What a revelation!

> Jesus answered and said to him, "Blessed are you, Simon Bar-Jonah, for flesh and blood has not revealed this to you, but My Father who is in heaven. And I also say to you that you are Peter, and on this rock I will build My church, and the gates of Hades shall not prevail against it. And I will give you the keys of the kingdom of heaven, and whatever you bind on earth will be bound in heaven, and whatever you loose on earth will be loosed in heaven" (Matt. 16:17-19).

We can glean two main principles from Jesus' words with regard to building: (1) You build out of revelation; and (2) you are given keys to see the fulfillment of God's kingdom purpose for your life.

Peter had a revelation of who Jesus was, and from that revelation the Church began to be built. Today, many in the Church want to build by beginning with revival, and many of these believe that revival grows out of repentance. But you can't repent without revelation. You've got to know who God is to see how far you've drifted from His character. Once you begin to see who God truly is, everything in your life will be built on that revelation of Him.

Revelation and authority are closely linked. Jesus says, "I will give you the keys, and you will be able to forbid or permit entry" (see v. 19). God is saying to us in this hour that He is ready to give us keys. These keys will unlock the supply we need to advance His covenant purposes. These keys will allow us to forbid hindrance to His purpose and to release His will on Earth.

When Jesus gave these keys to Peter, the scribes of the day had the authority to study the Scriptures and then communicate to the people what was written in the Scriptures. And yet Jesus knew that the scribes were not really communicating His building plan to the people. So what He was really saying to Peter was that He was taking the keys to the Kingdom from the scribes and handing them over to the disciples. He was giving them authority to forbid or permit (bind or loose) based on the revelation of His authority.

We know that Jesus eventually made His disciples into apostles, and they went forward unlocking the kingdom of God throughout the region. For this purpose God gave them the material resources needed to build His house in that day and season. We find this principle in Acts 4:32-37. This was the beginning of the harvest that occurred after the ascension of the Lord, and that harvest has continued down through the generations. The harvest has been more plentiful in some generations than in others. However, we are about to see the harvest accelerate, and we will need to have a mind for increase in the Kingdom if we are to be a part of this move of God.

Apostolic Authority:
Unlocking the Gates to the Harvest Fields

As we have stated, this is a *kairos*, or strategic, time for the Body of Christ to enter the harvest fields and begin to reap the harvest. It is a time to unfetter that which has been held captive and bound by the enemy. Now is the time to unlock the gates to fields and bring the harvest into the storehouse.

To unlock the gates, we must recognize and come against the illegal domination of demonic structures from region to region. To this end, prayer teams have traveled the world, praying and mapping these structures. But we must also arrive at an understanding of apostolic spheres and authority, for no illegal spiritual dominion will be able to stand against the Church if we embrace and implement God's design and authority structure.

Every field has the potential within to yield a harvest. Every farmer knows that in due season, there is a short window of opportunity in which to gather the crops of the field. I believe the Church is now entering into that window of opportunity for an unprecedented harvest of souls, and we must begin to pray accordingly.

When the Lord talks of harvest, He expresses His heart for harvesting a field of souls on Earth:

> But when He saw the multitudes, He was moved with compassion for them, because they were weary and scattered, like sheep having no shepherd. Then He said to His disciples, "The harvest truly is plentiful, but the laborers are few. Therefore pray the Lord of the harvest to send out laborers into His harvest" (Matt. 9:36-38).

To answer the Lord's call to harvest, we must have eyes to see the multitudes, a heart of compassion and a willingness to be sent to the fields the Lord has assigned to us.

Each of us has a field—the place to which the Lord has called us. In that field are many resources, the most precious resource being people. The Lord has also provided certain material resources that must be unlocked if we are to accomplish His call to harvest. Without the wealth necessary to cultivate and sow the land and harvest the crop, the field grows fallow. We will discuss this further later in the chapter.

In Matthew 9:36-38, Jesus commissions the disciples to go forth into the field. This is how apostolic authority begins. Remember, these were the Lord's disciples. The word "disciple" means "learner."

However, the word "apostle" (*apostolos*) refers to a special messenger, one commissioned for a particular task or one who is sent forth with a message. Apostolic authority must be established in a field if we are to reap the harvest of that field. Therefore, we find in Matthew 10 the Lord promoting and commissioning His disciples into a new apostolic realm, to go forth and cultivate the harvest in those places where He sent them.

In His commissioning of the apostles, we see the pattern for how the Lord cultivates and harvests a region.

1. *Jesus instructed His apostles concerning the scope of their mission.* He told them they were not called at that time to go to the Gentiles or to the Samaritans, but rather, they were called to the Jews (see Matt. 10:5-6). We must understand the scope, or boundaries, of what we are called to. Within those boundaries we will have apostolic authority.

   When we think of boundaries, it is good to think of it in terms of dominion. Dominion means the power to govern, or rule, forcing a territory to recognize and subject itself to an authority. Understanding dominion will help us to establish apostolic authority in a region.

   The apostle Paul spoke of apostolic boundaries and dominion. In 2 Corinthians 10, Paul is discussing spiritual warfare when he begins to declare the reality of his apostolic authority and the limit of its territorial boundaries:

   > We, however, will not boast beyond measure, but within the limits of the sphere which God appointed us—a sphere which especially includes you (2 Cor. 10:13, *NKJV*).

   The *New International Version* says, "We will confine our boasting to the *field* God has assigned to us" (emphasis added). Once boundaries are established, we

can unlock the inheritance that lies within those boundaries—and the harvest that lies within those fields.
Once we know our established boundaries, we have
full territorial authority to move within those
boundaries.

2. *Jesus instructed the apostles in the substance of their message.*
   The apostles were to preach that the Kingdom of heav-
   en was at hand (see Matt. 10:7).

3. *Jesus determined the works the apostles were to perform.* The
   apostles would have power over unclean spirits and
   cast them out. They were to heal all kinds of sickness-
   es and diseases. They were to cleanse lepers, and they
   were to raise the dead. Everything the Lord had shown
   them by example, they were to go forth and do in the
   fields to which they were sent (see v. 8).

4. *Jesus designated the equipment and supplies they were to take
   to each field.* Jesus wanted the disciples to be dependent on the people in the place to which they were
   going (see vv. 9-10). This would be one of the ways
   the Father would decide the unlocking of each
   region. If the people received the apostles and gave
   to them and provided for their needs, then the apostles would stay and bless the city (see vv. 11-13). If
   the people would not receive them, the apostles were
   to leave and not even take any dust from that territory (see v. 14). This would determine the Lord's
   judgment of the area (see v. 15).

5. *Jesus explained persevering, apostolic faith.* Disciples have
   to be willing to persevere even in the midst of persecution (see vv. 16-23). False apostles and governmental controls would come against the kingdom of God,
   and there would even be family members who resisted

their message. Without persevering faith, they could never hope to break open a territory.

Apostolic authority is a real key to seeing breakthrough in any region. Apostles have the ability to forgive that which has not been aligned with the purpose of God in a territory (see John 20:23). How apostles are received is a key measuring stick as to how the Lord will release blessings or judgments on a territory. Apostles also have authority over the demonic rulers of a region. They have the ability to demonstrate supernatural power that draws a whole region to our life-giving God.

Binding the Strongman

In Matthew 12:22-29, our Lord addresses the Pharisees concerning the deliverance of a man who had been blind and mute. The Pharisees accuse Jesus of being part of the ruling demonic structure that had blinded the man. But Jesus reminded them that a kingdom divided against itself cannot stand. If Jesus were of Satan's kingdom, then by casting out demons, Satan's own kingdom would be made powerless. Jesus' works, He explained, demonstrated that, in fact, the kingdom of God was among them. Then He sets forth an interesting principle in verse 29:

> How can one enter a strong man's house and plunder his goods, unless he first binds the strong man? And then he will plunder his house.

Jesus' illustration is tied in with prosperity and wealth. First He tells us there is a strong man who rules Satan's kingdom in any territory. This is where we see the Lord beginning to define the hierarchical structure of Satan's kingdom. He also tells us that if we bind the strong man, we can plunder his house and take his spoils.

As apostolic authority arises throughout the earth and aligns with strategic prophetic intercession through spiritual warfare,

I believe we will plunder the enemy's kingdom and unlock the wealth necessary to reap the harvest for the Kingdom in the days ahead.

A Prayer Journey to Unlock Harvest

Operation Queen's Palace, which we introduced in chapter 5, was a direct assault on what is perhaps one of the strongest spirits in Satan's kingdom, the Queen of Heaven. This strategic prayer initiative culminated in an event called Celebration Ephesus, which took place in Turkey. As the prayer leader, it was my job to mobilize prayer for this event. More than 5,000 individuals from around the world gathered to proclaim the kingship of Jesus Christ over this region. We worshiped and prayed for four straight hours in what was the most incredible event I have ever been a part of!

Celebration Ephesus was also the culmination of 10 years of praying through the 10/40 Window, an imaginary window that represents the area of the world most unreached by the gospel. During the event, I asked the Lord, *Where do we go from here?* I knew I was to submit this question to Peter Wagner, who had served as the apostle of the worldwide prayer movement during the '90s. Within two weeks Dr. Wagner had heard clearly from the Lord as to the next assignment for the intercessory leadership throughout the world. Their new assignment was to be the 40/70 Window, an area of the earth that spans from Iceland in the west to Great Britain, through northern and eastern Europe and including all of Russia. Turkey is the hinge nation in this window, the door from the south to this region. Some of the greatest financial wealth in the world is controlled from within this window.

We had confronted the Queen of Heaven where she resided in Turkey, but the 40/70 Window was now her greatest domain. Once Dr. Wagner declared that this geographic area was our new focus, I began to hear from the Lord about the intercessory keys necessary to transfer wealth from the Queen's domain to help fulfill God's covenant plan on Earth.

The questions I asked when inquiring of the Lord could also assist you in learning how to advance the Kingdom in the region you have been assigned to harvest:

Who Is the Strongman in this Region?

We knew that the ruling principality in the 40/70 Window was the Queen of Heaven. Who is the Queen of Heaven? This is a major demonic structure that has been worshiped almost from the beginning of human civilization. It gained power when people began worshiping what they could see—e.g., the moon and stars—instead of pressing in to know and communicate with our holy God. Satan empowered this type of worship through his demonic hordes. This god or goddess, depending on its manifestation, has been worshiped to ensure fertility, agricultural prosperity and material stability (see Jer. 7:18; 44:17). Such worship has long been a major influence in holding people captive to the devil's system.

How Is this Strongman Hoarding the Spoils of the Kingdom?

A biblical example is God's promise to Abraham concerning the Promised Land of Canaan. It wasn't until 470 years after the Lord spoke to Abraham and promised him total victory within these territorial boundaries that the Israelites entered the region to appropriate the promises. The assignment, or mission, that Joshua and the tribes of Israel were to accomplish was a *transference of the wealth* from the inhabitants of that region for the fulfillment of God's covenant Kingdom plan.

How Do We Bind the Powers and Take the Spoils?

As a part of Operation Queen's Palace, a team of 40 intercessors traveled to the original sites of all seven churches addressed in chapters 2 and 3 of the book of Revelation. When we were at Pergamum, Cindy Jacobs was leading the whole team in prayer when the Lord began to burden me concerning the issue of how a demonic structure was holding the wealth of this entire region and how the wealth of the region was being used for works of darkness.

What Is Our Plan of Advancement?

Joshua and God's covenant people needed strategy daily concerning how to advance and possess God's inheritance promised to Abraham. If they were going up against a city, they sought and received their instructions from the Lord as to how to take the spoils of war. Likewise, meditate on God's covenant vision that He has given you to accomplish.

The Plan to Plunder the Queen's Domain

How were we to see a transfer of wealth from the Queen's domain into the kingdom of God? The Lord showed me a path that would lead me to key cities around the world to pray for a release and transference of wealth from the Queen of Heaven. The Lord instructed me that if I would take a team to these places, I would see released the wealth necessary to affect the future harvest on the earth.

So in February 2000, I led a team of intercessors around the world. The purpose of our trip was threefold. First, we desired to connect with and cry out for apostolic leadership to rise up all over the earth. Our second objective was to test the communication system of intercessors that had developed during the previous 10 years. Our third and key objective of the trip was to meet with key leaders in each city and agree with them in prayer for a release of God's covenant wealth in their region.

Strategic prophetic intercessors paved the way for change with their prayers. We knew that if we broke down the spiritual forces that were holding back supply, the wealth needed for the harvest ahead would be released. As we traveled, we learned that there is much revelation and much supply that the Body will need in the days ahead to bring God's harvest plan for this season to completion. In other words, we are going to need money and resources combined with revelation from God in order to complete the task He has given us.

During our intercessory journey, we visited Frankfurt, London, Berlin, Warsaw, Zurich, Singapore, Chicago, Los Angeles, Denver and Colorado Springs. In each city we met with Church leaders, prayed, gave gifts and then went to key places within the city to make declarations of God's will to release wealth there for His kingdom purposes. God moved so mightily that one chapter cannot describe all that happened in every city, so I will recap just a few items to give you an idea of what we saw and learned.

Nazi Loot Returned

As we were traveling around the world, the issue of Jewish wealth stolen during the Holocaust came up, and the Lord led the team to visit Berlin, the seat of power of the Nazi government that orchestrated those horrible events during World War II. Next we went to Warsaw where much of the wealth had been taken from the Jews. From there we flew to Switzerland where much of the stolen wealth was stored.

In his book *The Swiss, the Gold and the Dead*, Jean Ziegler writes:

> Switzerland, the world's only neutral financial center of truly international standing, accepted Hitler's looted gold throughout the war years in payment for industrial goods or as bullion that was fenced and laundered and exchanged for foreign currency or traded off in other financial centers under new, "Swiss" identity.[1]

You can probably imagine the level of intercession this journey led us into. Immediate answers to prayer included the president of Germany asking for forgiveness for the Holocaust only days after we prayed. The Associated Press reported:

> Germany's president delivered an emotional address to Israel's parliament February 16, asking for forgiveness for the Holocaust. Johannes Rau, an Evangelical Christian, spoke to the Knesset in German, a historic first, saying he bowed his head before the 6 million victims, news reports said. Legislators applauded respectfully, but some stayed away in protest, saying they did not want to hear German spoken in parliament. A legislator who had watched Nazi

troops round up Jews in the Warsaw ghetto called German "the language of Satan."

Rau, a longtime friend of Israel, also toured the Yad Vashem Holocaust Memorial. He wrote in the guest book, quoting German clergyman and Nazi dissident Dietrich Bonnhoeffer, "Perhaps Judgment Day will be tomorrow. In that case, we would happily stop [working] for a better future, but not before."[2]

After our return home, we continued to see tangible answers to our prayers. *Time* that month carried an advertisement with the headline "Suppose Your Family Had a Holocaust Era Insurance Policy and You Just Didn't Know About It?" The ad provided information in 23 languages about the Holocaust claim resolution process.

About that same time British museum directors published a list of 350 art treasures displayed in their galleries that they believed may have been stolen by the Nazis during World War II. This first-of-its-kind report listed works worth tens of millions of dollars that may have been among the hundreds of thousands of paintings and sculptures once belonging to Jews and other victims of Hitler's Germany.

A Governmental Shift

The Lord also led our team to pray over the residual issues of Nazism as we were praying over the Holocaust. Another immediate and dramatic answer to prayer came when Jorge Haider, leader of Austria's Freedom Party, resigned amid criticism from the international community including the European Union and the United States. Haider had made public statements expressing admiration for Adolf Hitler's employment policies and describing the Nazi concentration camps as "punishment camps." His resignation helped to neutralize the divisiveness and violence that erupted after Haider's election, and many began to question the resurgence of Nazi ideologies.

These are just a few examples of what happens when we begin to release focused, strategic intercessory prayers and join with those who have been praying through the decades. If we pray, we will see miracles.

Transferring Wealth for Kingdom Advancement

An incredible history book called *The Wealth and Power of the Nations: Why Some Are So Rich and Some So Poor* by David S. Landes is a study of empires and how they gain wealth. Landes is an optimist. Even though many economic experts warn of coming depression, poverty, war, disease and ecological disaster—the horsemen of the apocalypse riding in to bring destruction—he believes there is an incredible future ahead, and I agree with his assessment. Where we differ is that I believe our future is in the hands of a holy God who wants His covenant plan accomplished on Earth.

> Every commandment which I command you today you must be careful to observe, that you may live and multiply, and go in and possess the land of which the LORD swore to your fathers. And you shall remember that the LORD your God led you all the way these forty years in the wilderness, to humble you and test you, to know what was in your heart, whether you would keep His commandments or not (Deut. 8:1-2).

This passage was the charge the Lord gave His people when the time had come for them to enter in and occupy the promise He had given to Abraham 470 years earlier. In every new season in the Church the Lord renews His vision, call and purpose to His Body. We are just maturing in the season God has had us in, and He is now calling His people to enter into the promises He has spoken over their territories to previous generations.

Every time we enter into a new season in the Church, the Lord does the following:

1. He releases new authority.
2. He commissions new leadership.
3. He causes people to desire a new level of His holiness.

4. He communicates new strategies for victory.
5. He transfers the power to gain wealth so that His kingdom purposes can be fulfilled.

Just as the Lord waited nearly five centuries before His people were ready to enter in and receive the promise He made to Abraham, I believe He is waiting for us today.

In every generation it is important to have apostolic leaders who understand the purposes of God and who know how to seek the Lord for revelatory strategy. Joshua led God's covenant people into the territorial boundaries declared in Genesis 15. Joshua received daily strategy for advancing the Lord's armies and possessing the inheritance that had been promised. He was God's leader for the season. If we are going to successfully overcome every obstacle—a city, a people or whatever—we must have individuals who inquire of the Lord and receive instructions from Him about how to advance. And we must know what we are to do with the spoils of war.

Deuteronomy 8:18 tells us, "And you shall remember the LORD your God, for it is He who gives you *power* to get *wealth*, that He may establish His covenant which He swore to your fathers" (emphasis added). "Power" means vigor, strength, force or capacity (whether physical, mental or spiritual). But what does the Bible mean when it speaks of wealth?

A Proper View of Wealth

The Bible has many things to say on the subject of wealth. Here are just a few:

- Wealth is a blessing from God (see Prov. 10:22).
- Wealth is a reward for obedience (see Deut. 7:12-13; Prov. 3:9-10).
- Wealth is a reward for wisdom (see Prov. 8:18,21).
- Wealth is a result of enterprise and useful work (see Prov. 10:4; 12:14; 14:23).

- Wealth is taken away from sinners and given to those who please God (see Prov. 13:22; Eccles. 2:26).
- Wealth is imperfectly distributed in this world, and it is sometimes gained through oppression and injustice (see Prov. 22:16; Amos 2:6; 4:1; 8:4-6).
- Wealth is not an end in itself (see Prov. 23:4; Eccles. 4:8).
- Wealth is potentially a deadly snare (see Eccles. 5:10,13; Matt. 6:24; Luke 16:13).
- Wealth is not guaranteed to believers at all places and all times (see 1 Sam. 2:7; Pss. 69:33; 82:4; 2 Cor. 8:2; Rev. 2:9).
- Wealth is to be shared with the needy (see Prov. 14:21; Eph. 4:28; Jas. 2:15-16; 1 John 3:17).
- Wealth is sometimes to be given away completely (see Luke 12:33; 18:22).

Wealth is generally acknowledged to be a blessing from God. All the patriarchs became very wealthy. Solomon's wealth was seen as God's favor. Job had wealth, lost it and then regained a double portion. Jesus' parable of the talents complimented the servants who multiplied their master's wealth (see Luke 19:11-27). However, He did warn us that the pursuit of riches and pleasure can keep our faith from maturing. Jesus warned us not to let money become a rival to God for our affections.

Christians should view wealth as a resource intended for the advancement of God's kingdom. With the approach of one of the greatest spiritual harvests ever, this is a season when wealth needs to be channeled into ministries that serve people and spread the gospel.

We must not fear the concept of wealth. We must not fear the idea of reaping what God has given us to harvest. We must not fear increase, for money in itself is not bad. The Bible says it's the *love* of money that is the root of all kinds of evil (see 1 Tim. 6:10). We must never confuse the abundance or lack of money with the attitude of our heart.

We must also resist the idea that to be poor is spiritual. This teaching has its roots in gnosticism, which states that matter is bad and the mind is good. Gnosticism has caused many problems in the Church, including the separation of the sacred and the secular.

We must also separate our worth from our possessions. That is, we must realize that we are worth far more to the living God than the monetary value of our wealth and possessions. What is important is our willingness to be good stewards of what God has given to us, to take appropriate risks and to make our possessions available to God to do with what He wants. Once we understand this, we are free to go forth into the harvest field that we are a part of and ask the Lord how we can best reap the harvest of that field. As faithful stewards, we will be given the vision and focus to overthrow anything that sets itself against the call of God on our life in our field.

Avoiding the Traps

As we consider matters of wealth, there are very real traps we must avoid. We must detect and repent of any of these patterns in our own lives, and we must stay in God's covenant timing.

When we go up against the enemy to fight for the transference of wealth into the kingdom of God, we must guard ourselves against the love of money. The Greek word *philarguria* in 1 Timothy 6:10 refers to avarice (the insatiable greed for riches) and covetousness (to desire the possessions of others).

We must also be wary of the deceitfulness of riches (see Mark 4:19). This can include the perceived power that comes with having money. Money can produce an attitude of heart that seeks to manipulate through false pretenses and appearances.

Money is good when it is made a servant to us. However, when we become a slave to its dominion, we are in trouble. Lot, Esau, Achan, Gehazi, Judas, Ananias and Sapphira are among those in the Word who were cursed by wealth and trapped by their own impure desires. As we prepare to move against the enemy, we must renounce every issue of covetousness that is tied to mammon.

The Lord says, "Take heed and beware of covetousness, for one's life does not consist in the abundance of the things he possesses" (Luke 12:15). The sin of covetousness is linked with uncontrolled, selfish emotional desire. The enemy attempts to lead us into illicit forms of idolatry because they misdirect our desires from a holy God toward flesh-filled, demonically inspired forms of lasciviousness. James 4:1 asks, "Where do wars and fights come from among you? Do they not come from your desires for pleasure that war in your members?"

Wealth Can Lead to Idolatry or Worship

Provision is necessary for building God's plan. In the book of Exodus, God remembered the children of Israel and raised up a deliverer to lead them into His covenant plan. However, God didn't just free the people and send them into the wilderness with nothing to show for 400 years of hard labor. Not only did He save His people, but He also provided for them! As the Israelites prepared to depart from Egypt, God prompted the Egyptians to give them all kinds of riches and goods:

> And the LORD had given the people favor in the sight of the
> Egyptians, so that they granted them what they requested.
> Thus they plundered the Egyptians (Exod. 12:36).

The Lord still wishes to give miraculous provision to His children today, as He breaks us out of the system we are in and points us toward the covenant blessings He has set aside for us throughout the earth.

God gave Moses a detailed plan for building His tabernacle in the wilderness, and we can surmise that some of what He had given the Israelites from the Egyptians would be used to fulfill that plan. God wanted them to build a tabernacle, or dwelling place, for Him so that they could worship Him and receive His vision for their future. Even as God was giving the plans for the tabernacle to Moses, the supply was already there to provide for its building.

Moses waited on God for every detail that was necessary for the future prosperity of his people. Unfortunately, the people did not wait on Moses. While he was on Mount Sinai receiving the plans, the people grew impatient. They took the provision that had been given them, and in their discouragement they wandered back to the very gods from whom they had been liberated:

> And [Aaron] received the gold from their hand and he fash-
> ioned it with an engraving tool and made a molded calf.
> Then they said, "This is your god, O Israel, that brought
> you out of the land of Egypt!" (Exod. 32:4).

Not only was this molded calf a familiar god of Egypt, but the calf was also worshiped in Canaan through the religious system that had been erected there. When we are discussing wealth, I don't think provision is the only issue in regard to God's covenant people and plan. There is provision all over the earth. However, worship and devotion to a holy God and His purposes do become an issue in the release and stewardship of wealth.

The Wisdom of an Ant

We must have a stewardship mentality before the Lord will release wealth. Proverbs 21:5 says, "The plans of the diligent lead to profit as surely as haste leads to poverty." We must persevere against all odds and enemy strategies. These are necessary characteristics of God's people that are needed to establish the Kingdom on Earth.

Proverbs 17:16 says, "Of what use is money in the hand of a fool, since he has no desire to get wisdom?" Therefore, if you are asking for money, ask for wisdom also. Recently I was on an airline flight when I shut my eyes and had a vision. I saw an ant. The Lord then quickened this passage to me:

> Go to the ant, you sluggard! Consider her ways and be
> wise, which, having no captain, overseer or ruler, provides
> her supplies in the summer, and gathers her food in the
> harvest. How long will you slumber, O sluggard? When
> will you rise from your sleep? A little sleep, a little slum-

ber, a little folding of the hands to sleep—so shall your poverty come on you like a prowler, and your need like an armed man (Prov. 6:6-11).

The ant is an example of the wisdom of providing in the summer for the wants of the winter. Not all ants store up seeds for winter use, but among the ants of Palestine there are several species that do. Their well-marked paths are often seen about Palestinian threshing floors and in other places where seeds may be obtained. Such paths sometimes extend for a great distance from the nest. *In every country in the world the ant is synonymous with industry.*

Here are some important facts concerning the ant for us to consider:

1. The ants of many countries lay up vast stores of grain in their nests.
2. To facilitate their efforts they place their nests as near as possible to the places where grain is threshed and stored.
3. The grain provides their food during the winter season.

From this example from the Word of God, we see that it takes diligence and perseverance to have the necessary supply to accomplish God's purposes.

Remembering God's Portion

I come from a family that had much potential to prosper. My dad was a creative, self-made man who probably felt the *lack* of money was the root of all evil. It seemed that whatever he touched met with success. He really didn't care about an impressive résumé; he just felt that whatever you put your hand to should prosper and multiply. Yet he never really mastered the power of money.

Money and wealth have inherent power; if you do not bring that power under the subjection of the Holy Spirit, it will overwhelm and ensnare you. My father fell into the covetousness and the strife of wealth. His ability to succeed drove him to forget God.

In forgetting God, he forgot God's portion. I believe this was his downfall.

You can read my testimony in *Possessing Your Inheritance*, a book about restoration. My dad allowed money to become his god, and the abundance that had been given him to steward was lost. When God showed me that He could restore what had been devoured by the enemy, He revealed to me the power of giving. I believe that giving of your resources—your money, your time, your mind, your heart—can unlock your destiny.

No matter what the generations of your family before you have done with their money, you can break the cycle of the sin of greed by confessing the sin of your bloodline and by the determination to no longer be ruled by the god of mammon. This will release the power for you to secure God's inheritance for your future.

Harvesting in Your Canaan

God is giving us strategy for reaping in the harvest fields. We have discussed how apostolic authority can overthrow the powers and principalities that are holding back the supply necessary to advance God's covenant purposes.

We also have seen how, in Deuteronomy 8:18, He spoke this principle to His people as He prepared them to enter into the land He had promised them. God knew they would be in for a spiritual war with the gods of the land of Canaan. Joshua and the tribes of Israel were to take the wealth from the inhabitants of that region for the purposes of God's covenant plan. Therefore, the gods of the land had to be defeated and their wealth plundered.

Just as there are two competing kingdoms in the heavenlies— God's and Satan's—there are two economic systems competing for the earth's wealth: God's and Satan's. Psalm 24:1-2 says that the earth and its fullness belong to the Lord because He, and He alone, is the sovereign Creator. Individuals, corporations, banks, lending institutions, markets, governments and international organizations are called to be stewards of God's resources in order to glorify Him and to demonstrate His righteousness and justice in the earth.

Jesus said, "You cannot serve God and mammon" (Matt. 6:24). "Mammon" was a figure of speech in Jewish literature, a way of personalizing inanimate wealth and riches. But this figure of speech points to a deeper truth. "Mammon" is an accurate description of the demonic personalities behind economic injustice and misery in the world.

The Scriptures teach that Satan is a usurper, a thief and, ultimately, a destroyer. Satan uses economic systems—individuals, corporations, banks, lending institutions, markets and governments—to subvert God's rule as part of his plan to get people to worship anything other than God. If Satan can get people to worship money or monetary systems, all the better. As "prince of this world" (John 12:31), Satan has a great deal of power he can exercise on Earth. But we must always remember that his power is limited, that it is nothing compared to the power of God and that Satan is ultimately an eternal loser. Nevertheless, Satan uses demonic forces, deception and human proxies to administer and control supply and distribution of wealth according to his agenda. Satan is a Machiavellian prince, not just of religions but also of economics.

Launch Out for a Transfer!

God is saying to His people, "Launch out!" The word "launch" means to send off, to send forth with force, to set in operation, to start on a new course or to throw oneself into an enterprise with vigor.

Fishermen in Jesus' day would take a circular net with weights attached to the perimeter and cast it out on the water. After the net sank, a drawstring was pulled and the catch was brought in. Simon Peter had been doing this all night and had caught nothing (see Luke 5:5). He was exhausted and frustrated. Jesus then gave him direction that was contrary to his thinking: "Launch out and go deeper!" (see v. 4). Peter doubted that Jesus could really understand his daily situation and the time-honored method of gaining the supply he needed. Nevertheless, he obeyed Jesus and he hauled in an overwhelming catch that supplied not only his need but his partners' needs as well (see v. 7). Then the Lord said, "From now on you will catch men" (v. 10). After this demonstration of power, the disciples went forth evangelizing. *A miracle overcame their doubt.*

The Lord is wanting to do miracles in our everyday lives. These miracles will cause supply to be released that will meet our needs. These miracles will cause faith to be released that will propel us forward to achieve God's purposes in our homes and our cities. As we see Him move in our lives, we can have faith that an entire region can be freed from the clutches of mammon and the power of covetousness.

God's Unfolding Revelation:
Managing God's Provision Responsibly

I believe one of the greatest wars ahead for the Body of Christ is with the god of Mammon. We will be a very frustrated and hindered people if we have all the vision of heaven but do not have the provision to accomplish God's purpose in this season. The war over the transference of wealth is intense.

God's people continue to prepare for this great transfer. One difficulty I see is that we have not understood this war. In *How to Minister Freedom* (Regal Books, 2005), edited by Doris Wagner, I wrote a chapter called "Unveiling the Evil Eye." It reveals the war we must fight as we resist Mammon's control.

In Deuteronomy 8:18, we read how the Lord spoke to His covenant people and prepared them to go into the land that He had promised. He told them that He would give them the power to get wealth, but He also warned them about the pitfalls of worshiping money (or mammon, which is wealth that has a debasing influence). God's assignment to Joshua and the tribes of Israel was to use their wealth for God's covenant Kingdom plan. To fulfill this assignment, a spiritual battle had to be fought, mammon had to be defeated and all riches had to be transferred to God's rule and stewardship plan. Proverbs 28:22 sheds some light by declaring that a man with an evil eye will greedily pursue earthly treasures. Matthew 6:24 further explains that no one can serve God and mammon.

We face a similar battle with mammon today. Have you ever looked closely at a dollar bill from the United States? An eye is imbedded right there in the paper. While the origin and meaning of this eye is debated, it clearly resembles the traditional evil eye. Moreover, in a wealth-driven world, people easily use their natural eyes to look upon money (mammon) with covetousness. Obviously we can't burn and destroy every dollar bill we have, so we must ask God how to deal with the presence of the eye.

Money is neither good nor bad in itself. The key issue for us is our relationship and dedication to the power behind money. We must guard ourselves against the *love of money* (see 1 Tim. 6:10). The Greek word for "the love of money," *philarguria*, refers to avarice, which is the insatiable greed for riches, or covetousness. It also means to inordinately or wrongly desire the possessions of others. If we are not careful, this covetousness is the fruit that money will produce in our hearts. Moreover, the *deceitfulness of riches* is an issue (see Mark 4:19). This is primarily a perceived power that comes with money. It produces an attitude of the heart that seeks to manipulate through false pretenses and appearances.

Envy is also linked with covetousness and the evil eye. When we look at something or someone else with an unholy desire, especially someone's riches, we fall under the power of this demonic grip. The power of envy is noted in Proverbs 27:4: "Who is able to stand before envy?" (*KJV*). To avoid this trap of the enemy, we must sanctify what God gives us and be satisfied with our portion (see Ps. 16:5; Phil. 4:11; 1 Tim. 6:8) . . .

Money often has curses attached to it. If we don't break the curses before we get the money, we will get the curse that comes with it. The Bible lists some people who were cursed by wealth or were driven by impure motives to gain it; Judas, Esau, Gehazi, Ananias, Sapphira, Lot and Achan are some examples. Each of these men and women were trapped by impure desires. One way we can break this curse is by tithing and giving offerings (see Mal. 3). These acts change our attitude about money. As we move forward against the enemy, we must renounce every issue of covetousness tied to mammon and break its curses . . . Money is good when it is a servant to us and to God. However, we can become slaves to its dominion. That is when it truly becomes an evil eye.[3]

The Transference of Wealth Has Begun

As we break the curse and defeat the spirit of Mammon, we will see money and other resources poured out for God's covenant purposes. This transference of wealth has already begun, and it will only increase in the days ahead. Here are two recent examples of this transference of wealth.

In January 2004, the estate of Joan B. Kroc, widow of McDonald's founder Ray A. Kroc, announced that it planned to give 75 percent of Mrs. Kroc's $2 billion estate to the Salvation Army. The bequest from the estate stipulated that half of the money would go for construction and operating costs of 30 to 50 educational facilities around the country, while the other half would be put into an endowment to pay for the operating costs of those facilities.

The Salvation Army received the $1.5 billion donation in an all-cash lump sum that was divided equally among the organization's four geographic divisions. Todd Bassett, National Commander of the Salvation Army, said, "Building the Ray and Joan Kroc Community Centers will be a major challenge for our organization, but they will have tremendous impact on communities. They could catapult the Salvation Army into a new era of exposure across the country." The centers will employ an estimated 9,000 more people than the organization currently has.[4]

A second example, although not directly related to the transference of wealth to a Kingdom-oriented business, involves Warren Buffet's decision to begin giving away approximately 85 percent of his wealth. Buffet, the world's second richest man at an estimated net worth of $44 billion, stated that he would begin giving the money away in July 2006. The decision represented a major change in Buffet's thinking. Although for decades he had said that he would like his wealth to go to philanthropy, he had always planned on this transfer to occur at the time of his death. "I know what I want to do," he now said, "and it makes sense to get going."

Buffet pledged to gradually give 85 percent of his wealth to five foundations. The majority of the money went to the Bill and Melinda Gates Foundation, an organization that focuses its efforts on issues of world health (such as fighting malaria, HIV/AIDS and tuberculosis) and on improving libraries and high schools in the United States. "The generosity and trust Warren has shown is incredible," stated Gates.[5]

In a paper titled "Sophisticated Philanthropy for Apostolic Distribution," Peter Wagner explains what is needed to increase the transference of wealth:

One of the salient characteristics of the Second Apostolic Age in which we now live relates to the availability of unprecedented quantities of wealth for the extension of the kingdom of God. It is one thing to generate the wealth through supernatural transfer or through God's empowering of individuals or groups to create the wealth, and it is another to see that this wealth is used responsibly according to the leading of God and for the purposes of God.

A term that encompasses what I believe to be a very productive approach to the task is "sophisticated philanthropy for apostolic distribution." Many are unaware that philanthropy is a specialized profession that requires knowledge, experience and skill, much as we regard law, engineering, medicine or physics. Although it may seem strange to those unaccustomed to handling large amounts of money, it is axiomatic that it is more difficult to give wealth away than it is to acquire it. Aristotle said that anyone can give money away, but only a few can give it to the right person, at the right time, to the right extent, for the right reason and in the right way. Unfortunately, history is full of horror stories relating to unwise transfer of wealth, starting with case studies of a disproportionate number of lottery winners.[6]

As we declare more and more money and resources for God's kingdom, let us also pray for an abundance of "sophisticated philanthropists" who will manage these blessings to empower the Body of Christ.

CHAPTER SEVEN

Lawlessness!

The fate of unborn millions will now depend, under God, on the courage and conduct of this army. Our cruel and unrelenting enemy leaves us only the choice of brave resistance, or the most abject submission. We have, therefore, to resolve to conquer or die.
GEORGE WASHINGTON (1732-1799)

The epidemic of world lawlessness is spreading.
FRANKLIN D. ROOSEVELT (1882-1945)

I grew up in a home that had both a godly and an evil inheritance. I was taught the Ten Commandments. I learned Bible stories. I had moral boundaries. However, in my home environment there was also corruption that had entered in to steal the covenant blessings God had intended for my family.

I came to know the Lord as a child, and I had a good understanding of some of His characteristics as I developed a relationship with Him. But as the corruption and violence intensified in our home, so did my confusion. I had a good idea of the way things should have been, but it was completely different from the way things actually were.

I witnessed my dad falling into lawlessness.

Even though as an older teen I was drawn away from the Lord and toward the enemy for a couple of years, my conscience could never tolerate lawless acts. I did plenty of bad things, but when I strayed into something of a lawless nature, it was as if alarm bells and red lights would go off inside me. The teaching and understanding that had been placed in me by a godly grandmother and mother protected me from straying too far outside of God's protective boundaries.

Daniel wrote of the Antichrist who in the last days will attempt "to change times and law" (Dan. 7:25). This is typical of the enemy's strategy. Satan tries to redefine law and pull us out of God's timing. If we are to win the future war of the Church, we must understand God's timing and the spiritual boundaries He has set for us. If we do not, deception will easily enter into our lives.

What Is Lawlessness?

Lawlessness means to be without regard for the principles and regulations established by a governing authority. It means to be uncontrolled, unruly, disorderly or unbridled. In spiritual terms lawlessness is a disregard for God's laws and His order. Why is it important to look at lawlessness as we discuss the future war of the Church? Because lawlessness and the Antichrist are linked together:

> Don't let anyone deceive you in any way, for that day will not come until the rebellion occurs and the man of lawlessness is revealed, the man doomed to destruction. He will oppose and will exalt himself over everything that is called God or is worshiped, so that he sets himself up in God's temple, proclaiming himself to be God.
>
> For the secret power of lawlessness is already at work; but the one who now holds it back will continue to do so till he is taken out of the way. And then the lawless one will be revealed, whom the Lord Jesus will overthrow with the breath of his mouth and destroy by the splendor of his coming. The coming of the lawless one will be in accordance with the work of Satan displayed in all kinds of counterfeit miracles, signs and wonders, and in every sort of evil that deceives those who are perishing. They perish because they refused to love the truth and so be saved (2 Thess. 2:3-4,7-10).

As lawlessness increases, we will need to learn strategies to overthrow the enemy behind it. In chapter 2 we discussed five specific ways in which the antichrist system operates: anti-Semitism, abuse of the prophetic gift, oppression of women, ethnic domination, and sexual perversion. Each of these has its roots in lawlessness, and each bears the fruit of lawlessness.

The Spirit of Lawlessness—A Modern Example

April 20, 1999. With the sun rising to a cloudless blue sky and a springtime chill in the air, the day dawned much like any other in the quiet and beautiful Colorado suburb of Littleton. But this day would not end as any other. Before the setting of the sun, two young men who had plotted and schemed for months would bring terror and destruction to the high school they had attended. Fifteen would lie dead and several others would be hospitalized, as the shock of the worst school shooting in American history would begin to sink in for a horrified nation.

On May 27, 1999, Darrell Scott, father of one of the slain victims, was invited to address the House Judiciary Committee's subcommittee on the matter. The transcript of Mr. Scott's address reads in part:

> Since the dawn of creation there has been both good and evil in the hearts of men and women. We all contain the seeds of kindness or the seeds of violence. The death of my wonderful daughter, Rachel Joy Scott, and the deaths of that heroic teacher and the other 11 children who died must not be in vain.
>
> I am here today to declare that Columbine was not just a tragedy; it was a spiritual event that should be forcing us to look at where the real blame lies! Much of the blame lies here in this room. Much of the blame lies behind the pointing fingers of the accusers themselves. . . .
>
> We have refused to honor God, and in so doing, we open the doors to hatred and violence. And when something as terrible as Columbine's tragedy occurs, politicians immediately look for a scapegoat such as the NRA. They immediately seek to pass more restrictive laws that

contribute to erode away our personal and private liberties. We do not need more restrictive laws. . . .

Political posturing and restrictive legislation are not the answers. The young people of our nation hold the key. There is a spiritual awakening taking place that will not be squelched! . . . As my son Craig lay under that table in the school library and saw his two friends murdered before his very eyes, he did not hesitate to pray in school. I defy any law or politician to deny him that right! I challenge every young person in America and around the world to realize that on April 20, 1999, at Columbine High School, prayer was brought back to our schools.

The chill of the Columbine High School shooting hit me especially hard because, at the time, I lived less than 50 miles from Littleton, and I had two children of my own in high school. Yet in the aftermath of Columbine, I was constantly reminded of the vision I had in 1985, which I described in some detail in chapter 1. In that vision I saw a structure that was called Lawlessness. In the vision I saw acts of violence and murder taking place in schools, churches, shopping malls and supermarkets.

While I was shocked and grieved by the Columbine incident, as I had been by several school shootings that had taken place in recent years, I cannot say that I was completely surprised. Just as I had seen in my vision many years prior, Satan was carefully constructing a structure of lawlessness designed to capture an entire generation. What then is his strategy, and how is he able to do this?

Tolerance, Grace and Justice

In chapter 4 we discussed how Satan creates a confederation of demons to establish a throne of iniquity. He uses the same tactic to create lawlessness in a society. Demons will work together to remove the understanding of the law from every structure of society. If the demonic confederation is successful, the lines between right and wrong become so blurred that the people will not act with any moral conviction.

Take, for example, the shift toward tolerance of sin in our society. Adultery, divorce, fornication, witchcraft and homosexuality seem to be more socially acceptable than ever. Homosexual behavior, which God has clearly called an "abomination" (Lev. 18:22), is now commonly termed an alternative lifestyle.

Because of relaxed moral standards in our nation and our failure to understand the true nature of grace, we have managed to pervert justice. In an article titled "United, We Fall," Matt Daniels writes:

> The activist gay legal strategy is to legalize marriage in one state, then attack traditional marriage laws in the rest of the country. In July [2000], Vermont becomes the first state in the nation to recognize homosexual "unions". . . .
>
> With 70% of Americans viewing marriage as uniquely and essentially the union of a man and woman, homosexual activists have instead turned to the courts to implement an end-run around popular opinion. In Vermont, a decision from the state's highest court forced the state's legislature to either grant marital status to homosexual couples or institute a statewide domestic-partnership scheme. The legislature opted to develop a system to provide all of the benefits and privileges of marriage to homosexual couples. In an effort to prevent the transfer of such "civil unions" to other states, many states have made efforts to protect the institute of marriage by specifically defining marriage for purposes of state law as the union of a man and a woman.
>
> But there's a problem. Proponents of same-sex "marriage" are hoping that, after their first state-court victory, the resulting legal and social conflicts at the state level will encourage the federal courts to intervene in the emerging debate over marriage. Using another round of specious legal arguments, homosexual activists will demand that the federal courts remove all of the remaining state-law barriers to same-sex marriage. Although family law has

traditionally been a matter for state law, past federal intervention in the abortion debate—striking down all state laws protecting unborn human life—provides ample evidence that the federal courts may well do the same to marriage law.[1]

Of course, we have the freedom to sin. God has made the human race able to choose, and He allows us to choose the path of the destroyer if we wish. However, it is a very scary situation when government authority and ruling powers attempt to force a mainline society to conform to the choices of others' sin.

Two consenting adults should have the freedom to form a relationship of their mutual choosing. However, if they elect to form a relationship that falls outside the boundaries established in God's Word, their beliefs should not be imposed on a society founded on the moral standard of God's Word. I believe that anyone who chooses to orient themselves in a wrong direction sexually should be shown the love that Jesus would show them as well as the right to choose and prosper in this nation. But their own choice of orientation should not change the course of the justice system of America.

A failure to understand grace leads us to set our own boundaries so that we can satisfy our soulish natures and carnal desires. Those who dare to suggest that homosexuality is a sin and that God has the power to transform a homosexual are now viewed as intolerant and homophobic at worst or politically incorrect at best. Because the lines of right and wrong have been virtually erased in our culture, those trapped by the enemy in these types of sins are encouraged to embrace their sins rather than feel conviction. If they never come to repentance, the Lord cannot lead them back into the best that He created them to experience here on Earth.

As demons confederate to infiltrate a society through attitudes and politics that shift the culture away from God's law, society declines and Satan is able to establish his rule and capture an entire generation. Such was the case with the children of Israel who were led out of Egypt. Rather than acknowledging God's salvation and allowing His rule to be established among them, they allowed themselves to be seduced into idolatry and debauchery.

As a result, God allowed Satan to capture the entire generation and postpone God's will for the nation of Israel. The trip to the Promised Land should have taken no more than a few weeks from Egypt. Instead, they wandered for 40 years until the defiled generation had completely died off and God's law could be reestablished through Joshua.

The Law Versus the Kingdom

Lawlessness is more than just breaking a law or standard; it is rebelling against a holy God. The Bible talks about the sin we can fall into once we stray outside of God's ordained boundaries (see 1 Pet. 4:3).

The Law was a revelation of the will of God in the Old Testament. But we find that with their traditions the elders of Israel tried to add to the law and establish an incredible narrowing of the boundaries to God's covenant people and plan. The central idea of the Law was that these were instructions received from a superior authority on how to live. One thing that is missing many times from our understanding of the Law is that this was also the story of God and His heart toward the human race.

The covenant agreement between God and His people at Mount Sinai provided the foundation for Israel's future. They were to stay within the boundaries God had set for them so that they could be saved from the power of Egypt from which they had been delivered. The Law would provide health and wholeness to the covenant community. This Law would also develop a judicial system and establish policies for what was to occur if the Law was violated.

Approximately 2,000 years later, Jesus presented the law of the Kingdom to the people. To present the law of the Kingdom, He had to fulfill the Law of the Old Testament (see Matt. 5:17; Rom. 10:4). Jesus then set a new standard of judgment and even gave a new commandment: "A new command I give you: Love one another. As I have loved you, so you must love one another" (John 13:34).

Here we see the principles of the Law transferred into the Kingdom law being established by Jesus. For instance, being rightly related to God should compel us to be rightly related to our neighbor. Jesus tells us to love our neighbor as ourselves (see Matt. 22:39). Likewise, in the Ten Commandments the Lord tells us not to covet anything that belongs to our neighbor (see Exod. 20:17).

But Jesus violated the traditions of the elders, particularly those concerning what could or could not be done on the Sabbath. Jesus said He didn't come to destroy the Law, but rather, to fulfill it (see Matt. 5:17-20). Jesus transferred the Law from an external, legalistic domain into a spiritual one. He moved the emphasis from outward appearance to inward living (see Matt. 5:21-22). Jesus called attention to the spirit of the Law and thus moved the Law into a deeper level of meaning.

Jesus said in Matthew 22:37, "You shall love the LORD your God with all your heart, with all your soul, and with all your mind." Love can never be adequately portrayed through rules or teachings; it must be demonstrated through the heart, as seen in the life, death and resurrection of our Lord.

Paul had a lifelong struggle with the Law. In Romans 7, he writes about the law of sin and the law of faith. Paul recognized that the Mosaic Law had been given for a good purpose—its demands were not evil but were for the purpose of making us holy. However, in Galatians 3:10-13, he writes that the Law became a curse instead of a blessing. If we were going to be true children of God it wouldn't be by keeping the Law but rather by getting free from its requirements and coming into a level of faith that would produce an overcoming power within us. The only way this could be fulfilled was through love and by the Spirit of God. Whereas the Law was given to help reveal the nature and life of God in Christ, we could never enter into the fullness of Christ without embracing Him, His death and His resurrection life.

Lawlessness Versus Legalism

You have to understand the law in order to understand how lawlessness operates. Yet in order to operate in the Spirit of God, we must understand grace. Grace is undeserved acceptance and love received from someone else. God provided this through salvation in Jesus Christ. The Greek word for grace, *charis*, is related to joy, pleasure or something attractive in a person. Therefore, grace is linked with favor, kindness and thankfulness.

God is kind to us in many ways when we make mistakes. This doesn't give us liberty to do wrong; instead it shows that He has an understanding about our ability to choose that allows us to operate in freedom. In the days ahead we are going to recognize and receive a superabundance of God's grace. This is what propelled the Early Church forward, and it will propel us forward. Grace leads us into communion with God, and communion leads us into revelation.

With lawlessness on the rise, it's hard to find our balance in the operation of grace. We tend to respond to lawlessness by setting much more stringent boundaries than the law of love ever intended us to. Therefore, not only will lawlessness be a problem in the coming days, but so will legalism.

There is a major difference between legalism and faith. Legalism leads to obsession, which leads to destruction. Obsession, the domination of one's thoughts and feelings by a persistent desire, keeps you from seeing your sin. The prophet Malachi would tell the people that they had violated God's law by robbing God, and they would respond by saying, "How have we done this?" (see Mal. 3:8). They could not stay in touch with the reality of God through the Law. Consequently, they couldn't hear the voice of God and fell into 400 years of darkness.

Apostle John Kelly gives a great example of how legalism works in the Church:

A friend of mine was saved in a very legalistic Pentecostal church. Everything in that church was called sin—except breathing. Going to movies was sinful, wearing certain kinds of clothing was sinful and long hair on a man was sinful. As a child he went to see the movie *Mary Poppins*, and it took him six months to get over the guilt feelings. When he was older and was called to preach, he preached and acted in the same fashion he had been raised in. Inside the place of worship he never told any jokes, and outside the church sanctuary he was never lighthearted or frivolous because for him such things were nothing less than sin. What a powerless and joyless way to live in Christ!

God wants to send forth an army with His anointing that will smash the strongholds of hell, enter strong-walled cities and shatter the power of the enemy. Sad to say, God's army, the Church, is often crippled by legalism. This attitude makes it hard for people to be genuine with each other.

In Christ's day the religious, legalistic phonies were a type and shadow of the Dark Ages to come. When Emperor Constantine declared Christianity to be the religion of the state, the Church began to lose its genuine power and joy. The moment the Church stopped being an enemy of the world, it became a submitted friend of the world. The Church gradually lost all its power, and its priesthood became not all that different from the priesthood of the Greco-Roman Empire. Even the secular historians call it the Dark Ages which means "the light is not among us." The Church was a political entity—powerless, joyless, only a shell.[2]

Legalism in the world is not much different from legalism in the Church. In December 1999, *Time* ran an article by John Cloud called "The Columbine Effect." The article states:

It's understandable that school officials are unsettled these days. Polls show that most Americans favor "zero tolerance" policies for campus violence, and many parents demand tough-minded, short-term solutions even as they wait for the results of more complex approaches like better mentoring and earlier intervention for troubled children.

It may seem silly to go after a kid whose only crime is manicuring during school hours. But how do you know whom to treat sympathetically at a time when 11-year-olds commit murder? And how do you decide which kids are just morose and creative—and which ones are plotting to kill? A zero-tolerance approach ends the guesswork. In the early '90s, schools began adopting one-strike-and-you're-out policies for kids who secreted weapons or drugs on campus. . . . But by definition, zero tolerance erases the distinctions among student offenses. . . .

The consequences for rule breaking are getting harsher. What's new is that even pranks can land kids not just before the school board but before a judge.[3]

We must not allow legalism to overtake us in the midst of lawlessness. If we do, legalism can easily cause us to adopt obsessive behaviors and create an abundance of rules that can lead to our destruction rather than propel us into our future. We need to understand the boundaries that God has set for us and determine to live by the spirit of the law (which is a picture of Jesus) rather than the letter of the law (which Satan can easily pervert and use to bring us into bondage).

Revelation of Lawlessness from a Group of Boys

One of the ministry assignments God gave me several years ago was to be the executive administrator of the largest children's home in Texas. My role was to bring order to the administration of this large home. After Pam and I and our 18-month-old son moved to the campus of this home, some interesting things happened.

The home housed boys who were predominantly fatherless. The complex was divided into 12 staff homes. Each staff home had 8 to 10 boys living in it. There was a separate campus for girls. The house parents of the home where the older teen boys lived had left abruptly. Therefore, my wife and I had to become the house parents of this home for a season. This home was known as the "seat of Satan" for the whole campus. In this home were eight tough high-school boys. After moving there I began to realize what a challenge this home was. One night I discovered a small hole in the wall between my closet and one of the boys' bedrooms. I saw all kinds of things happening in that bedroom that should not have been happening. These boys were indeed lawless. Not only was this house affecting the whole campus, but certain vile things happening in this particular dorm cottage were affecting the whole community.

I was in a quandary. I wanted to protect my wife and son from what was going on there, but I was also trying to set order in the home. After about three months, the struggle had worn me out. I felt paralyzed from dealing with the lawless spirit that permeated the house. One night I had a group of friends and intercessors over for my birthday, but I was so wearied that my guests actually had to come into my bedroom and minister to me. LaCelia Henderson, a dear friend of mine and a very mature intercessor and teacher, rose up over me and began to bind the spirit of antichrist and lawlessness that was trying to overtake me. I was a little clueless as to what she was talking about, but my spirit began to come alive again.

My wife then told me just to rest the next morning, something I had not done in several months; she assured me she would take care of getting the boys up and off to school. Pam rose early, started preparing breakfast and then got the boys up. It was then that a transformation began to occur. The boys came out with their same terrible attitudes and disrespect. Pam had breakfast prepared and waiting for them. I was watching from my office, and I heard her say, "I do not have the same out-of-balance mercy that Chuck has toward each one of you. You are required to get your beds made before you leave for school. In case you get killed on the way to school today, I don't want to have to make your bed. That is not my role in life. So get your bed made before you leave. I will have dinner waiting for you when you get home."

A wave of shock went through those eight tough boys. My wife showed mercilessness in the face of their lawlessness. When they came home that evening there was a difference in them. She was in the kitchen preparing dinner when one of them confronted her. She backed that young man into the wall and began to tell him what she would require in their relationship from that point on. She then said, "Over the next three weeks you will be cooking dinner with me, and you and I will get to know each other." When we came to dinner that night, one of the boys (sort of the ruler of the house) pulled me aside and said, "We'll change if you won't leave us to her all the time."

The Lord began to break into that cottage. All but one of the boys got radically saved. To this day we have relationships with most of them. I was speaking in Houston in a televised message when the station managers received a call from one of the boys whom I had not heard from for several years. He had been freed from his lawlessness and was living a Christian life.

I have seen how lawlessness works. I now have faith to see how it can be overcome.

Our Youth at Risk

Satan would use lawlessness to capture the entire generation of young people now arising. While every generation has had to deal with some form of lawlessness or rebellion, it seems the youth of today have been particularly targeted. Teens are dealing with issues that parents couldn't have imagined 25 years ago. High schools are installing security cameras and metal detectors, and college campuses are swarming with armed guards. Juvenile courts are overflowing, and family therapists are booked solid. Sure, parents have been dealing with troubled teens for centuries, but it is obvious that Satan is escalating the war against this generation.

Fatherlessness

One of the ways Satan draws kids into lawlessness is through fatherlessness. Our young people must have fathers in the days ahead. My father died when I was 16. Since that time the Lord has always made certain I had a spiritual father in my life. I have always submitted to these father figures whom God brought into my life to help grow me into the destiny for which I was created.

My wife, Pam, was able to deal effectively with the spirit of lawlessness because she herself had also been, in essence, abandoned

doned by her mother and father, who fell into alcoholism when she was just a child. Pam has told me stories of how she would wander the streets of Houston and Los Angeles. Thank God for His grace! She was adopted when she was 12. The father who adopted her was a chief master sergeant in the Air Force, so you can imagine how he set for her proper boundaries and influenced her growth.

The statistics linking fatherlessness to lawlessness are very real. Here are some recent statistics published at a website called KidsNeedDads.com:

- 63 percent of youth who commit suicide are from fatherless homes.
- 90 percent of homeless and runaway children come from fatherless homes.
- 85 percent of all children who exhibit behavioral disorders live in fatherless homes.
- 71 percent of all high school dropouts are from fatherless homes.
- 75 percent of all adolescent patients in chemical abuse centers come from fatherless homes.
- 70 percent of juveniles in state-operated institutions come from fatherless homes.
- 85 percent of all youths now in prison grew up in fatherless homes.[4]

The statistics also tell us that children from fatherless homes:

- Are 5 times more likely to commit suicide than children from single-father households;
- Are 20 times more likely to have behavioral problems;
- Are 20 times more likely to become rapists;
- Are 32 times more likely to run away;
- Are 10 times more likely to abuse chemical substances;
- Are 9 times more likely to drop out of school;
- Are 33 times more likely to be seriously abused;

· Are 73 times more likely to be fatally abused;

· Are 10 times as likely to be in a juvenile prison.[5]

Another study examined specifically the link between fatherlessness and crime:

> A recent study on young men growing up in homes without fathers revealed that these men are twice as likely to end up in jail as those who came from traditional two-parent families. Researchers at the University of Pennsylvania and Princeton University found that those boys whose fathers were absent from the household had double the odds of being incarcerated—even when other factors such as race, income, parent education and urban residence were held constant.
>
> Surprisingly, those boys who grow up with a stepfather in the home were at an even higher risk for incarceration, roughly three times that of children who remain with both of their natural parents. The study also found that young men whose parents part ways during their adolescence were roughly 1-1/2 times as likely to end up in jail as children from intact families—faring slightly better than boys who are born to single mothers. Furthermore, juveniles sent to jail were three times more likely to commit a violent crime than those who were sent to other programs.[6]

Satan has a plan to ensnare our young people through an epidemic of fatherlessness. God's remedy for this—a spirit of adoption—is wrapped in His plan of redemption for the entire human race. God is neither an abusive father nor an absent father. He is an ever-present Father who has provided a great inheritance for His children. Romans 8:15 says, "For you did not receive the spirit of bondage again to fear, but you received the Spirit of adoption by whom we cry out, 'Abba, Father.'"

The spirit of adoption releases us from a spirit of bondage and fear, which is often caused by fatherlessness. Therefore, the

Church needs to cry out for the spirit of adoption to invade the nations of the earth.

God's Cure for Lawlessness

> But the end of all things is at hand; therefore be serious and watchful in your prayers. And above all things have fervent love for one another, for "love will cover a multitude of sins." Be hospitable to one another without grumbling. As each one has received a gift, minister it to one another, as good stewards of the manifold grace of God. If anyone speaks, let him speak as the oracles of God. If anyone ministers, let him do it as with the ability which God supplies, that in all things God may be glorified through Jesus Christ, to whom belong the glory and the dominion forever and ever. Amen (1 Pet. 4:7-11).

The heart of this passage as it relates to God's cure for lawlessness is the fervent love that covers a multitude of sins. Here are five principles that will help us dismantle a spirit of lawlessness:

Prayer
We are to be serious and watchful in our prayers. The prayers outlined in chapter 5 will help us to overthrow thrones of iniquity, including lawlessness.

Love
Faith works by love. Therefore, the power of love, through faith, will dismantle the power of lawlessness.

Understanding God's Timing
At the beginning of this chapter, we saw that the antichrist spirit will try to change timing. To dismantle lawlessness, we must understand God's timing and be vigilant against Satan's plans to throw us off. In his book *Spiritual Timing*, Roberts Liardon writes:

One of the things that Jesus came and produced for us at Calvary was the ability to perceive and regain the correct timing of God. By receiving His redemption and walking in the Spirit, we can come back into it. We can fine-tune our spirits to know when to be in the right place at the right time, or to stay out of the right place at the wrong time. Through knowing God and His ways, we can build the character within ourselves that will position us strategically in the proper season. When you live in the Spirit, time is lovely. Time is a blessing. A Spirit-filled man can walk in step with God and work the works of God without stress or strain. He understands time.

To a Spirit-filled man, time means stability and nurturing. Time matures and heals. It brings understanding and abilities. Time expands and deepens our insight. When we walk with time, we walk with patience. As a result, we have the ability to possess our whole man, physically, emotionally and spiritually. Walking securely in the timing of God alleviates fear. There is no fear or doubt in the proper timing of God. Godly timing produces courage, boldness, security and strength.[7]

Purity

God's cure for lawlessness is not legalism but rather purity—purity of heart and mind. Purity does not mean that we stringently follow a strict set of rules (legalism) but rather that we are so sensitive to the leading of the Holy Spirit and so aware of the law of God written on our hearts that we know when we are moving into an area that does not please Him and we choose to turn back. Legalism produces bondage of heart, whereas purity produces freedom of heart.

The people of God should never fall prey to Satan's trap of militancy. Only love, grace and purity of heart will lead individuals out of a harsh, legalistic, hate-filled religion to embrace the good news of a living Christ.

Operating in Spiritual Gifts

As we each learn to operate in our gifts, the Body of Christ will function as it was meant to. No demonic force, including lawlessness, will be able to stand against a fully functioning Body of Christ. Operating properly in the gifts will lead us back to love (see 1 Cor. 13:1-10), where we can work together according to the heart of God.

God is ready in these days to display His power through the gifts He has given us so that His glory can be manifested on Earth. As we, the Church, come together to demonstrate God's power, even those who are caught in Satan's trap of lawlessness will be able to see the unmatchable and awesome glory of God!

God's Unfolding Revelation: Warring Against Lawlessness

This is a season in which we have seen much headway in turning "the hearts of the fathers to the children, and the hearts of the children to their fathers" (Mal. 4:6). Without family and authority structures being restored in our lives and society, we will continue to see lawlessness arise in the earth. All antichrist systems are tied into lawlessness. The city of New Orleans after Hurricane Katrina provides a powerful case study.

A year to the day before Hurricane Katrina struck the Gulf Coast, the Lord led me to prophesy that a wind of purification would blow from the south and that water would overtake New Orleans. The prophecy was actually addressed to Baton Rouge and said that the city should prepare to be the first refuge city in our nation. Katrina, which means "purification," occurred one year later. The waters overtook New Orleans and the population of Baton Rouge doubled overnight. During this crisis, lawlessness began to reign, and it has continued to reign in that city to this day. This is a warning for us about the lawlessness that will come with other crises in the days ahead.

As lawlessness began to reign in New Orleans and surrounding areas, the publisher of The Elijah List, one of the most extensive prayer networks in the United States that communicates to more than 150,000 people worldwide, asked me how to pray. I believe my response to him is still important for us as we look to the days ahead.

Stand and War

This is a major call to "stand and war." We must take a clear stand in the spirit for what is going on in this coastal tragedy. This disaster is a warning that times are changing rapidly, and we must have an immediate shift in the spirit. Only by crying out for a Holy Spirit revival in our nation will we see evil restrained.

We must pray and intercede on behalf of those traumatized along the Gulf Coast areas. When I wrote *The Future War of the Church* to explain the antichrist system and lawlessness, many criticized and scoffed at the concept of the level of warfare that we would be encountering in the days ahead. We are now entering into a level of warfare in the earth that is beyond our present mindset and paradigm. We need supernatural grace to deal with lawless structures in the upcoming days.

Please, please prepare yourself for these next three years. Begin to engage spiritual forces in ways that you may not have understood in the past. The following prophetic word is from the revelation that came forth on August 12, 2005, two weeks before the storm hit landfall:

To the United States of America: Today this nation is being realigned. Get ready, for refuge cities will begin to arise throughout this land. They will rise up from state to state to state, along the East Coast, along the Gulf and along the West Coast.

I AM raising up refuge cities. Florida is resisting the development of My plan, but I will cause a strong remnant to arise in this state. I AM beginning to train those in cities that will know how to move forward. Many of you have wondered, Why am I not involved here or there—why do I seem to be shelved? *I will assign you to be a part of those groups that will aid My next move in the earth.*

This will come because of great shakings, floods and disease structures that are forming. I AM assigning you now to spread My good news because I AM *moving over those with ears to hear My grace. There is a shifting now of compassion and mercy, for I need My healers to be ready to be released throughout the land.*

To those in law enforcement and public authority: Lawlessness is beginning to rise and escalate. Many of you who have prayed will become discouraged as you see statistics change. Lift up your heads. I will divide and expose the true source of covenant breaking and violence that is seething in this land. I will give you strategies for how to defeat major lawless structures . . . Remain on alert from this day forward.

The following are 10 principles for praying against lawlessness:

1. Ask God to teach you about lawlessness.
2. Ask the Lord to build a shield of faith around you.
3. Ask the Lord to help you become more responsive to prophecy.[8]
4. Don't lean on your own understanding. We are entering into a supernatural dimension.
5. Bind the accuser who is working in the earth realm to bring division in the midst of crisis.
6. Set a bloodline barrier on a 150-mile radius around the victimized area. Decree by the Spirit of God that there is a supernatural shield set so that the enemy's plan cannot invade that barrier. Cry out for angelic forces to visit individuals who are crying out in these areas. Ask for angels to help in the structure of lawlessness operating in that part of the earth.
7. Pray for those areas serving as cities of refuge: Houston, Baton Rouge and others.
8. Let God show you areas in your life that need to be purified. Ask God to purify areas where we have allowed the enemy to take control.
9. Pray for supernatural, unexplained healings to start occurring in individuals.
10. Ask for the Holy Spirit to invade this situation.

Many times in the midst of disaster, we need to seek God to find if there was an entry point that allowed the disaster to occur. For instance, in regard to the situation that occurred in New Orleans, you could ask the following questions: Could this be a result of the Gaza Strip crisis in Israel? Could this be a result of the spiritist decadence that goes on in New Orleans? Could this be a result of the gambling along the coast line? Could this be a result of the circuit court system in New Orleans taking a stand on behalf of abortion in the land?

Regardless, the issue right now is to let the Spirit of God rise up within us and for us to begin to cry out in the midst of the situation in a way that we have never cried out before. Job 22:30 says, "He will even deliver the one [for whom you intercede] who is not innocent; yes, he will be delivered through the cleanness of your hands" (*AMP*). Once you have lived through severe trauma, you realize that pointing a finger is not necessary! You actually realize that it is by the grace of God that any of us are not in more of these situations. Pray that the spirit of man will withstand this major wound and infirmity in this nation (see Prov. 18:14).[9]

The Refuge of God's Grace

Despair and lawlessness overcame the Gulf region and especially New Orleans in the aftermath of the Katrina crisis. The Brookings Institution's "Katrina Index" for early 2007 reported that there were 9 murders in the first 10 days of the year. "With the highest per-capita murder rate in recent memory, a sense of lawlessness abounds, helped along by the knowledge that police are still working out of trailers and the fact that jail space is scarce, court dockets are overflowing, and only a handful of public defenders remain in the city," the report said.[10]

When we experience trauma in our lives, we either enter the refuge of grace or the trauma hardens us through our anger and confusion. Given the sharp increase of violent crime along the Gulf Coast since the storm in 2005, it is evident that many people have chosen resentment and disorder over the refuge of God's grace. Iniquity and perversity are byproducts of lawlessness, and this threefold cord can overtake a society.

But God! Lawlessness abounds, but there are also many victories occurring around the nation. Lou Engle, Ché Ahn, Dutch Sheets, Karen Wheaton and others are leading a major effort to align and connect the generations. Lou is responsible for what is known as The Call, a movement to cause a divine restoration in the upcoming generation. Thousands have met in auditoriums and stadiums throughout the nation. Mike Bickel is challenging young people to pray and worship in what is known as the 24-7 Prayer Movement.

I see a generation arising. I see dark getter darker and light getting lighter. Evil will be overcome by good if we will allow the Holy Spirit to work in our lives.

CHAPTER EIGHT

The Modern-Day "-Ites"

There is no neutral ground in the universe: every square inch, every split second, is claimed by God and counterclaimed by Satan.
C. S. LEWIS (1898-1963)

And when the war broke out, its real horrors, its real dangers . . . were a blessing compared with the inhuman reign of the lie, and they brought relief because they broke the spell of the dead letter.
BORIS PASTERNAK (1890-1960)

God longs for His children to know and enjoy intimate contact with Him. If we will humble ourselves before Him and pray and seek His face and repent of our wicked ways, He will bring restoration to our Father-child relationship and release a new measure of childlike faith among His people. Places and position will begin to be restored. Health and joy will be restored. Our inheritance, covenant relationships and portions that have been taken from each of us by the enemy will be restored. God will begin to make us whole, not only individually but also corporately. These things will cause a breaking forth of evangelism worldwide.

Let us pray together:

> *Lord, let the hope of Your kingdom begin to dawn on all mankind. Let a worldwide knowledge of God begin to sweep the earth. Establish Your kingdom in fullness. May You rule in fullness, and may the manifestations of this fullness be demonstrated. Establish the love of God throughout the earth. And may the order of everything that is not aligned with Kingdom purposes be changed. Remove all the veils that would stop us from seeing Your redemptive plan.*

Of course, in order for us to pray this prayer with understanding and hope of fulfillment, we must also recognize there are opposing forces that will resist any and all attempts to manifest God's kingdom on Earth.

Just as the Church is building so that God's kingdom rule can be seen in the earthly realm, there are other motivated forces who, under Satan's rule and influence, are also building. These forces are working against the plan of God. We cannot avoid confrontation with these forces in the coming days. This confrontation will occur physically as well as spiritually.

Many Christians live with a naïve worldview, thinking they can and should avoid any sort of conflict or confrontation. That is not so. That is why we see the doctrine of persecution throughout the Bible. Now God is shaking His Church into a level of reality.

We are called to abide with our Lord in the throne room. However, we can't just sit and bask in God's presence forever. From the throne room we receive revelation and instruction for effecting God's plan on Earth. Therefore, we cannot be so heavenly minded that we're no earthly good. We must bring the revelation we receive in the throne room back down to Earth to battle as the Lord instructs us. This is how God's will is done on Earth as it is in heaven. I call this process apostolic ascending and descending.

This apostolic ascending and descending includes worship, war, exercise of territorial responsibility, and manifestations (including signs and wonders) of God's purposes in the earthly realm. This process allows us to participate with the Lord until the harvest is full and in the storehouse. We are called to reach the entire world as collaborators with the Lord; therefore, our demonstrations of Kingdom life should produce a fullness of times and accelerate what the Lord is doing through His covenant people.

Our Jewish Roots

There is no question that the Jews are God's covenant people. They are His firstfruits. It is easy for those of us who are Gentiles to forget that we are the ones who have been grafted onto the vine. Paul, speaking to the Gentiles, says:

For if the firstfruit is holy, the lump is also holy; and if the root is holy, so are the branches. And if some of the branches were broken off, and you, being a wild olive tree, were grafted in among them, and with them became a partaker of the root and fatness of the olive tree, do not boast against the branches. But if you do boast, remember that you do not support the root, but the root supports you.

For I do not desire, brethren, that you should be ignorant of this mystery, lest you should be wise in your own opinion, that blindness in part has happened to Israel until the fullness of the Gentiles has come in. And so all Israel will be saved, as it is written: "The Deliverer will come out of Zion, and He will turn away ungodliness from Jacob; for this is My covenant with them, when I take away their sins" (Rom. 11:16-18,25-27).

God loves His covenant people, and He has not forgotten them. We would be wise to remember that, no matter where our forefathers came from, if we are part of God's covenant plan through Jesus Christ, our spiritual roots are tied in with His covenant people, the Israelites.

Dan Juster, author and messianic leader in the Body of Christ, recently declared six things the Church (especially those of us in America) must repent of in order to move forward in the days ahead:

1. *Repent for sharing a partial gospel message.* We have preached a partial and therefore false gospel. Salvation through the sacrifice of Jesus is only part of the gospel, although it serves as our entrance into the Kingdom. The true gospel is the good news of the Kingdom that releases the power of God within us to resist the power of the enemy. The power of God is manifested in healing, deliverance and restored relationships. The Kingdom is revealed in our behaving and discipling people to live according to the law of the Kingdom (see Matt. 5).

2. *Repent of tolerating personal peace and affluence with Jesus being presented as the means to that end.* Many of us in America are epicurean Christians, meaning we have luxurious tastes or habits. We are comfortable and contented to be so. But it is through *suffering* that the Kingdom is extended. Though we never want to have a martyr syndrome and seek out suffering, and while it is true that we can enjoy what the Lord has provided for us materially, we also have to know that in the days ahead persecution will cause the Kingdom to advance. If we are committed to be a people of Kingdom advance, we also have to be ready for whatever it may cost us personally to accomplish God's purposes.

3. *Repent for our failure to perceive and pursue the fullness of the Church.* American churches have long sought growth for their own sake, even at the expense of other churches. Church in our nation is often perceived as a social club or a place to get a touch of God once a week. But God does not want us to just go to church in the traditional sense. The question should not be "Where do you go to church?" but rather, "Where are you submitted for training for the work of ministry?"

4. *Repent for backsliding from the Holy Spirit.* When we do not acknowledge the Holy Spirit in His fullness, we do not have the power to truly advance God's kingdom.

5. *Repent for failing to uphold righteous standards in the Church.* We discussed in the previous chapter how tolerance and lawlessness are linked. For example, we have sometimes tolerated divorce by not calling it what it really is: covenant breaking.

6. *Repent for abandoning our responsibility to pray for and evangelize the Jewish people.* Israel's "reingrafting" in the final days will mean life from the dead for the Gentiles. We need to respond to God's covenant people with deeds of love, kindness, intercession and giving in order to reveal Christ.[1]

Repentance changes our minds so that we can have the mind of Christ. We must make many changes in our thinking processes and paradigms if we are to unleash the next dimension of grace that God wants demonstrated on Earth. In his article "Paradigm Shifts for the 21st Century," Jim Goll wrote:

> A wave of "identificational repentance" will overwhelm a remnant of the Gentile Church, causing her to repent of her historical wrongs against the Jewish people. In response to this, a revelation of the "sabbath rest" shall be released from the throne of grace that will be non-legalistic and result in healing to many.
>
> There will be a great harvest among the Jewish people, which will escalate. This will particularly affect the Russian Jews around the world. There will be what some missiologists term "a people movement" among them. There will also be a parallel persecution of the Jews in the "land of the north" and potentially other lands that could occur. It is the devil's strategy to precipitate another type of holocaust; but God will raise up trumpeters like Mordecai who shall prepare the corporate Esther (the Church) for such a time as this. Radical prayer will open a window of escape for those Jewish people who feel called to leave and a hedge of protection to those who are temporarily called to stay (see Jer. 16:14-16).[2]

In their book *Israel, the Church and the Last Days*, Dan Juster and Keith Intrater share the following prophetic observations concerning the Church and the Jewish people:

> Although the world system around us will grow more evil and dark in the end times, we as the people of God will be growing more pure and bright. As society and culture around us turn against God, they will begin to persecute the true believers even more viciously. But in the midst of that attack, we will be getting stronger spiritually. The Church,

or Bride, that Yeshua is coming back for is described as glorious and without any spot or blemish (see Eph. 5:27). While the pagan nations of the world may turn against Israel (see Zech. 14:2), there will be a greater unity and mutual understanding between Jew and Gentile within the Body of Christ (see Eph. 2:14).

False Christianity will fall prey to spirits of anti-Semitism and anti-Zionism, but the true believers will develop a greater awareness of the Jewish roots of the faith (see Rom. 11). There is a special release of power in the Body of believers when we enter into the correct cooperation between Jew and Gentile. As the correct interaction between male and female provides zest and romance within a marriage, so does the distinctive relationship between Jew and Gentile provide a certain spiritual dynamism within a New Covenant congregation. Wisdom and revelation will flow as we bring out of our treasure and heritage things new and things old (see Matt. 13:52).[3]

So let us now turn our attention to the world systems around us—the "-Ites"—that Satan would use to try to thwart reconciliation between Jew and Gentile and, thus, the advancement of God's kingdom. Again, -Ites refers to the world systems and religions we will have to overcome, much like Joshua had to overcome the -Ites of Canaan—the Canaanites, Hittites, Amorites, Perizzites, Hivites and Jebusites—in order for the Israelites to advance into their Promised Land.

Anti-Semitism and the Church

Christianity is rooted in Judaism. All of the Early Church leaders were Jewish. In fact, the entire first-century Church was Jewish before several visions and dramatic experiences led Peter to take salvation to the Gentiles.

Some Jewish believers at first didn't understand why Peter had done this, but Peter convinced them there was a new work happening beyond the household of Israel. Paul continued this new work to the Gentiles and multiplied it. The early Gentile church affirmed its Jewish roots and even blessed the Jewish community in Israel (see Rom. 15:25-27). The apostle Paul clearly taught that global redemption and restoration depended upon God's plan to rightly relate Jews and Gentiles in the Body of Messiah:

> He Himself is our peace, who made both groups [Jews and Gentiles] into one, and broke down the barrier of the dividing wall . . . that in Himself He might make the two into one new man, thus establishing peace, and might reconcile them both in one body to God through the cross (Eph. 2:14-16, *NASB*).

Satan hates this "one new man" concept. He hates Israel because she brought forth the Redeemer of the human race, and he hates Gentiles and Messianic Jews who work together to continue God's redemptive purposes on Earth (see Rev. 12:17). The antichrist system hates everyone but is especially determined to annihilate God's covenant plan displayed in the Word through the nation of Israel.

Remember, Paul warned Gentiles in Romans 11:17-18 not to be arrogant toward the Jews or to boast of our position in God's family. Yet we have seen the anti-Semitic spirit rise up repeatedly throughout history. Martin Luther brought great reform to the Church concerning faith; unfortunately, in his failure to convert the Jews, he also penned some hateful rhetoric against the Jewish people—words that have haunted German society ever since. Consequently, anti-Semitic religious theology invaded modern society.

It was never God's call on the Church to replace the Jewish people in His heart. As to their rejection of Christ, Paul wrote of the Jewish people:

> Did [the Jews] stumble so as to fall beyond recovery? Not at all! Rather, because of their transgression, salvation has come to the Gentiles to make Israel envious. But if their

transgression means riches for the world, and their loss means riches for the Gentiles, how much greater riches will their fullness bring! (Rom. 11:11-12).

Sadly, we find in Western history that Christians have too often driven the Jewish people *away* from their Messiah. Marty Waldman's article "Historic Issues: Jewish Roots of Christianity" helps us to understand this issue more fully:

The Church has also propagated a more subtle form of anti-Semitism through particular doctrines such as replacement theology and dual-covenant theology. Replacement theology disregards Israel's chosenness as well as its irrevocable calling by God (see Rom. 11:28,29). "The Church is Israel" has been the theological position of the Roman Catholic Church and was further adopted by John Calvin as well as other Reformers.

Dual-covenant theology disregards the need for Jewish people to receive Yeshua as their Messiah, stating that they are saved through their father Abraham. Many Christian Zionists and other well-meaning Christians who want to build a bridge of communication with the Jewish community have adopted dual-covenant theology. This insidious doctrine robs the Jewish people of salvation in their own Messiah. It also magnetically draws the Jewish and Christian communities back to the original stronghold of agreement that a Jew cannot remain Jewish and believe in Jesus. That stronghold rejects the validity of the Messianic Jewish community.

Many Christians hold this theology today even though it is a ploy of the enemy to divert attention away from the fact that God is faithfully grafting the Jewish branches of Romans 11 back into their own olive tree. The Spirit of God is moving through the hearts of many believers today, and the Church is beginning to recognize the hand of God in the Jewish community, particularly as He draws the remnant of Israel back to Himself.[4]

The Amalekite Spirit

The Amalekites provide the best example in the Word of the link between anti-Semitism and lawlessness. In his book *In That Day*, Rabbi David Levine states:

> The spirit of Amalek typifies all those who oppose the Jews and God's plan to use the Jews. This spirit has motivated many people under widely different circumstances, but always toward the same goal: the destruction of the Jewish people (see Exod. 17:8-15; Num. 24:20). Sometimes the battle has been waged politically, sometimes militarily. Other times it is fought on the cultural front, or philosophically, or religiously. Pharaoh was motivated by the spirit of Amalek, as was Haman, and of course, Hitler too, so motivated that he destroyed six million Jews on his way to the final solution.[5]

Exodus 17:8-16 chronicles the first time the Israelites went to war as a group after they had left Egypt. The Amalekites tried to prevent them from progressing in the path that God had ordained for them. Notice how the pattern the Israelites had to operate in to defeat the enemy is still important to us today. The apostolic type of leader (Moses) had to take his stand. The priest-pastor type (Aaron and Hur) had to hold up his hands, while the prophetic-warrior type (Joshua) had to go forth into battle. This proper alignment was necessary for God's people to see victory.

> So Joshua overcame the Amalekite army with the sword. Then the LORD said to Moses, "Write this on a scroll as something to be remembered and make sure that Joshua hears it, because I will completely blot out the memory of Amalek from under heaven." Moses built an altar and called it The LORD is my Banner (Exod. 17:13-15).

When we see the Messianic Jewish Church arising and coming into proper apostolic/prophetic/intercessory alignment, we will see a sweeping move of God across the earth. This should be one of our key prayer points as we pray for God's covenant people. In his book *Kneeling on the Promises*, Jim W. Goll lists seven scriptural reasons to pray for Israel:

1. Israel is still the apple of God's eye and His inheritance—a people close to His heart (see Deut. 32:9-11; Pss. 33:11-12; 148:14; Zech. 2:8; Rom. 11:29).

2. God says that His servants should pray with compassion concerning Israel's condition (see Ps. 102:13-14).

3. God commands us to give Him and ourselves no rest until He has established Jerusalem and made her the praise of the earth (see Isa. 62:1,6-7).

4. God's heart will travail through us for Israel's salvation (see Rom. 9:2-3; 10:1).

5. God commands us to seek the spiritual and physical good of the Israeli people and to pray for the peace of Jerusalem (see Ps. 122:4,6,7,9; Rom. 1:16; 2:9-11; 15:25-27).

6. The Jewish people's acceptance of Jesus as Messiah will lead to life from death—a worldwide revival of unprecedented magnitude (see Isa. 27:6; Rom. 11:15).

7. Jesus linked His second coming to Israel's national turning to Him (see Matt. 23:39).[6]

The Growing Gap Between Religion and Reality

Let no one deceive you in any way; for [the day of the Lord] will not come unless the rebellion comes first and the lawless one is revealed, the one destined for destruction (2 Thess. 2:3, *NRSV*).

Clearly, there will be a remnant group alive at the Lord's coming who have seen the Antichrist. We will understand his workings fully before we see Jesus face to face.

A time is coming when lawlessness will be given full reign on Earth. Presently, lawlessness has been restrained because the Church is willing to war. During what remains of this restraining time, however, we are going to see an increasingly visible contrast and battle forming between false religions and the reality of God. Certain political systems will align themselves with these false religions. When that happens, a new dimension of the antichrist system will be working in the world. These politically powered religious systems will establish themselves against religious freedom and the movement of God's Spirit on Earth.

The spirit of religion has already begun a last-ditch offensive to deceive multitudes and to divert them from true faith in the only head of the Church, Jesus Christ. As the war intensifies, we can expect religious deception to become increasingly more common and more intense.

Not only will the gap widen between false religions and those who are operating in the reality of God, but also entire religions and the people and governments connected with them will be used by the antichrist spirit to try to gain control of the earth and its resources.

The -Ites and -Isms Are Shaking

In his book *The Queen's Domain*, C. Peter Wagner writes:

> In 1990 the four major anti-Christian forces on Earth were Communism, Buddhism, Hinduism, and Islam. Literally millions of believers were praying that the grip that these ungodly focuses had on people's lives and destinies would be broken once and for all. High-intensity initiatives involving spiritual mapping, prayer journeys, prayer expeditions, published prayer guides, and strategic-level spiritual warfare specifically targeted one or the other of these obstacles to the gospel year after year.

What were the results?

Communism, for all intents and purposes, is gone! The grandiose Marxist experiment as a savior for society has failed. Its theology of atheism never could and never will capture people who are made in the image of God. Even nations which have retained Communism politically are no longer able to stem the tide of the gospel. Communist China is seeing the greatest harvest of souls in all of Christian history with an estimated 20,000 to 35,000 people being born again every day. Professing atheist [and Cuban dictator] Fidel Castro, who ruthlessly persecuted Christians before the 1990s, found himself in a front-row seat in a crowd of 100,000 singing, dancing, banner-waving evangelicals in Havana's Revolution Square before the end of the decade. Even in North Korea the opposition to the gospel is not so much political and ideological Communism as it is "Juche," an idolatrous worship of the leader, Kim Jong II.

The spirits empowering Buddhism are now on the run! Buddhism no longer has the strength it once had in China and both North and South Korea. Thailand used to be one of the most resistant nations to the gospel, but dramatic changes have taken place in this decade, and churches are now multiplying among Buddhists who are coming to Christ. Buddhism has lost its grip on much of Southeast Asia. In 1998 the Dali Lama called a high-level conference of Buddhist leaders in Kyoto, Japan, with the main item on the agenda: What are we going to do about all our Buddhists—especially our youth—becoming Christians?

The spirits empowering Hinduism are badly battered! In Nepal, the world's only Hindu kingdom, there were only a few thousand believers at the beginning of the decade. Jail sentences were the price that many of them had to pay for following Jesus. However, by the end of the decade some were estimating that there were 500,000 believers, and some considerably more. George Otis Jr.'s Sentinel Group has just removed Nepal from its strategic list of "Target Group 20" countries. North India was spiritually stagnant until the 1990s. Now the gospel is spreading with signs and wonders following all through the region. Some say the formerly resistant region of Sikkim is no more than 20 percent Christian.[7]

Wagner goes on to discuss Islam:

The spirits empowering Islam are extremely nervous! Islam was still the most formidable barrier to the gospel at the end of the 1990s. More than one billion people continue to be held in spiritual darkness by these principalities and powers. Prominent among them is the Queen of Heaven, frequently disguised as the Moon Goddess. But this fortress of darkness has developed widening cracks. For example, Indonesia is the largest Muslim country in the world. For years, however, the government has refused to publish their religious census because of their embarrassment over the unrestrained growth of Christianity. During the 1990s panicking Indonesian Muslims burned more than 1,000 Christian churches, but God used each one to advance, not to restrain, the spread of the gospel. Numbers of Muslim conversions are being reported in the Middle East as a result of visions, dreams, and miraculous healing where outward preaching of the gospel is forbidden.[8]

Although the spiritual forces behind Islam are being challenged, the religion's influence within American society is increasing. *Christianity Today* recently focused on the rise of Islam in mainstream America. Examples of this growing cultural and political influence include a Detroit hospital that offers copies of the Koran to Muslim patients; the Denver International Airport, which features a chapel for Muslim pray-ers; the United States

Senate's inviting a Muslim cleric to open its session in prayer; the military's hiring of four Muslim chaplains, and the White House's sending greetings on the feast that ends Ramadan. Muslims have begun to exercise the rights and freedoms available to them in the West, while at the same time Islamic regimes brutally persecute Christians in Muslim countries, denying them the same freedoms. From 1989 to 1998, the Muslim population in the United States grew by 25 percent.[9]

We must also recognize the building of Muslim political muscle in America. With a growing population through immigration and conversion comes growing influence. Increasingly, Muslims are entering the nation's political process, seeking to use their increasing numbers to influence policy, particularly with regard to the Middle East.[10] In February 1999, the State Department began a series of roundtable discussions with about 20 Muslim leaders, culminating in a request for more Muslim applicants for U.S. government positions.[11]

An article in *Christianity Today* tells us:

> Further debates over future U.S. policy in the Middle East will certainly contain an increasingly strong Muslim voice. Furthermore, with the mentality that they have a mandate from God that the whole world must come under the banner of Islam, we can only expect to see their influence rise. The Muslim religion particularly understands the concept of possession; Muslims believe they are to possess and occupy the land where they live. *Jihad*, or appeal to battle, is one means to accomplish this. Another is the more patient approach of supplanting the dominant religion over a period of many years [as in Egypt and Indonesia].[12]

The Islamic understanding of this principle of geographic domination is very similar to God's apostolic principle of authority discussed by Paul in 2 Corinthians 10:13.

The apostle Paul, however, was under the Kingdom law of love and grace. Islam is a religion of duty and submission in which human effort is thought to lead to salvation. There is no plan of redemption. This creates a driving, dominating need to perform. Without a provision for the remission of sin and without grace, the whole religion is based on works.

So how should we view the role of Islam in society? In his book *Is Fanatic Islam a Global Threat?* Victor Mordecai writes:

> The Moslem religion (Islam) is both a religion as well as a society, religion and state as one. Whoever is not a member of this religion is considered a foreigner and outsider. According to Islam, at least for the foreseeable future, no pluralistic or democratic society can exist. Islam cannot and must not agree to any non-Islamic rule. Just as Islam is considered citizenship, it is also the House of Islam; all lands on which Moslems live or were ever conquered by Moslems are considered part of the House of Islam.
>
> Today, the geographic entity known as Palestine is considered WAKF, or Moslem trusteeship (land ownership) . . . a principle that the Jews also hold regarding Palestine. In Saudi Arabia, for example, it is forbidden to build a Christian church or to bury a Christian, simply because it is forbidden to profane Moslem soil. The call to prayer is also territorial: It must be heard throughout all the neighborhoods of the city. Since the Moslems are not capable at this time of implementing a homogeneous Islamic society on the entire nation regarding a way of life, legislation of laws, they are attempting to "Islamicize the land," i.e., that the land be property of Moslems.[13]

Islamic powers are unable to grasp the rebirth of the Jewish state of Israel. This was a sovereign move on God's behalf. Militant Islamic powers do not want to submit to the covenant boundaries set by God.

So how are we to fend off the advance of Islam? We can only do this by defeating the demonic powers and principalities behind this false religion. Only then can we hope to fully penetrate this people with the good news that our Lord died to extend grace and salvation to the Muslim people, too. His Spirit is quite capable of infiltrating the strong, militant stronghold that has captured this entire people group. The Lord is going to extend His grace to this people and surprise them with His Spirit!

When I pray for the Islamic people, I ask for the Lord to visit them with signs, wonders, dreams and visions of Himself. And He is doing that all over the world. However, to date we have not seen the power of His visitation change an entire Islamic nation. Therefore, we must keep crying out to God that these people would be saved from Satan's snare.

Those who attempt to convert Muslims to Christianity are going to battle discouragement many times. You can't win this people with arguments and debates; the religious spirit is much too strong. Conversion will only come through key relationships that break down these religious barriers.

For example, there is also a gender wall in Islam that makes it possible for a Muslim woman to relate more closely to a Christian woman than her husband can to Christian men. I believe this is a great key that will allow Christian women to penetrate Islam with the gospel in the coming days. Of course, there are still difficult cultural and spiritual hurdles to overcome.

Among all the 99 names of God in Islam there is no name that conveys that He is capable or willing to grant us an intimate relationship like the one we enjoy with our Abba Father. A Father-child relationship with God is incomprehensible in this religion. This defies the apostolic call of God as we know it; therefore, there can be no true fathering of sons. As we have seen, fatherlessness breeds frustration, terrorism, loneliness, rejection and hate.

Terrorism and the Seeds of Hate

Hate breeds hate, and violence breeds violence. I was in Oklahoma City in April 1995, the week before the worst terrorist attack ever perpetrated on United States soil up to that time. I remember knowing when I was there that something was not right in the spiritual atmosphere over that city. God sometimes burdens His people to let them know that things are not the way that He would have them be and that there is danger on the horizon.

I began to pray.

I told several spiritual leaders in Oklahoma City how I felt. I also shared my feelings prophetically at a church service on Wednesday, trying to mobilize the people in prayer. I have seen the power of corporate prayer, and I knew that if enough intercessors would rise up at that strategic time, they could change the atmosphere over their city. However, I was unable to muster enough intercessory strength to sound an effective alarm. Consequently, I was shocked and overwhelmed and even jarred into a new reality when the tragic event of the Oklahoma City bombing occurred the next week.

Terrorism is on the rise. *Project Megiddo*, a recent report on terrorism released by the FBI, warned of terrorist activity that may be instigated from within our own borders:

> The majority of growth within the militia movement occurred during the 1990s. There is not a simple definition of how a group qualifies as a militia. However, the following general criteria can be used as a guideline: (1) a militia is a domestic organization with two or more members; (2) the organization must possess and use firearms; and (3) the organization must conduct or encourage paramilitary training. Others terms used to describe militias are Patriots and Minutemen.[14]

We must be on alert, people! Once hate has embedded itself in a group, its author, Satan, will devise a strategy to demonstrate the power of this hate. *USA Today* reported:

> The 1993 bombing of the World Trade Center shook our nation's sense of security and awakened us to the fact that terrorist acts could also occur within our borders. Whereas foreign crises are predominately handled by the

State Department, lines of authority are far less clear in domestic terrorist attacks. Now that nontraditional threats are no longer a matter of if but when, a whole new debate has emerged, spurring fundamental changes in national security strategy. Federal, state and local governments will need to partner in new ways if our nation is to effectively plan for and respond to the formerly unthinkable.[15]

We must continually apply the Lord's principle of division toward hate groups in particular. Remember, when He was discussing Satan's house, Jesus said that if there were division in the devil's kingdom, it would fall into desolation (see Matt. 12:25-29). When I pray for the members of these hate groups, I pray that the organizations would begin to divide and fragment so that Satan's strategy may not come to fruition.

There is a powerful religious spirit behind terrorism and hate-motivated violence. The *Project Megiddo* report tells us:

> The general trend in domestic extremism is the terrorist's disavowal of traditional, hierarchical, and structured terrorist organizations. Even well-established militia, which tend to organize along military lines with central control, are characterized by factionalism and disunity. While several "professional" terrorist groups still exist and present a continued threat to domestic security, the overwhelming majority of extremist groups in the United States have adopted a fragmented, leaderless structure where individuals or small groups act with autonomy. . . .
>
> Religious motivation and the NWO conspiracy theory are the two driving forces behind the potential for millennial violence. . . . Numerous religious extremists claim that a race war will soon begin, and have taken steps to become martyrs in their predicted battle between good and evil. Meanwhile, for members of the militia movement, the new millennium has a political overtone rather than a religious one. It is their belief that the United Nations has created a

secret plan, known as the New World Order (NWO), to conquer the world beginning in 2000. . . .

Religiously based domestic terrorists use the New
Testament's book of Revelation—the prophecy of the end
time—for the foundation of their belief in the Apocalypse.
Religious extremists interpret the symbolism portrayed in
the book of Revelation and mold it to predict that the end
time is now and the Apocalypse is near. . . .

To understand the mindset of why religious extremists
would actively seek to engage in violent confrontations
with law enforcement, the most common extremist ideologies must be understood. Under these ideologies, many
extremists view themselves as religious martyrs who have a
duty to initiate or take part in the coming battle against
Satan. Domestic terrorist groups who place religious significance on the millennium believe the federal government will act as an arm of Satan in the final battle.[16]

Hate crimes are defined as unlawful acts of violence, vandal-
ism, harassment and intimidation directed against individuals on
account of their race, religion, ethnicity or sexual orientation. Hate
crimes are frequently based on ancient ideologies that get repack-
aged in every generation. Gays, Jews, Christians, Muslims, Arabs—
any group can be the target of hate and hate crimes. Terrorism is
not the answer to bring change to this world. It is another -Ism that
stands in opposition against the kingdom of God.

Secret Societies

Members of these so-called extremist groups are often linked together by their participation in some secret organization that appears very
religious.[17] One of the most famous secret societies is Freemasonry. In
his book *Unmasking Freemasonry*, Selwyn Stevens says:

Many authorities, both Masons and others, have stated
that Freemasonry is just the religious belief of paganism.
Paganism has been defined as "the occult worship of

Nature, attributing to gods and goddesses aspects of nature." This is primarily understood to be a revival of the ancient Egyptian, Greek and Babylonian mystery religions.[18]

Stevens quotes M. Haywood, founder of the Masonic Study Club, as saying, "The religious cults in the Greco-Roman world—Egypt, Greece, Rome, etc.—were known as the Ancient Mysteries. These powerful fraternities had many things in common with our own craft."[19]

When the Israelites came out of Egypt, the Lord told them that He alone would lead them:

> You shall not bow down to their gods, nor serve them, nor do according to their works; but you shall utterly overthrow them and completely break down their sacred pillars. So you shall serve the LORD your God, and He will bless your bread and your water, and I will take sickness away from the midst of you (Exod. 23:24-25).

I believe that if we repent of the idolatry of secret societies, we will see some major breakthroughs in our nation. Freemasonry traces its roots all the way back to Egypt. As this idolatrous system is overturned, we will see—as a sign—healing break forth in this land.

Prejudice

Kelley Varner defines prejudice as "anything that separates us from God and each other":

> Prejudice is learned behavior. Men have discovered how to build all kinds of walls. Prejudice is hate, and it is based upon the spirit of fear. Its underlying essence is insecurity—the fear of rejection, of not being accepted. Prejudice is "pre-judgment," an opinion formed before the facts are known. It is unreasonable bias. Prejudice is bigotry, discrimination, intolerance, narrow-mindedness, opinion, partiality. Prejudice is poison.

Prejudice is the innate, corrupted character of the old Adamic nature that causes men to choose whom they love. Prejudice has to do with character, the heart condition of the inner man. Prejudice is engrained in us. It is the thing that knots up in our gut and really upsets us when we hear the truth. Prejudice pushes our buttons and rings our bells. Prejudice can never be surmounted by human means. The only real, lasting cure for this unholy spirit is the love of God. The single antidote for this spirit of antichrist is the supernatural, dynamic, life-changing power of the Holy Spirit. The only remedy for this universal human need is the personal and collective experience of the love of God—being forgiven, accepted in the Beloved, safe and secure in Christ. Simply stated, prejudice is "pre-judgment."[20]

According to Varner, the three main prejudices are based on gender, race and religion. In the next chapter we will take a look at the issue of gender, particularly with regard to women. First, however, know that God has no regard for our differences; He sees all who would believe as heirs, and He has an inheritance for each one of us:

> For you are all sons of God through faith in Christ Jesus. For as many of you as were baptized into Christ have put on Christ. There is neither Jew nor Greek, there is neither slave nor free, there is neither male nor female; for you are all one in Christ Jesus. And if you are Christ's, then you are Abraham's seed, and heirs according to the promise (Gal. 3:26-29).

God's Unfolding Revelation: The Holy City

In an article titled "Anti-Israel/Anti-Jewish?" Peter Hirsch writes, "People like to think they can be against the state of Israel, but still not be anti-Jewish, or anti-Semitic. It's simply not possible. I must quickly add that there is a huge difference between being anti-Israel and being against some of the policies of the Israeli government. . . . But let's be clear. Anyone who supports the destruction of the state of Israel, or who wants to limit Israel's right to exist through diminished security is an enemy of the Jewish people. Of course, anti-Zionists will claim that they simply oppose the nation, not the people, and in fact Judaism is not a nationality but a religion. That is mere rationality. The Jewish nation is an essence of Judaism since Biblical times. It must be stated that supporting Israel does not mean being against Arabs. . . . There are many instances, even in Israel, where Jews and Arabs are friends and living in peace because they share a deep commonality. That is, faith in Jesus as Messiah. Only through Him will there be a true and lasting peace."[21]

Key Prophetic Revelation from June 2005

I attempt to make a trip to Israel at least once a year. While I am there, I usually minister to the Messianic Body and then travel to key places to pray. In June 2005, the Lord led me and the team traveling with me to the Temple Mount. While I was there, I began to prophesy the following:

> For this is a time that heaven is resounding and My voice is descending to bring forth victory in the earth. I will have a joyful house of prayer for every ethnos people. This is a day of extension, for I am extending Myself to places in the earth that have never received My joyful sound. Nations are in the Valley of Decision, choosing their altar and object of worship. I will watch how they worship. I will come down and review their houses of worship, and I will reconcile all nations back to My land of Israel and the city of Jerusalem. Nations who have never known My Sprit will have an opportunity to experience Me in days ahead. As you stand upon this hill [the Temple Mount], you are standing where the nations of the earth will choose their alliance. This is the place My watchmen will come into conflict over. My glory will cover the earth, but My glory will enter in through the Eastern Gate and I will establish Myself as King over the earth.

Be still and know that I am God. This is a time of conflict. This conflict will decide who will stand with Me as the nations align. This is a time of contending for the portal of heaven to be opened over this city and this place that you stand. My watchmen will contend in the nations that are contending for Me. The conflict that is occurring in the heavenlies will begin to penetrate the earth. The next three years will reflect the level of conflict. Many will have opportunity to know Me and align with Me. Others will turn away and harden their hearts. One nation at a time will be reconciled with My covenant plan. I am raising up those who are watching with Me. These will gain the strategies over how to realign entire people groups with My plan for days ahead. I will create a sound of praise that will be contagious. My house will be filled with joy. Those who resist the joy of My house will also lose their strength as a nation.

This will be a season of descending. You must first go to the low place to win the high place. My Son first descended before He ascended. You will learn to worship in your low places. You will learn not to fear the hell around you. You will worship in unusual places. But when you worship in the low places, I will rend the heavens and come down and I will raise you up, level your path, make your crooked places straight and produce a way out of the wilderness. I will teach you to worship in new ways. Therefore, adversity will not capture you. I am calling you to stand in new ways. If you will journey with Me and be willing to face the enemies that have attempted to defeat you in the past, I will place you in the cleft of My rock. I will surround you, weaken their ability and send you forth to break their cycles. This is a time of recovery!

This is a time of procession. I am coming close to you to lead you in a new way. Submit, resist and follow me for I am drawing very near to you. I am drawing near to this city. As you say, "I will come near," you will begin to hear My voice in a new way. I am ready for you to hear My voice at the gates. There is a sound beginning to be released at the gates. I am putting a prophetic anointing within your mouth to speak what I am speaking. Open your mouth and I will fill it. I will take you from gate to gate and place to place. You will record the sound and sing the songs of deliverance that will open up the gate. For each gate has a sound that heaven is releasing. This is a time that My armies are responding to your singing in the earth realm. I am ready to send help to establish you at the gates of your lives and cites. I am ready to establish Myself at the gates of Jerusalem. Hear the song—sing and watch the hosts of heaven align themselves to assist you at the gates.

The War Over the Temple Mount

The Temple Mount in Jerusalem has always been a place of war, both physical and spiritual, and it is the place where the war of all worship wars will be fought. To understand the war that is coming, it's important to have a clear picture of the Temple Mount's history and the wars that have been fought for millennia over its control.

Although David was a worshiper, he was a man of war and was not allowed to build the Temple. However, he was permitted to gather the materials for it and to organize the project (see 1 Chron. 22). The actual work began "in the four hundred and eightieth year after the children of Israel had come out of the land of Egypt, in the fourth year of Solomon's reign over Israel" (1 Kings 6:1). Solomon began to reign about 971 B.C., so his fourth year would have been about 967 B.C. The Temple was completed about 960 B.C., seven years later (see 1 Kings 6:37-38).

In biblical times, three temples were built on the same site: Solomon's, Zerubbabel's and Herod's. Solomon built the Temple on the east side of Jerusalem on Mount Moriah, "where the Lord had appeared to his father David, at the place that David had prepared on the threshing floor of Ornan the Jebusite" (1 Chron. 21:28; 2 Chron. 3:1). The highest part of Mount Moriah is now the site of the building called The Dome of the Rock.

During the reign of Solomon's son Rehoboam, the Temple treasures were taken to Egypt (see 1 Kings 14:26). Asa used the Temple treasure to buy an ally (see 1 Kings 15:18) and stop an invader (see 2 Kings 16:8). Manasseh placed Canaanite altars and carved images of Asherah, a Canaanite goddess, in the Temple (see

2 Kings 21:4,7). Ahaz introduced an altar patterned after one he saw in Damascus (see 2 Kings 16:10-16). By about 622 B.C., Josiah had to repair the Temple (see 2 Kings 22:3-7). He overthrew his predecessors' false altars and restored true worship back to Judah. (Notice these cycles.) After robbing the Temple of its treasures and gold during his first attack, the Babylonian king Nebuchadnezzar looted, sacked and burned the Temple in 587 B.C. However, God's people still came to the site to offer sacrifices (see 2 Kings 24:13; 25:9,13-17; Jer. 41:5).

After the Temple was destroyed during the Babylonian captivity, the Ark of the Covenant was never recovered, and so the Second Temple (and Herod's Temple) had no Ark. Nor were Solomon's 10 lampstands ever recovered. One seven-branched candelabra, the table of showbread and the incense altar stood in the Holy Place of the Second Temple (as they did in Herod's Temple), but these were taken by Antiochus IV Epiphanes, who defiled the altar in 167 B.C.

Jesus showed great respect for the Temple and referred to it as "the House of God" (Matt 12:4) and His "Father's house" (John 2:16). He taught that everything in it was holy because it belonged to God, and He was angry when it was defiled. Jesus purged the Temple of the moneychangers (see Mark 11:15-17; John 2:16). He wept and proclaimed its destruction prophetically (see Mark 13:1; Luke 19:41-44). Jesus' actions in the Temple disclosed Him as Messiah, which is one of the reasons the Pharisees wanted His death. At the moment of Jesus' death, the veil of the Temple was torn from top to bottom (see Matt 27:51; Mark 15:38; Luke 23:45). At the crucifixion, Jesus opened a new way for the presence of God to be attained. A new order and a new covenant were released in the earth. No longer was the Temple in Jerusalem to be the only place where mankind worshiped God. God is Spirit, and those who worship Him must worship Him "in spirit and truth" (John 4:21-24).

Many temples have been built on the Mount, including a temple of Jupiter, which was destroyed at the Roman emperor Constantine's direction. He despised the place and made it into a dump. Many years later, an Islamic caliph approached the Byzantine ruler of Jerusalem to ask for a place where the Muslims might build their mosque. The ruler gave the caliph permission to build a mosque on a dump filled with rubbish and trash—the Temple Mount! A church leader actually gave the Temple Mount away!

We must open our eyes to see the war, both physical and spiritual. The Mount is truly a portal of heaven and a gate of hell, with hidden occult powers working underground to hold the whole Mount captive. On the corner of the Temple Mount is now the largest underground mosque in the Middle East, which can accommodate more than 30,000 people. This signifies how the war has shifted from being above ground to underground. The Islamic leadership is also hoping to bring water from Mecca to store in the underground cisterns on the Temple Mount, which would give the Muslim faithful the option of taking their *hajj* to the Temple Mount and give the Mount status similar to Mecca. There is much contention over who will rule this place. *Can you see the war?*

The first Christians, converted Jews, continued to worship at the Temple (see Luke 24:52; Acts 2:46; 3:1; 5:12,20-21,42), but persecution and powerful works caused new wineskins to be developed in other areas such as Antioch, Ephesus and Corinth. We should each realize that we are new temples, but we must also realize that nations are aligning and God's Living Body is at war with antichrist covenant forces that want to control our worship. By asking the Lord to return in His power to the Church, the war over the Temple Mount will begin to escalate.

Shakings and Skirmishes Will Increase!

Anti-Israel sentiment will continue to grow as time advances. Exodus 15:17 says, "You will bring them in and plant them in the mountain of your inheritance, in the place, O Lord, which you have made for your own dwelling, the sanctuary, O Lord, which your hands have established."

Israel took the Mount from Jordan 40 years ago in June 1967, claiming sovereignty over it. However, the Israelites allowed a contingent of police from Jordan to "oversee" the Muslim holy sites alongside Israeli troops. This will eventually result in a great war. The kingdom of Jordan has developed plans to build a fifth minaret on the Temple Mount in Jerusalem, which will be placed at the Eastern Gate. With the other four already on the Mount, they will symbolize the so-called "Five Pillars of Islam."

On February 1, 2007, Islamic officials at Al Aqsah Mosque on the Temple Mount unveiled a new wooden stairway and pulpit in the mosque. The pulpit is a replica of one donated to the mosque by Saladin after he conquered Jerusalem from the crusaders in 1187. The original was burned in 1969 by an Australian, a follower of Herbert W. Armstrong, who believed that destroying the mosque would speed the coming of Messiah. As a goodwill gesture, Israel allowed the pulpit to be replaced, and the Jordanian government reportedly paid some $1 million for its construction. According to some of our contacts, one official in the mosque saw its replacement as an important sign that Jerusalem will soon be liberated from the Jews.

Tensions are continuing to build over the Mount. Several years ago, a fault, probably caused by an earthquake, caused the ramp that non-Muslims take up to the Mount to begin to collapse down into the women's area of the Western Wall (the Wailing Wall). Israel constructed a temporary ramp, which has now been used for more than a year. Israeli officials now want to build a permanent one, but Israeli law requires that before construction, there must be an archaeological dig under the area to ensure there isn't something important that will be permanently covered up. The area is totally outside the parameters of the Temple compound, but Muslim leaders both within and outside Israel are using this as a pretext for stirring up violence, claiming that Israel is threatening Al Aqsah. They are calling on their followers to flood the area with demonstrations and are even threatening to blow up Jewish synagogues if Israel continues digging.

The -Ites are withstanding God's glory, but will eventually bow to His will!

Praying for Israel and Understanding God's Covenant Plan

Throughout Scripture we are encouraged to pray, but in all of Scripture there is only one *place* for which we are specifically called to pray—that place is Jerusalem.

How do we do that? As we go about our lives being His people and His vessels in our nations, in our cities, in our neighborhoods, in our families and in our churches, how do we "pray for Jerusalem"? How is a connection made? How do we hear the heart of the Lord for a city located very far away from most of us?

Throughout the Word of God, Jerusalem always occupies a central place. Abraham in obedience built an altar on Moriah (a mountain in Jerusalem) to offer Isaac unto the Lord. David brought the Ark of the Covenant to Jerusalem, and his son Solomon built the Temple there. When Yeshua (Jesus) walked this earth, Jerusalem was clearly a heart issue with Him. Both Matthew and Luke record Yeshua lamenting that Jerusalem kills her prophets!

Wars have been fought over this city. It has been in the hands of the Jebusites, of the Jews, the Romans, the Persians, the Crusaders, the Ottoman Turks, the British and the Jordanians. From 1949 until June 1967, the Old City was divided, with part being under Jordanian rule and part under Israeli sovereignty. Jerusalem is known as the City of the King. A small area is known as the City of David. The Jews pray at the Western Wall and the Muslims pray on the Temple Mount. If we could but see the angels and demons that hover over this city, we would all be amazed!

Books have been written about Jerusalem, songs have been sung about her, blood has been spilled on her and battles fought over her. Before time comes to an end, there will be more books, more songs, more blood and more battles. So how do we pray? How do we stand? How do we become "watchmen" on her walls? I offer a few points at this 40-year (a "generation") anniversary of the return of Jerusalem to the Jews:

1. Pray for the Messianic remnant in the Land. Pray for those Messianic believers who live here, work here, minister here—that their lives will be strong lights in a dark place. For the bond of *shalom* to be preserved between them, in this city rife with religious contention. Pray for them to have positions and to gain favor in their jobs, in the government, in their communities and in the army.

2. Pray for Arab Christians in Jerusalem, for God's revelation concerning His purposes in His City. Pray for unity, both among themselves and between themselves and their Messianic Jewish brothers and sisters. Pray for love and courage and vision. For protection from Muslim Palestinian Arabs who hold them in contempt. For prosperity in their businesses and grace and provision for their families.

3. Pray for the Gentile believers whom God sends to minister here. Pray for them to have wise boldness in their ministries and to build relationships with Israelis. Pray for visas and for favor with the Ministry of Interior. Pray that the gates will be open for those whom the Lord sends, that they may go in and out without harassment.

4. Pray for the city government. A mayor is needed who is open to the Messianic Body and will give them a voice and a place in the City.

5. Pray for the national government—for all corruption to be exposed and for the fear of the Lord to come on those who have positions here. Israel is presently undergoing the greatest crisis of exposure of corruption and impropriety among her elected leaders in her present-day history.

6. Pray for the true prophetic to be released in Jerusalem and throughout Israel. Pray for false prophets to be silenced and true ones to be recognized and given a voice. Pray for the leaders of the nation to cry out for the voice of God, and for the voice of the prophet to gain credence as in the days of Elijah and Elisha!

7. Pray for the Body of Messiah in the nations to have wisdom in how to give finances to Israel. Many desire

to bless Israel, but they give ignorantly to organizations they encounter in sentimental ads on television—unaware that these are generally run by the ultra-Orthodox who hate Messianic believers. Or they gave to nationalistic causes, which are fine—but the Body here is poor! Pray that there be greater discernment in giving.

8. Pray for the youth. Pray for revival to come to Israeli youth who are looking to Eastern religions and empty philosophies for fulfillment. Pray for the believing youth to be bold in their friendships and love.

9. Worship as you watch! "Your watchmen shall lift up their voices, with their voices they shall sing together; for they shall see eye to eye when the Lord brings back Zion" (Isa. 52:8) There is a huge battle over who will be worshiped in this city—the God of Israel?—or Allah? Worship the God of Israel as you stand with her!

10. Psalm 122:6 says "pray for the peace [*shalom*] of Jerusalem." In Hebrew the word for "pray" is *sha'a*—to request, demand, beg, desire earnestly. This *shalom* is not something we gently request—it is something we cry out for with all of our hearts!

11. Isaiah 62:1 says that we will not hold our peace and not rest until the righteousness of Jerusalem shines forth. Interestingly, the words translated "hold our peace" and "rest" in the Hebrew mean "I will not be quiet." So praying for Jerusalem is not a "quiet" thing. It is something we must do aloud. It is something to declare, to speak forth. *THE MESSAGE* puts it this way: "Regarding Zion, I can't keep my mouth shut, regarding Jerusalem, I can't hold my tongue until her righteousness blazes down like the sun and her salvation flames up like a torch." Pray Isaiah 62.

12. Pray for the Holy Spirit to grant you the revelation and grace to love Jerusalem—with the Love that God Himself has for her. The prosperity of the Lord rests on those who do so. In blessing Jerusalem and the descendants of Abraham, we release grace and blessing back into our own families, cities and nations (see Ps. 122:6; Gen. 12:3)![22]

But God! Jerusalem is His city, the place where He has put His name. His mountain is here! "I will return to Zion, and dwell in the midst of Jerusalem. Jerusalem shall be called the City of Truth, the Mountain of the Lord of hosts, the Holy Mountain" (Zech. 8:3). Over the doors of the Dome of the Rock are written passages from the Koran declaring that "Allah" has no son. Psalm 2 of the Hebrew Scriptures states that YHVH the Lord of Hosts laughs—that He not only has a Son but also has ordained that that Son will reign on His throne on this very mountain. A confrontation of beyond epic proportions is coming!

CHAPTER NINE

Women Arising Now

Village life ceased, it ceased in Israel,
Until I, Deborah, arose,
Arose a mother in Israel.

JUDGES 5:7

Women are called to be a great power in the future.
JOSEPHINE BUTLER (1828-1906)

Thus far we have seen that the Church is in a real spiritual war. There is much oppression and conflict ahead, but if we will step up into the authority God has given us for this season, we will see great victory. One of the areas of oppression most commonly linked with the antichrist system worldwide concerns the oppression of women.

Recently I read the following in the *Dallas Morning News*:

A woman in Afghanistan was recently beaten for eating ice cream in public after buying it from a street vendor. Among the thousands of reports on human rights [concerning] abuse of Afghan women, this is certainly not the worst, according to Eleanor Smeal [president of the Feminist Majority Foundation, a research and advocacy group]. But she says it is emblematic of the human tragedy occurring in the rugged mountain recesses of central Asia. Now feminists are joining arms with Hollywood celebrities to step up a three-year campaign against the ruling Muslim fundamentalists now ruling most of Afghanistan.

The goal is to connect Americans with underground schools for Afghan girls, and to make the plight of Afghan women the human rights focus of the new millennium.[1]

The Seduction of Women

Not only will there be increasing oppression of women in the coming days but there will also be a seduction of the world's women to lead them away from their God-ordained direction.

In *World* magazine, Bob Jones IV wrote that the long-standing debate over gender equality is broadening in scope. No longer are education and equal-pay-for-equal-work the only issues. In addition to their liberal stand on reproductive rights, the United Nations is promoting "the right to free choice of profession and employment," including the legalization of prostitution. The Convention for the Elimination of Discrimination Against Women (CEDAW) is one avenue by which the UN is redefining global opinion and acceptance of prostitution as an inherent freedom.[2]

This seduction of the female is nothing new. There is a wonderful book called *Bad Girls of the Bible* by Christian author Liz Curtis Higgs. In this book, Higgs takes from Scripture each key woman who deviated from God's perfect plan for her life and analyzes her mistakes. She discusses Eve, Potiphar's wife, Lot's wife, Jezebel, Rahab, Michal, and others. Higgs shows how several of these deviated from and never returned to God's perfect plan, perhaps even setting a poor pattern for others to follow. Other biblical women, such as the woman at the well, are shown to have recognized their true identity and turned from a horrible season of life toward a new destiny.

The enemy will oppress and attempt to stop women from becoming all that God has created them to be. And if he is able, Satan will enslave them to accomplish his will on Earth. But despite the enemy's efforts to oppress and seduce women, we are about to see women of the Church arise and influence the world in a way they have never done before!

Women on the Rise

In a recent article in *SpiritLed Woman*, Judy Jacobs examines how "the kingdom of heaven suffers violence, and the violent take it by force" (Matt. 11:12). She writes:

> "The violent take it by force" means that an energetic force takes for itself what is rightfully its own. . . . This is a season where violence is required to get things accomplished in the supernatural that could never be done in the natural. . . . This requires a new level of courage, determination, perseverance and unwavering faith. Women who have never felt violent will now arise in faith and believe God for the impossible.[3]

We are about to see faith-filled women arise and change the course of history.

With the apostolic Church rising and the apostolic gift being restored in the Body of Christ to produce a new order, the question of how women fit into God's plan for the days ahead is key. I believe this question is going to be as big as the Acts 15 ordeal over circumcision. In this passage, Gentiles were beginning to come into the Kingdom, and the Church (which was mostly Jewish at the time) was trying to determine whether the Gentiles would have to obey the Jewish laws in order to experience salvation. A key meeting was held and a binding decision was made that salvation was a gift by grace and that the Gentiles could be welcomed into the saving grace of God without observing the law of circumcision.

Today, we must ask how God wants to raise up women to influence the Kingdom and the world. We must also recognize how Satan's plans depend on the continued oppression of women. Our understanding of these two issues will help us to determine the progress of the Church in the future war.

Undoubtedly, women are one of the Church's most untapped resources. David Yonggi Cho, senior pastor of the 700,000-member Yoido Full Gospel Church in Seoul, has said:

For 5,000 years in Korea, women had no voice at all. They were only to cater to the needs of men. Then Christianity came and set women free. Especially in the church, women are free. . . . In ministry, they are equal to men. They are licensed; they are ordained. They become deacons and elders, and they become cell leaders. . . . [If pastors will train women and delegate ministry to them] they will become tremendous messengers for the Lord. . . . [Although some argue that women should be silent in church] once women are called into ministry, they no longer belong to the category of women. They are messengers of the Lord.[4]

Women of Faith Transforming Society

I remember seeing a TV commercial that declared, "There's never been a better time in history to be a girl." Even though great oppression is occurring in certain areas against women, they are also enjoying more opportunities than ever to become all that God created them to be—to let their lights and gifts shine.

As we have said, the new millennium is revealing a new order in the Body of Christ. The law of order says that there is a sequence of events arranged in a definite plan and time that causes the proper functioning of systems, resulting in victory. Order is also linked with authority.

Women have become recognized in the Church as prayer warriors but not particularly for their ability to exercise God's authority on Earth. During the past decade I have had the opportunity to work with great women of faith. Through my position among the leaders in the global prayer movement, our Lord has brought me into relationship with several gifted women who know how to wield great authority on their knees. This authority, through spirit-filled praying, brings heaven to Earth and changes the course of the world.

God is renewing and restoring the apostolic gifting in the Body of Christ. He is raising up leadership for the future. He is releasing an anointing for spiritual breakthrough against the kingdom of darkness from region to region. This is a season when our Lord's apostolic order and authority are being established in a new, fresh dimension. Part of God's order for this hour is the establishment of godly women with an authority and a sphere of influence that will revolutionize societies throughout the earth.

Many prophets are declaring that there will be a great move of the Holy Spirit among women. I believe that many women are being called to preach, teach and evangelize cities and nations. These women will find themselves released and liberated to go forth proclaiming, "The kingdom of our Lord is at hand!"

So what role will women play in the future transformation of society? And just where do women fit in the apostolic reformation of the Church that is now occurring?

Spiritual Mothering

When apostolic authority is established in a territory, the vision of today is thereby passed to the succeeding generations. Most of us think of the gift of apostle, the first gift God recognizes as necessary for His order to be established on Earth, as being a *fathering* gift. This is definitely true. However, there is another dimension of transgenerational vision and apostolic gifting that includes spiritual *mothering*. Without both mothering and fathering, the next generation of believers becomes dysfunctional. Mothers have many times determined the course of history. God is raising up spiritual mothers in this hour.

I have always had a heart and a great respect for women who endured and overcame their circumstances. It is easy for me to relate to the Scripture in 2 Timothy 1:5 when Paul encourages Timothy "to remember the genuine faith that is in you, which dwelt first in your grandmother Lois and your mother . . . and I am persuaded is in you also." I look back at the difficult circumstances of my youth and it is with great joy that I reflect on the faith of a godly grandmother and the endurance of a mother who imparted future strength to me.

Passionate Conception

The Bible gives us many examples of women operating in faith who changed the direction of the human race. *Women of faith receive strength to conceive the seed of the future.* The first woman of faith we find recognized by God was Sarah:

> By faith Sarah herself also *received strength to conceive seed,* and she bore a child when she was past the age, because she judged Him faithful who had promised (Heb. 11:11, emphasis added.).

Sarah gave birth to Isaac when she was 90 years old. She overcame her physical inability because she judged God to be faithful to His promise that she would be the mother of nations and that kings would descend from her (see Gen. 17:15-16; 18:10).

The Hebrew word *yacham* ("conceive") means to get hot. There is a passion that God is about to release upon His Church. We are going to see the passion of God rise up in His women of faith. Although Sarah's womb was dead, it got hot as God produced within her the faith to lay the foundation of our covenant future. This is God's time for passion to hit women—a godly, holy passion that will cause the foundation of the future to come into being.

These are days of supernatural conception and birthing, and women understand and model conception and travail better than men. I believe God is asking the question today, "Where are my Sarahs?" He is saying, "I plan to conceive My purpose to bring forth My inheritance in the nations in this hour. I need Sarahs filled with faith who can conceive and bring forth this plan."

Overthrowing Enemies

Women who have been disciplined and prepared have faith and boldness to overthrow an enemy bent on destruction. Esther was such a woman (see chapter 2). Even though she was an adopted orphan, through preparation and discipline the favor of God rested upon Esther, as she was willing to be used by a holy God to save an entire people. By receiving the spirit of adoption that the Lord Jesus Christ has offered us, we will be prepared for what is ahead in the future. Even if you feel totally abandoned, know that the Lord can raise you up and prepare you for that special moment when He will use you for the advancement of His kingdom.

We are seeing a generation of Esthers arising—godly, obedient, grace-filled women who are being positioned to overthrow the enemies of the future.

Transforming Cities

Women of faith bring transformation to cities. In 2 Samuel 20 we find the story of two nations at odds. This story has rebellion, anarchy, betrayal—many of the same issues we see between nations in the world today.

The rebel Sheba had led an uprising against David that threatened the entire kingdom. One of David's mighty men, Joab, pursued Sheba to Abel of Beth Maachah, the city where Sheba was holed up. Joab's men surrounded the city and, bent on destruction, began battering the walls to bring them down.

> Then a wise woman cried out from the city, "Hear, Hear! Please say to Joab, 'Come nearby, that I may speak with you.'" When he had come near to her, the woman said, "Are you Joab?" He answered, "I am." Then she said to him, "Hear the words of your maidservant." And he answered, "I am listening" (2 Sam. 20:16-17).

Faith has a voice and wisdom that can produce change. I really like this passage because it never gives the woman's name.

This lady recognized that her city was headed for destruction. So she said to Joab, "I am among the peaceable and faithful in Israel. You seek to destroy a city and a mother in Israel. Why would you swallow up the inheritance of the LORD?" (v. 19). This statement stopped Joab and made him rethink his course of action. Why should he destroy a whole city just to overtake one rebellious individual? So he said to the lady, "Deliver Sheba into my hands, and I will depart from the city." The woman responded, "Watch, his head will be thrown to you over the wall" (v. 21). Then the woman in her wisdom went to her people, and they cut off the head of Sheba and threw it out to Joab. This caused the army to withdraw from the city.

Wow! One woman's wisdom and influence prevented the destruction of an entire city. God is now raising up unknown women who are filled with faith and who carry the Word of God in their mouths. They will become like two-edged swords, ready to speak wisdom that will alter the plans of destruction for our cities.

There are many more biblical examples of women who exercised authority that resulted in historical change. Lydia in Acts 16 is a great example of women operating in the marketplace who caused the evangelization of a nation to occur. I also love Moses' mother, whose faith saved an entire nation. Deborah was an established warrior who led an entire generation (see Judg. 4). Jael was just a normal young girl with a ready weapon in her hand who brought the final blow on the enemy of her people (see Judg. 5:24-27). Mary of Bethany displayed extravagant devotion in the midst of rebuke to practice servanthood upon our Lord (see John 12:1-8).

Women in past seasons have known they had a call to influence and transform society. Unfortunately, some attempted to enter into this authority outside the boundaries and timing of God, producing confusion and a measure of reproach upon the whole of the female gender. However, *this* is a time and season when God is preparing women leaders and spiritual mothers who will step up and enter into authority according to His perfect plan, His order and His timing. These are the women who will change the course of the world.

Arise, women of the faith, and transform your families, cities and nations!

Jesus Changed the Status of Women

In the Old Testament and under the Old Covenant, women were essentially relegated to the task of keeping the home. But God in His sovereignty would raise up women leaders from time to time. When He did this, these women often had an incredible apostolic anointing. They exercised great influence and in some instances ruled better than the men of their time. God is able to break into a culture that subjugates women to men, and He will raise women to positions of leadership, empowering them to accomplish His purposes on Earth.

Indeed, in the New Testament, we see Jesus doing a new thing: He changes the status of women! Our Lord caused society to recognize women in a different way. Let's look at the incident in which a woman caught in an adulterous act was brought before Jesus:

> The scribes and Pharisees brought to Him a woman caught in adultery. And when they had set her in the midst, they said to Him, "Teacher, this woman was caught in adultery, in the very act. Now Moses, in the law, commanded us that such should be stoned. But what do You say?" (John 8:3-5).

Cindy Jacobs shares that she could "only imagine the thoughts that ran through Jesus' mind" during this confrontation:

> One immediate thought would have been that the Scribes and Pharisees had only quoted *part* of the law on adultery. Leviticus 20:10 says that both the adulterer and the adulteress shall be put to death. The woman alone had been "caught in the act"; the guilty man was getting off scot-free. Many other double standards had evolved in the society since the law had been given. Of course, the eternally present Son of God and lawgiver knew. His next statement ripped the covers off the hidden places of their hearts: "He who is without sin among you, let him throw a stone at her first" (John 8:7).[5]

Jesus demolished the double standard that had been established by tradition and culture. This was not just a matter of a woman being judged for her sin; this was a societal issue concerning gender! Christian tradition has it that this woman later became an incredible influence within the Lord's ministry to the society that surrounded her. The same thing happened after Jesus spoke with the Samaritan woman at the well. Once she met the Lord, her testimony helped to transform her entire city (see John 4:39-42).

If the people of God are to march forward in this season, we must see and expect the redemptive power of God that came to Earth when the Lord Jesus visited. He literally liberated women! Yet in society we keep going back to the old ways. We simply cannot go back in this season. Know that the enemy is afraid of the woman! The first redemptive promise found in the Word of God is that although Satan would bruise the heel of her seed, her seed would crush the head of Satan (see Gen. 3:15). This is an incredible redemptive promise.

The enemy has so many believing women cowering in fear. Consequently, they have lost sight of the fact that their seed will one day crush the enemy's head. Ladies, now is the time to ask the Lord to make your ministry strong. Shake off the bruising you see and feel, and confess that the heels of your physical and spiritual sons and daughters will soon crush the enemy!

Satan's View of Women

Many women struggle to understand all they are in Christ. They have been told over and over, "Here's your role." The enemy has used this religious spirit to steal women's hope and confine them to a place the Lord never intended.

One reason I have such a heart for women is that I grew up in a home where my mother was abused. My dad fell into corruption, and I saw a man who had so much potential instead take an abusive path. I watched him violate everything he knew to be right.

I remember the first time I took a stand against this behavior in our home. I ended up receiving the abuse as well. This began a cycle of destruction set against both my mother and me. Eventually I asked the Lord, "Why is this happening?" I had to come to an understanding of why there was such enmity between the woman and the seed of Satan.

Male and female roles and relationships are so clearly defined in the first couple of chapters of Genesis. Truly, whatever seeks to demean, enslave or dominate women is contrary to God's original plan and purpose for humankind. Man and woman are created equal in all aspects. They are one in Jesus Christ.

Man and woman, who are made in God's image and likeness, share a unique position and relationship in God's created order. God gave two commands to the first couple: Be fruitful and rule over the earth (see Gen. 1:28). These commands were given to both the man and the woman. And yet, as Jim Davis and Donna Johnson tell us in *Redefining the Role of Women in the Church*, "there has been a persistent tendency . . . to apply the command to procreate to woman, but to exclude her from the command to exercise dominion, or rule, over the earth."[6]

Somehow Satan has managed to deal devastating blows to male-female relationships in the Church. Rather than collaboration in unity and harmony to accomplish God's purposes, we have instead had separation and domination. Many of God's people have indulged in evil practices, including adultery, divorce, polygamy, abuse, unfaithfulness and the breaking of covenant.

I first came to know the Lord when I was 11, but it was not until I was 16 that I really began to *seek* Him. It was then I recognized Satan's hatred of women. I can't say I ever had any bitterness toward my dad, because I had experienced the love of God and I knew the Lord also loved my father. But I knew another force was controlling him. Through him I could see the power of Satan. I saw in my father more than just abuse; I saw wrath.

I repeat, Satan hates women with great wrath. One way you can always determine the level of the antichrist spirit and his operation is how you see women being treated in a region. Similarly, how you see women being treated in the Church displays the level of the freedom of God in that region. The two are in direct correlation with each other.

Because of the abuse and destruction in our family, our family had to be realigned with Father God. Part of that realignment occurred because my mother did not just write off all men; instead, after my father's death, she married a godly man who helped to break the power of dysfunction that was in our family.

I mentioned earlier how the apostolic call to the Church is to both spiritual fathers and mothers. Larry Kreider, in his book *The Cry for Spiritual Fathers and Mothers*, explains the three keys to spiritual parenting: (1) initiate a relationship, (2) build a relationship and (3) release your children into their own relationship so that they, too, can produce spiritual children. Kreider also explores God's nurturing mother heart. I highly recommend this book to anyone who wants to learn how to break down the dysfunction in a family's life, whether it be a spiritual family or natural.[7]

God is calling His people to a balanced spiritual life that includes spiritual mothering as well as fathering. I believe Satan hates the realignment of fathers and mothers, both spiritual and natural, even more than he hates the female gender itself.

NOW Women Rising

In her book *Women of Destiny*, Cindy Jacobs writes:

> Of one thing I am certain: God is calling women today in a greater way than He ever has before. Major prophetic voices are prophesying all around the world that this is the time to find a way to release women into the ministry.[8]

It is of utmost importance that we understand the role of women in the new place to which the Lord has called His Church. The women He is raising up in this hour are what I call NOW women. This designation has nothing to do with the feminist organization (the National Organization of Women), but rather, refers to *women who have been called and prepared for such a time as this.*

Past apostolic movements in the Church did not bring the gifts of God in women to their fullness, usually because women were not considered by men to be equal in their giftings. This did not stop the gifts of God from moving through women; instead it caused their gifts to be developed outside the four walls of the local church. As a result, we have seen Christian women's organizations spring up all over the world to help release women in their giftings, the largest being Aglow International.

In this new move of God, this will not be the case. We are coming into a new dimension in the Body of Christ in which the women of God will be given great authority and great influence in the Body.

NOW Women Initiate the New Thing

This is a NOW season on Earth. What we do NOW will dramatically affect our future. It is a new season for women, as the Lord is beginning to call forth NOW women for His purpose. This is the time for NOW women to rise up. (This is also a slogan of the feminist movement. But God has a way of revealing His truth, even when the world and the devil try to pervert it.)

What does a NOW woman look like? The account of Jesus' first public miracle—turning water into wine—provides some insight:

> There was a wedding in Cana of Galilee, and the mother of Jesus was there. Now both Jesus and His disciples were invited to the wedding. And when they ran out of wine, the mother of Jesus said to Him, "They have no wine." Jesus said to her, "Woman, what does your concern have to do with Me? My hour has not yet come." His mother said to the servants, "Whatever He says to you, do it" (John 2:1-5).

This is an incredible Scripture passage. Jesus looks at His mother and basically says, "What does this wedding have to do with Me? I'm not ready to display My glory." Notice His mother's reaction: She didn't seem to listen to Him. The mothers that God is raising up in this hour just know when it's time for something to happen. NOW women initiate the new thing.

Mary said to the attendants, "Whatever He says to do, do it." Here is an example of a woman initiating the new thing. Based perhaps on what His Father wanted to do as revealed by His mother, Jesus submitted and began to give instructions to create the wine that would bring fulfillment to the wedding. He told the servants to get water pots and fill them up. Then He said to them, "Draw some out *now*, and take it to the master of the feast" (v. 8, emphasis added).

Mary initiated this NOW event. Many times women are called to initiate the next move of God on Earth. Have this mindset about you even though society may not see it this way.

After Jesus changed the water to wine, the host said to the bridegroom, "Everyone brings out the choice wine first and then the cheaper wine after the guests have had too much to drink; but you have saved the best till *now*" (v. 10, emphasis added). The best is yet to come, and women are going to be on the front line, initiating the best in the days ahead. Remember, this was Jesus' first sign that He demonstrated to Palestinian society. It was the first time they saw His glory revealed—and it was initiated by a woman.

NOW Women Conceive the New Thing

We've already discussed Sarah from the standpoint of birthing what God wanted to do on the earth. But let's look at her from the standpoint of conceiving. In Hebrews 11:11 (interestingly, 11 is the number of judgment), we read, "By faith Sarah herself also received strength to conceive seed, and she bore a child when she was past the age, because she judged Him faithful who had promised." NOW women conceive the new thing. As we have seen, the Hebrew word *yacham* ("conceive") means to get hot. Passion comes alive, and from this conception begins to occur.

If there is one thing wrong with the Church, it is that we've lost the passion to be able to properly conceive the new thing that God wants to do on Earth. However, we are now on the verge of one of the greatest women's movements ever. This new movement will not be perverted, and it will not be out of sync with God's purpose and timing. It won't be conceived by the flesh, and the enemy won't motivate it. The Lord is raising up passionate women who are filled with faith and who are about to conceive this new thing.

Early one morning on the way to a conference, Cindy Jacobs suggested we stop at a Krispy Kreme (a great doughnut shop). If you know anything about Krispy Kreme, you know to look for a neon sign in the window that says "Hot." When you see this, you know that the doughnuts have just come out of the oven, and that's when they taste incredible! On this day we saw the sign flashing in the window, so Cindy and I pulled into Krispy Kreme. There were huge lines because everyone there had come to get in on the very best. That's what God wants to do in the Church! He wants that "Hot" sign to come on in the Church, and when it does, this will draw people from all around. They will be lined up, trying to get in! And it will be the women who have the ability to conceive and release that passion.

NOW Women Announce the New Thing

The Gospel of Mark reveals another characteristic of NOW women. After we learn that the stone had been rolled away from Jesus' tomb and that He had risen from the dead, we read:

> Now when [Jesus] rose early on the first day of the week, He appeared first to Mary Magdalene, out of whom He had cast seven demons. She went and told those who had been with Him (Mark 16:9-10).

Jesus chose a woman to be the person to whom He first appeared. This woman would be a prototype of the believer spreading the good news of salvation to the world. So just because you've been demonized in the past does not mean you're not a forerunner for the future. You, too, could revolutionize the world! Mary Magdalene went and told the mourning and weeping disciples that Jesus was risen indeed!

NOW women announce the new thing. Not only do they initiate and conceive it, but NOW women also announce the new thing. Jesus' handpicked disciples were too filled with fear and unbelief; they were not ready to announce His resurrection. As it was, they didn't believe Mary Magdalene when she made her announcement. But she knew she had seen the Lord. Women are about to become the next trumpeters of faith throughout this land.

Men Should Position Themselves to Receive NOW Women

The story of Rebekah at the well in Genesis 24 reveals a different dimension regarding NOW women that God wants us to understand at this time. If you remember, Isaac had been given Abraham's heritage. However, Isaac could not perpetuate this inheritance by himself. Consequently, Abraham sent his servant to find a suitable bride for Isaac. In Genesis 24:10, we find that "the servant took ten of his master's camels and departed, for all his master's goods were in his hand." That means the servant had access to anything his master had, so he chose camels laden with gifts to begin his search for Isaac's wife. What the servant was really looking for was the release of the inheritance of God on the earth.

When the servant arrived in Mesopotamia in the evening, he made his camels kneel down outside the city of Nahor by a well of water. The time of day is important, as evening was the time when the women of the city came out to draw water. Knowing this, Abraham's servant arrived at the well at the right time so that he could watch for a suitable bride among the women. Then the servant prayed to the God of his master and asked for success on this day in his mission:

> Behold, here I stand by the well of water, and the daughters of the men of the city are coming out to draw water. Now let it be that the young woman to whom I say, "Please let down your pitcher that I may drink," and she says, "Drink, and I will also give your camels a drink"—let her be the one You have appointed for Your servant Isaac. And by this I will know that You have shown kindness to my master (Gen. 24:13-14).

These men positioned themselves to receive a NOW woman. This is a very important point. Abraham's servant was looking and listening carefully for a woman to fulfill God's prophetic command at that time. And when the NOW woman said the right thing, he knew she was the one.

We have a concept in our society that men always lead. Yet many times it's the women who fulfill the destiny of God. When we hear the right thing coming from a woman, we need to begin to acknowledge that woman. Are you recognizing how great a role women play in the course of society and in the course of God's inheritance? There is a perfect timing for everything, and this is a time that women and men must position themselves properly.

Rebekah came out to the well with her pitcher on her shoulder even *before* the servant had finished praying (see v. 15). This is an hour when you need to get to the well to which God is calling you. And you need to have those vessels ready to fill up what needs to be filled.

When Rebekah appeared, the servant ran out to meet her and asked if he could have a little water to drink. Rebekah said, "Drink, my lord," and lowered her pitcher so that he could get a drink (v. 18). She also offered to give water to his camels. This lady was at the right place at the right time and said the right thing. As a result, she ended up marrying the richest man in the region. Many times when you come to the right place at the right time, there are all sorts of blessings waiting for you there.

Earlier, in Genesis 24:5, the servant questioned Abraham, saying, "Perhaps the woman will not be willing to follow me to this land." But Rebekah was ready to make a move. She chose to move forward into the inheritance of God, and she ended up fulfilling the destiny of God. Because Abraham's servant was positioned correctly to receive this NOW woman, all of God's generational blessings were opened to Isaac and his descendants. NOW women have great influence, and men are now being positioned to receive them.

NOW Women Intervene on Behalf of Foolish Men

The life of Abigail exemplifies influence as well as another attribute of NOW women. In 1 Samuel 25, we learn that Abigail was married to Nabal, a very wealthy businessman and landowner in Carmel. David and his men were camped in the area, and they sought refreshment from the household of Nabal. David's men came with a right spirit to this man, but Nabal replied foolishly and denied their request. Often women live with foolish men, but that should not stop them from being who they're supposed to be.

When Nabal rejected the opportunity to refresh David and his troops, he also rejected the opportunity to receive promise. David's encampment had actually been forming a wall around this foolish man's territory and protecting everything he had. Consequently, when David asked for blessing, he thought that Nabal would gladly reciprocate.

Given the wealthy man's scornful response, David decided to go in, take what he and his troops needed and kill all the men in Nabal's household. So Nabal's wife, Abigail, "made haste and took two hundred loaves of bread, two skins of wine, five sheep already dressed, five seahs of roasted grain, one hundred clusters of raisins, and two hundred cakes of figs, and loaded them on donkeys" (1 Sam. 25:18). She bypassed her foolish husband in order to save him and his household from the wrath of the renowned warrior and his men.

When Abigail went out to meet David, she bowed her face to the ground and said, "On me, my lord, on me let this iniquity be! And please let your maidservant speak in your ears, and hear the words of your maidservant" (v. 24). It doesn't matter who your husband is; a NOW woman can intervene on behalf of a foolish man. Abigail positioned herself correctly; she humbled herself and interceded for her husband. Notice the results: David received her intercession and bade her go in peace.

When Abigail told her husband the next morning what she had done, "his heart died within him, and he became [paralyzed, helpless as] a stone. And about ten days after that, the Lord smote Nabal and he died" (1 Sam. 25:37-38, *AMP*). Abigail later married David.

God has placed many women in difficult situations and has given them the ability to intervene correctly. When a NOW woman intervenes correctly before the Lord, know that the Lord will intervene on her behalf.

NOW Women Know the Time for Change

Naomi is another example of a NOW woman. The name "Naomi" means "pleasant," but the Word of God says she was bitter (see Ruth 1:20). Here is a woman who lost her husband and both sons while the family dwelt in a foreign land. Following their deaths, Naomi chose to leave Moab and return home to Bethlehem. After they had already set out for Bethlehem, she spoke with her sons' widows (Orpah and Ruth, both women of Moab) and gave them a choice: They could remain with her and move on to a new place or they could go back to Moab. One daughter-in-law, Orpah, did the expected and returned to the familiar. The other, Ruth, did the exceptional and went forward with her mother-in-law.

Ruth chose to keep covenant with Naomi. Together they would try to rebuild their lives. Once in Bethlehem, Ruth did everything Naomi asked of her, and one morning her mother-in-law woke up and said something like this: "We've got to make a change, and we've got to make a change *now*! Daughter, if you do what I tell you to do *now*, you shall secure your future" (see Ruth 3:1).

NOW women know the time for change. And if they move in God's perfect timing, they will secure their future. Why is this important? Because if women begin to rise up as NOW women and begin to pray in accordance with what God is doing, we will begin to see these things manifest.

Naomi told Ruth, "Boaz, whose young women you were with, is he not our relative? In fact, he is winnowing barley tonight at the threshing floor" (Ruth 3:2). There's a law of redemption Naomi had learned about long ago, and she recognized that the time was now to activate that law of redemption. There are things in each one of us that need to be activated in this NOW time. God is just waiting to redeem and bring to fullness your redemption, and NOW is the time to activate that.

Let's look at the instructions Naomi gave to Ruth:

Wash yourself and anoint yourself, put on your best garment and go down to the threshing floor; but do not make yourself known to the man until he has finished eating and drinking. Then it shall be, when he lies down, that you shall notice the place where he lies; and you shall go in, uncover his feet, and lie down; and he will tell you what you should do (vv. 3-4).

First, Ruth was to wash herself and get cleaned up. Second, she was to get a new anointing. Third, she needed to put on her best garment. The widow's outfit she'd been wearing since they left Moab was to be taken off since that represented the grief of the past season. Fourth, she needed to wait for the proper timing before moving ahead. Finally, she was to lay at Boaz's feet. Ruth was required to fully submit to what God wanted to do.

So Boaz got up and blessed her. He acknowledged that there was a closer relative that had a right to Ruth before he did. But if that man did not perform his duty, then Boaz would do it and move in the law of redemption.

Do you see what this means for us? When you do that which God is asking you to do in His perfect timing, then one way or another you will receive your blessing. If we know the time for change and go through the scenario of cleansing ourselves, receiving the new anointing, changing and removing those garments of grief, moving at the right time and submitting ourselves to the full purpose of God, then we will receive blessing. Be sure you understand this: There is a way for women to receive what God is doing in the Body of Christ.

NOW Women Need to Be Patient for the Next Move of God

Women are often more intuitive than men to what is going on around them. Because women are intuitive and "know" when certain things need to happen, sometimes they get impatient.

John 11 tells the story of Mary and Martha and the death of their brother, Lazarus. We must understand that Jesus had already tried to tell His disciples that Lazarus's sickness had a greater purpose about it. Lazarus passed away before Jesus reached Bethany, and many of the Jews joined with the women around Martha and Mary to comfort them concerning their brother. When Martha heard that Jesus was nearing town, she went to meet Him; but Mary remained sitting in the house.

> Martha said to Jesus, "Lord, if You had been here, my brother would not have died" (John 11:21).

So many times, we think we know more than Jesus, and this passage should serve as a real caution. The passage continues:

> "But even now I know that whatever You ask of God, God will give You." Jesus said to her, "Your brother will rise again." Martha said to Him, "I know that he will rise again in the resurrection at the last day." Jesus said to her, "I am the resurrection and the life. He who believes in Me, though he may die, he shall live. And whoever lives and believes in Me shall never die. Do you believe this?" (vv. 22-26).

That's an incredible question!

> She said to Him, "Yes, Lord, I believe that You are the Christ, the Son of God, who is to come into the world." And when she had said these things, she went her way and secretly called Mary her sister, saying, "The Teacher has come and is calling for you" (vv. 27-28).

The Teacher is now visiting the earth in a new way. The Holy Spirit is moving in a new way, and He's calling for His women to come forward NOW.

> As soon as [Mary] heard that, she arose quickly and came to Him. Now Jesus had not yet come into the town, but was in the place where Martha met Him (vv. 29-30).

Here's something important to understand about visitation. Jesus did not need to go into Bethany for what He was going to do. Therefore, He called the women to come to Him outside the city gates so that He could talk to them. Some women today are waiting for Jesus to visit them in their homes. Others are waiting for Jesus to visit them in their churches. Others are waiting for Jesus to visit them in their cities. Yet all the while He is saying, "Come outside the gates, and I will visit with you here."

Then the Jews who were with her in the house, and com-
forting her, when they saw that Mary rose up quickly and
went out, followed her, saying, "She is going to the tomb to
weep there" (v. 31).

The neighbors didn't understand what she was doing. They
thought she was going to weep and mourn, but in reality she was
going outside the gates to meet Jesus. Similarly, we see people today
frequently misunderstand what God is doing with women.

Then, when Mary came where Jesus was, and saw Him, she
fell down at His feet, saying to Him, "Lord, if You had been
here, my brother would not have died" (v. 32).

In our sermons and studies, we tend to put Mary on a pedestal
and leave poor Martha hanging out to dry. But Mary did the same
thing Martha did. They both told Jesus that had He been there, their
brother would not have died. Do you see how they shifted the blame
to Jesus? Have you ever done that? We just rail on Him, telling Him
that if He hadn't done certain things, then we wouldn't be in the fix
we're in.

The Bible teaches us to take credit for our own actions. I have
a beautiful redheaded wife, and sometimes she will turn and rail
against me. My daughter is a blonde, and she also lets me have it at
times. Occasionally, I just sit there and wonder if they'll ever get
quiet so that I can say what I need to say.

Therefore, when Jesus saw her weeping, and the Jews who
came with her weeping, He groaned in the spirit and was troubled. And He said, "Where have you laid him?" (vv. 33-34).

And so they went to the tomb, where Jesus raised their brother,
Lazarus, from the dead.

Then many of the Jews who had come to Mary, and had
seen the things Jesus did, believed in Him (v. 45).

NOW women need to be patient for the move of God. God is about to raise women up in an incredible way in this land, but women must wait for His timing. Many want to know something before it's time to know it. NOW women, if they are patient to watch for the movement of God and enter at the proper time, will see the glory of God revealed.

Women, Awake!

This is a time of awakening for the women of God's people. Deborah was such a woman who woke up to God's purposes. According to the *Dictionary of Biblical Imagery*:

> The general concept of "awakening" captures the notion of either rousing oneself or being aroused in order to take action, as in the call of Deborah to "wake up" in song (Judg. 5:12, *NIV*). Such calls to action are usually accompanied by urgency and intensity, as seen in the empathic repetition "wake up, wake up!" (Judg. 5:12; cf. Isa. 52:1).[9]

During the time of the judges, each tribe of Israel thought they knew best how to secure and maintain their territory. All these separate interests and opinions produced disunion and jealousy. Governmental leadership was needed to bring unity to Israel, and God awakened Deborah to do just that.

Deborah judged Israel before she planned the war against Jabin. Most of the judges were men who procured justice, or right, for the people of Israel, not only by delivering them from the power of their enemies but also by administering the laws and rites of the Lord (see Judg. 2:16-19). Judging in this sense was different from the administration of civil jurisprudence and included the idea of government such as would be expected from a king (see 1 Sam. 8:5-6; 2 Kings 15:5).[10]

The Hebrew warrior Barak, who fought so valiantly and provided outstanding leadership to the armies of Israel, had to be shaken out of his weak acquiescence to the Canaanite bondage.

Once Barak was jarred out of his despondency, Deborah called on him to assist her in changing the nation. When the time came to wage war against Jabin and Sisera, "Barak refused to go without a prophetic complement; namely, the presence of Deborah":

> Barak should not be judged as lacking faith at this point. He merely wanted the one who could give divine guidance and help for such an important occasion. He was quickly reminded by Deborah that the victory which God would give would not come as a result of his genius, but it would be a victory brought by the Lord.[11]

Before the mass of the people could be revived, there had to be a stirring in the hearts of those with the qualities of leadership, including Deborah. Deborah had characteristics that I see God awakening at this time in women all over the world. Descriptions of these characteristics are provided in Dr. Herbert Lockyer's *All the Women of the Bible*:

She Was a Prophetess

Deborah is one of several females in Scripture distinguished as being endowed with the prophetic gift, which means the ability to discern the mind and purpose of God and declare it to others. In the days of the Old Testament, prophets and prophetesses were the media between God and His people Israel, and their gift to perceive and proclaim divine truth stamped them as being divinely inspired. Such an office, whether held by a male or female, was a high one.

She Was an Agitator

As one meaning of "agitation" is to stir up or excite public discussion with the view of producing a change, then Deborah was an effective agitator who stirred up Israel's concern about its low spiritual condition. The land was debauched and well-nigh ruined, and under the rule of the

Canaanites, liberty had been lost. The people were dejected
and afraid, for their spirits had been broken and all hope
of deliverance had vanished. But Deborah did more than
prophesy; she aroused the nation from its lethargy and
despair. Here was a fearless and unsolicited devotion to the
emancipation of God's people, and she awoke in them a
determination to free themselves from their wretched
bondage and degradation.

She Was a Ruler
[This is the type of apostolic leader God is raising up at this
time.] Deborah was the fifth of the leaders, or "judges," of
Israel raised up by God to deliver His people from the
bondage their idolatry had caused, and both in word and
deed she fulfilled her rule as Judge, at a time when men tried
to do right in the sight of their own eyes. As the position of
woman in those days was of a distinctly subordinate character, Deborah's prominence as a ruler is somewhat remarkable. All Israel was under her jurisdiction, and from the
palm tree bearing her name . . . called "the sanctuary of the
palm," she dispensed righteousness, justice and mercy.

She Was a Warrior
Having fought with words she went forth to throw off the
oppressor's yoke with swords, and what a fighter this patri-
otic and inspired heroine proved to be. Deborah sent for
Barak, the son of Abinoam of Naphtali, and told him that
it was God's will that he should lead her forces and deliver
the country. Long slavery and repeated failures made
Barak hesitate, but ultimately he decided to lead the army
provided Deborah, the brave-hearted and dauntless ruler,
went with him. Barak felt he could face the foe if his ruler
were at hand, and out they went to meet Sisera, a mighty
man of war, who had terrorized Israel for many years.
Great were the odds against Deborah and Barak, for their
army consisted of some 10,000 men. Sisera commanded

100,000 fighters and had 900 iron chariots. When the eventful moment of combat came, the dauntless spirit of Deborah did not quail. True, tremendous odds were against them, but Deborah had God as her Ally and "the stars in their courses fought against Sisera" (Judg. 5:20, KJV). A fearful hailstorm overtook the land, and the Canaanites were almost blinded by the rain, and were ultimately overwhelmed in the swollen river of Kishon. Sisera escaped but was killed by Jael while asleep in her tent. Thus Deborah gained undying fame as the female warrior who rescued her people from their cruel foes.

She Was a Poetess
[God is today creating the gift of psalmist in women.] The prose and poem of Judges 4 and 5 are associated with the same historic event, and reveal that Deborah could not only prophesy, arouse, rule and fight, but also write. It was said of Julius Caesar that he wrote with the same ability with which he fought. This observation can also be true of Deborah, who, after her victory over the Canaanites, composed a song which is regarded as one of the finest specimens of ancient Hebrew poetry, being superior to the celebrated song of Miriam. This song of praise, found in Judges 5, magnifies the Lord as being the One who enabled Israel's leaders to conquer their enemies. Out of the contest and conquest came the moral purification of the nation, and the inspiring genius of it was a woman daring and dynamic in the leadership of her nation.

She Was a Maternal Figure
The last glimpse we have of Deborah is as "a mother in Israel."

> The inhabitants of the villages ceased, they ceased in Israel, until that I Deborah arose, that I arose a mother in Israel. (Judg. 5:7, KJV)

Commenting upon our Lord's action in taking up little children into His arms and blessing them as being a father's act in Hebrew custom, Bengel says, "Jesus had no children that He might adopt all children." Perhaps it was so with Deborah who, as far as we know, had never experienced actual motherhood but yet became as a mother to all in Israel, and the source of this spiritual motherhood was her piety. Above all of her remarkable gifts was her trust in God, which is ever the source of any woman's highest adornment. As she sat under her palm tree to rule in righteousness and translate the revelation of God, her heart was filled with that "grace divine which diffused itself like a sweet-smelling savor over the whole land." Hers was a brilliant career because of a heart that was fixed in God.[12]

NOW Women Must Be Properly Align and Positioned

Miriam is an interesting study. Not only is she a picture of the NOW woman, but she also provides us with an illustration of proper apostolic-prophetic alignment. Miriam was a prophetess and one of the key individuals in the scenario of God gathering His people and leading them out of bondage in Egypt.

However, we find a situation in Numbers 12:1-10 in which Miriam questioned her brother Moses' right to be the sole leader of the movement of God's covenant plan. Miriam seemed to have a problem with pride in her gift of prophecy. Moses, by contrast, is referred to in the Word of God as "humble" (v. 3).

Miriam did not align herself with Moses. Together with Aaron she complained and murmured against Moses for marrying a foreigner. God became angry and summoned the three of them into His presence. There He affirmed Moses and rebuked Aaron and Miriam for their actions. Miriam was immediately covered with leprosy, and she might have suffered for the remainder of her life had her brothers not beseeched God to restore her. God did heal her, but, according to the Law, she had to remain outside the camp for seven days before she could be restored to fellowship.

John Walton and Victor Matthews point out that the camp waited for Miriam to complete her waiting period before they moved on:

> "And the people did not journey." The decision on when to journey depended solely on when the pillar of cloud lifted (see Num. 9:17). Our verse indicates, however, that the people had decided to honor Miriam by remaining at the camp until she could join them.[13]

This was very unusual that God would stop the entire movement of the people until Miriam was positioned properly. Prior to this, the fire and cloud had been the indicator for movement. But now God was using this woman and her proper alignment with apostolic authority as an indicator of how the whole group would move forward.

Women and the Future War of the Church

Women, you are more important than you know in God's future. In his book *Satan's Subtle Attack on Woman*, Dr. J. G. Morrison makes an appeal to liberated women to lead the way in devoted service and sacrifice for the One who has freed them from bondage:

> The advent of Jesus Christ saved womanhood. Not only saved souls of those who accepted and believed on Him, but brought the whole human race to see, at least wherever the gospel light has spread at all, that woman's place is not at man's feet, but is at his side. . . . [Christian] women, do not forget your heritage. You are the spiritual descendants of the Sarahs, the Deborahs and the Hannahs of the Old Covenant. Your line is renewed again in the New Testament in Mary who gave birth to Jesus Christ; Elizabeth who mothered His great forerunner; in Mary of Bethany, who

anointed His precious head and feet; in Mary Magdalene, who was last at His cross and first at His empty tomb; in the host of women who in the early gospel days, gave their hearts, homes and deepest toil to the cause of the Master.

Your line is again renewed in church history, until for faithfulness, devotion, heroism, martyrdom and all else that pleases the heart of the great Christ, woman has . . . borne the brunt, shared the vigils, preached with life and lip and handed the cause on to the next age with its banners proudly breasting every gale of opposition! . . . Remember then, sisters, your marvelous heritage and your amazing responsibility.[14]

We will not win the future war of the Church without women coming into place for what God is doing in this hour. Now is the time, dear sisters, for you to understand your invaluable worth, to come into the alignment God has for you and to exercise the unique gifts and callings the Lord has for you at this strategic time in history. If you will do so, great victory lies ahead for the Church of Jesus Christ!

God's Unfolding Revelation: Women on the Rise

One of the greatest changes in the Body of Christ over this last decade has been the release of women into ministry. The call to women is changing throughout the world. I honestly believe that without women and men joining hands, we will not see God's purpose fulfilled in the earth realm.

Look for more and more women empowered by God's Spirit in civil as well as religious structures in days ahead. In *God's Bold Call to Women,* Barbara Yoder, pastor of Shekinah Christian Church in Ann Arbor, Michigan, writes the following:

Woman, this is the day for which you were born—for such a time as this. It is a day of freedom, a day of boldness, when we can come out of a place of hiding and begin to connect with our apostolic mandate. This book is written to motivate and encourage women to move into the place of significance to which God has called us. This is a day in which the whole Church is being freed and is arising to take its rightful place. As you read this book, let it both heal and empower you for this new day.

How did this book come about? I recognized people were addressing women's issues through books and conferences. They either spoke on how to be a better woman or laid out an apologetic explaining why women could do anything in addition to being a wife or a mother. Many great books have been published on the subject, and I have listed some in the Suggested Reading section; however, I found nothing written to specifically motivate women to break through into their apostolic mandate. I chose to host a conference addressing the apostolic call on women. From that conference, it became clear that the Body of Christ would benefit greatly from a book written directly addressing the topic, and that collaborative effort would offer a well-rounded point of view.[15]

In *Rise to Your Destiny, Woman of God,* Barbara Wentroble, a key apostolic leader who heads an international network that includes both women and men, writes the following:

> Today, the walls that have kept men and women from walking together in full partnership are crumbling and falling as surely as the walls that once separated Eastern and Western Europe. Jesus came to tear down *every* dividing wall and to set people free to serve Him and to minister in His name. "For He Himself is our peace, who made both groups into one, and broke down the barrier of the dividing wall" (Eph. 2:14).

Oppression and cruelty toward women is also crumbling. God is empowering a new generation of men and women to walk side by side and press into every area of life with great victory. A shift has taken place in the earth. A tsunami of God's Spirit is crumbling every wall that keeps men and women from fulfilling His purpose. Together, men and women are arising in partnership to bring transformation to the nations of the earth!

God is calling out to women today to arise. Arise out of your captivity! Arise out of religious restrictions! Arise out of traditional mindsets that are contrary to the will of God for your life! Arise with a new freedom that allows you to explore God's plan for you, in a similar way that explorers search out new territory.[16]

There are several champions of women who are bridging the gap between the genders in this hour. One of those champions is Lee Grady, author of *10 Lies the Church Tells Women*, in which he relates several lies the Church has told women to keep them in spiritual bondage, including: God created women as inferior beings destined to serve their husbands (lie #1); women are not equipped to assume leadership roles in the Church (lie #2); a man needs to "cover" a woman in her ministry activities (lie #5); women are more easily deceived than men (lie #7); and women must obediently submit to their husbands in all situations (lie #10). I also recommend *Women of Destiny* by Cindy Jacobs, an incredible book that helps people come into a right perspective of women in ministry.

Just like Esther and Mordecai, women and men must work together to expose the enemy's plan. This will become a great pattern to watch in days ahead. You will see key leaders, both male and female, working as one in the kingdom of God.

CHAPTER TEN

The Best Is Still Ahead: Pressing Toward Prophetic Fulfillment

Ten thousand times ten thousand
In sparkling raiment bright,
The armies of the ransomed saints
Throng up the steps of light;
'Tis finished! All is finished,
Their fight with death and sin:
Fling open wide the golden gates
And let the victors in.

HENRY ALFORD (1810-1871)

Eye has not seen, nor ear heard, nor have entered into the heart of man
the things which God has prepared for those who love Him.

1 CORINTHIANS 2:9

To change and prosper in the days ahead, the Church will have to take some risks. It would be all too easy for us to stick with that which is familiar and miss all that we could have obtained had we entered into the new thing God has for us. The Lord gave me this word recently while I was ministering:

I am giving My people the opportunity to go backward. Many will be as Orpah and return to the familiar and the known. This will be a season that many will do the expected. Others will be like Ruth, making decisions to move forward into the unknown. They will make exceptional decisions and be known as those who will do the exceptional in the future. Those who decide to do the exceptional

will go through much testing in the unknown waters they are
charting and fields they are pioneering. However, the unknown
will soon become familiar. From this place they will prosper and
gain new favor. Fear not these crossroads, for there is a great grace
to move forward at the crossroads. Even though your emotional
soul will want to go backward, I say press into the New Covenant
relationships that I have for you and you will prosper.

This word caused me to look again at the book of Ruth. Ruth
is a good example of the kind of risk takers we need to be in the
coming days. Even though she was a Gentile, she aligned herself
properly with God's covenant people around her. There is coming
a great alignment between Gentile and Messianic believers that
will bring a fullness of God's purpose to the earth.

In her covenant relationship with Naomi, Ruth was willing to
work and obey in order to see the purpose of Naomi's life fulfilled.
She did not fear her future but rather made necessary changes at the
important crossroads of her life. When Naomi saw that it was time
for Ruth to enter into her future, she said to her, "My daughter, shall
I not seek security for you that it may be well with you?" (Ruth 3:1).

Security means rest and protection within one's own home or
boundary. How can we enter into the rest of God and enjoy His
promise in our own homes, families, churches and cities? I believe
that we, like Ruth, need to recognize the time for change, get a
plan for change and have an obedient heart to move forward. This
is key to our future.

Get Off the Dead Horse!

The tribal wisdom of the Dakota Indians, passed on from one generation to the next, says, "When you discover you are riding a dead
horse, the best strategy is to dismount." Many of us, however,
would rather stay on the dead horse and be comfortable rather
than go on to a new thing.

The war to change an old wineskin or government in the
Church is unbelievable. That war occurs because the mind must

shift to a new way of processing and thinking. Instead of remaining entrenched in one paradigm, we must allow God to move and position us in a new place of revelation and authority. From this new position, we can more effectively influence, govern and rule our surroundings.

We may feel that we cannot change, but God created us to do so! The brain is incredibly flexible, able to constantly undergo physical and chemical changes as it responds to its environment. The brain is not a hardwired unit that learns from a preset, unchangeable set of rules. We *are* capable of changing. We have been made to adapt. When the Great Architect is ready to alter the building plans of His kingdom, we should readily receive new revelation and shift our way of thinking. We are capable of making any shift that God requires of us.

The problem is not that our brains cannot change, but that our mind, which is the flesh, is often unwilling to move with God. Romans 8:7 says, "The mind set on the flesh is hostile toward God" (*NASB*). We would remain rigid, set in our old ways of doing things rather than change to suit God's building plan for the future. But we must stay dependent on the One who made us. This will cause us to receive His revelation not only for our personal future but also for the overall future of the Church.

As we prepare to move into the future, there are several things we need to understand about the new season. The following are eight key characteristics of the coming days.

1. This Will Be a Time of Realignment and New Order

At the dawn of the new century, the Lord began to speak to me the word "realignment." He said, "*I have been gathering my army. Now I will align and realign them for victory. I will accelerate the development of My new order on this earth. For the earth is Mine and I desire to see the fullness of My purposes made manifest. From this order many territories will be liberated.*"

I immediately looked up several of these words to better understand what the Lord was saying. To realign means to bring into a straight line or to rearrange so that an agreement and close cooperation can occur. This word also means "an arrangement of events that produces a proper plan." Realignment is linked with timing and place. "Order" is a mathematical and military term used to define the law of arrangement. Order is also linked with authority. When someone in authority gives a decree, order is produced, events are aligned and victory occurs.

In this new season, many in the Church who have felt displaced will find themselves connecting with leadership. Some leaders will find themselves connecting with segments of the Body different from those they have associated with previously. The Lord is aligning and connecting the gifts of His Body in such a way that a new maturity will be displayed in His kingdom to the world. This alignment will loose wisdom in the earth. As we have said before, wisdom dismantles demons and releases harvest. Be careful not to resist God's adjustments.

2. This Will Be a Time for Release of God's Power and Demonstration

The order described above is a functioning order of giftings that will result in power evangelism. Signs and wonders will follow us! Once we are in God's order—first apostle, second prophet, third teacher—then miracles and healings will occur (see 1 Cor. 12:28).

The Bible tells of times when one healing, one miracle or one deliverance caused an entire region to be liberated. For example, the gospel spread rapidly after Aeneas was healed (see Acts 9:32-35). He had been bedridden for eight years, until Peter decreed, "Jesus Christ heals you!" He immediately arose, and all of Lydda and Sharon then turned to the Lord. We will be a people who operate in signs, wonders and miracles to accomplish God's purpose here on Earth.

God invites His people to ask for signs and wonders. A sign is like a road marker; it points you in the right direction toward what God is doing. A sign may occur through an object or daily activity. It is a visible illustration that brings you into agreement with God's path and purpose for the future. Wonders describe God's supernatural activity and can serve as a sign of a future event. When He manifests His power in this manner, it produces awe on Earth. Wonders cause people to marvel.

Miracles are linked with God's ability to come from the supernatural into the natural and rearrange events, time sequences and orders. Miracles are not really contrary to nature, but rather, they bring nature into harmony with God's purpose. Human knowledge and ability have limited perspective. So God does miracles to help us comprehend higher laws that we have either strayed from or missed in our daily lives. Miracles will also attract the unsaved to a powerful God.

3. This Will Be a Time of Increased Discernment

If we do not develop discernment, we are in trouble indeed. The first thing we must do to gain discernment is to meditate on the Word of God. As we hide His Word in our hearts (see Ps. 119:11), how we view and process the world around us is interpreted by the Word within us. There is no reliable discernment apart from the Bible.

Discernment also comes by the Spirit of God. A gift of the Holy Spirit called "discerning of spirits" allows us to see when an evil spirit may be orchestrating an event, sign, wonder or lying tongue (see 1 Cor. 12:10). It takes both Word and Spirit to discern properly, to bring us into the reality of God. The Word of God says in John 4:23 that those who worship in spirit and truth will experience the reality of God. Without worship, we will miss the best that God has for us.

4. This Will Be a Time of Increase in God's Glory That Will Produce Harvest

When God's glory manifests, harvest is released. John 2 is a record of when Jesus first began to display His ministry and miracles on Earth. He did this to manifest His glory and propel His kingdom forward. Glory is the manifestation of God's attributes and perfections, or a visible splendor that represents His attributes or perfections. Be ready. Be expectant. Be filled with joy! Transformation of society is on the way!

The key to our future is our embracing the glory of God. Each of you reading this book has a future, but your future is linked to a release of His glory from within you. The Word of God says:

Arise, shine, for your light has come! And the glory of the
LORD is risen upon you (Isa. 60:1).

This promise was meant to provide tremendous hope and
comfort to the defeated and exiled people of Israel, promising the
everlasting establishment of Zion filled with God's glory. The
Church, which the Word says comes to the heavenly Zion and cannot be shaken (see Heb. 12:22,28), has every reason to also rejoice
in this promise. I love the *Amplified Bible*'s expanded translation of
Isaiah 60:1:

Arise [from the depression and prostration in which circumstances have kept you—rise to a new life]! Shine (be
radiant with the glory of the Lord), for your light has
come, and the glory of the Lord has risen upon you!

Isaiah 60 is a chapter on hope! Hope is an important element we
need in order to face the future ahead. This glowing prophetic
promise includes:

- The glory of God resting on us (see v. 1)
- The darkness around us submitting to the glory on us
  (see vv. 2,14)
- The Gentiles being drawn to this glory (see v. 3)
- Wealth being released because of the glory (see vv. 5-13)
- Violence being removed from the land because of this
  glory (see vv. 17-18)
- An acceleration of God's purposes on Earth because
  of this glory

We were created to carry or wear God's glory. Until we allow
His glory to be seen through us, the identity and purpose that He
created us for can never be fully revealed to those around us.

His glory is honor. His glory is strength. His glory is power.
His glory is wealth. His glory is authority. His glory is magnifi-
cence. His glory is fame. His glory is dignity. His glory is riches. His

glory is excellence. His glory is a visible splendor. His glory is coming! We must wear His glory if we are going to have favor and enter into our future with faith.[1]

5. This Will Be a Time of Changing Methods

When God's glory manifests, our environment cannot remain the same and there may be confusion until a new order forms and is understood. Once God invades, people must use their gifts of administration to develop a new order. Within the new order, new methods and strategies arise to make the Church's part in the move of God more efficient and understandable to the people of God. Martin Luther, John Calvin and John Wesley are just a few who have brought new order, methods and strategies to the Church.

Of course, Satan has his own plans and strategies. Once he sees the pattern of our methods, he will develop strategies to keep us stuck in those methods. That is why God invades again and again, bringing with Him new strategies for advancement. If we are not willing to accept the next move of God's glory, if we prefer to stay comfortably with last season's methods, a deadness will set into the Church, inhibiting God's plan for the earth. This is how religious spirits work!

We must be a people willing to change and adopt God's new methods in order to advance His kingdom.

6. This Will Be a Time of Revolution Brought On by Breakthrough Believers

God is raising up a new generation of apostolic breakthrough believers. Breakthrough believers do not conform to the ways of the world. Methods of past systems do not hold them from moving into God's purposes for the future.

Romans 12:2 says, "Do not be conformed to this world, but be transformed by the renewing of your mind, that you may prove what is that good and acceptable and perfect will of God." The word "conform" means to have the same focus or to act in accordance with the prevailing standards, attitudes and practices of a society or group. God always has a remnant group that does not conform to the world or the religious system around them.

Breakthrough believers display the following characteristics:

- They pioneer new moves of God. They are willing to enter uncharted regions and territories and bring the gospel of the Lord Jesus Christ. Loneliness does not overcome them, for the Spirit of God refreshes and leads them on a daily basis.
- They face off against existing religious structures.
- They are able to move forward, even under intense pressure. Despite any satanic onslaught against them, the pressure of the enemy just leads to more anointing.
- They retain the standard of truth learned from their mentoring leaders, yet they move in what God is doing today.
- They have a deep desire to impact new cities and territories.
- They break through personal fears of other believers, cultural limitations and prejudice to advance the gospel.

Breakthrough believers are the reason we can see breakthrough in our cities. Breakthrough believers create revolution. In his article "Revolution," Rick Joyner says the following:

> A revolution is coming to Christianity that will eclipse the Reformation in the sweeping changes that it brings to the Church. When it comes, the present structure and organization of the Church will cease to exist, and the way that the world defines Christianity will be radically changed. What is coming will not be a change of doctrine, but a change in basic church life. . . . For a time this transformation will release a life force that will be so great that it will dominate the news around the world. The Church will truly be the light of the world and the salt of the earth. The light of the gospel will shine through the Church to the degree that the whole world will see it, and the gospel will be clearly and powerfully presented to every nation on earth.
>
> The armies of God in heaven and on earth are mobilizing now. When they march, it will be the most awesome

and fearful sight the world has ever seen. In some places, this army will appear so fast that it will seem to have come out of thin air. . . . To those who are unaware of what is now taking place, it will be like peacefully going to sleep and waking up the next morning to the fact that your entire city, and in some cases, nation, has been occupied by a foreign army. . . .

This will happen suddenly because Christians will begin to stand up for the Lord, for the truth and the gospel. Instantly, the Church will become an overwhelming spiritual force. Whole cities will be taken for Christ before the evil forces of those cities even suspect an attack against their strongholds. This will be accompanied by great rejoicing and celebrations, large worship services, generosity and extraordinary miracles. But just as the light will become lighter, so also the dark will become darker. Wherever the great spiritual awakenings and revivals are not happening, evil will be released in a much more concentrated force. In many places, lawlessness will increase so that there will almost be a complete breakdown of order and justice. In the end, where love does not prevail, fear will.[2]

David is a historical type of a breakthrough believer and revolutionary. In 1 Samuel 17, he goes to visit his brothers on the battlefield and finds that Saul and his army have conformed to the taunting accusations of Goliath. Goliath is a type, or prophetic representation, of the strong man Jesus spoke of in Matthew 12:29. For 40 days Goliath had repeatedly told the Israelites that the Philistines would overcome them. David finds the whole troop believing this. David rises up and says, "I will not accept this same mindset." In 1 Samuel 17:29, he says, "Is there not a cause?" (*KJV*). When you have breakthrough in your heart, you never conform to the way of the world; instead, you see the cause of God at hand.

Breakthrough believers are by no means just adults. In her newsletter *GI News*, Cindy Jacobs says, "This Davidic spirit is certainly being expressed through the young people of the nations of the earth. They are revolutionary and passionate for the cause of Christ."[3] This is a time for the next generation to arise! They are a revolutionary generation of young people who will connect with the generation before them and cause great breakthrough to occur in all the earth.

7. This Will Be a Time to Overcome the Spirit of Fear

To be revolutionaries we must be a people of boldness. Even though evil abounds around us, we must be bold! Daniel prayed three times a day and was thrown into the den of lions for his faithfulness because of an unjust law. He persisted in boldness and ended up ruling over his enemies.

The opposite of boldness is fear. Fear can be an emotion and/or a demonic spirit (see 2 Tim. 1:7). When we agree with the spirit of fear and allow it to become embedded in our emotions, we grow confused and unstable. The voice of fear says, *There is a lion in my path, and I must hide out.* This effectively stops us from advancing. Fear agrees with a spirit of poverty, a spirit that whispers to our souls, *God is not able to deal with what I see and hear looming ahead on the path.* Yes, terrorism, financial instability, increasing litigation and government oppression may be lurking around the bend, but Almighty God says we *can* advance with confidence!

Eleanor Roosevelt once said, "You gain strength, courage and confidence by every experience in which you really stop to look fear in the face. You must do the thing which you think you cannot do." In other words, we can advance with confidence, but we must have overcoming hearts. Revelation 12:10-11 says:

> Then I heard a loud voice saying in heaven, "Now salvation, and strength, and the kingdom of our God, and the power of His Christ have come, for the accuser of our brethren, who accused them before our God day and night, has been cast down. And they overcame him by the blood of the Lamb and by the word of their testimony, and they did not love their lives to the death."

To have an overcoming spirit, you must come to a place of intimacy and deep communion with God. This causes what God is trying to birth on the earth to be conceived deep within you. Overcoming Christians understand travail. Once something has been conceived in them, they know they must travail until it has been birthed. This is not a time of fear but rather of overcoming and birthing.

A person with an overcoming spirit produces breakthrough. God is releasing an overcoming anointing for spiritual breakthrough. In *The Breaker Anointing*, Barbara Yoder writes:

> The breaker anointing affects individuals, churches and cities. When the breaker anointing comes into an area, it results in changes not only in individuals, but also in churches and socio-political structures and belief systems of the city. . . . To accomplish the mission of transformation this breed of radical shakers and movers that will affect society in days ahead needs a new anointing. . . . The breaker anointing is that anointing that breaks one through every kairos challenge.[4]

Micah 2:13 says, "The Breaker [the Messiah] will go up before them. They will break through, pass in through the gate and go out through it, and their King will pass on before them, the Lord at their head" (*AMP*). The breaker anointing is the anointing of any forerunner ministry. It will break fear away from us as we move into the future.

8. This Will Be a Time of Holiness and Humility
The only way that we can be a holy people is to be in a holy array.

> O sing to the LORD a new song!
> Sing to the LORD, all the earth. . . .
> Proclaim the good news of His salvation from day
>   to day.
> Declare His glory among the nations,
> His wonders among all peoples.

> Oh, worship the LORD in the beauty of holiness!
> Tremble before Him, all the earth (Ps. 96:1-3,9).

Sergio Scataglini writes that 98 percent holiness is not enough in these days:

> Many believers have experienced only the blessing of the Lord up to this point in their lives. And His blessings are wonderful. But in order to be used mightily by Him, we must also be cleansed. The same Lord that loves us and blesses us is coming to do surgery in our heart. We cannot be in the ministry and have evil habits in our private lives. Some have said, "Well then, I will get out of the ministry." No! Get the evil habits out of your heart.[5]

In his book *Radical Holiness for Radical Living*, C. Peter Wagner writes:

> Holiness is a godly quality that we cannot internalize without a fundamental understanding of what the Bible has to say about it. Since standards have not gone out of style, and since we have a deep need to know what the standards for our life are, where do we find those standards? Do we seek a human leader and expect the leader to set standards? If so, we might end up with a Joseph Stalin or Adolph Hitler. Do we take a vote and agree that the consensus of the majority sets the standards? We've tried that and ended up with mass abortions, homosexuality as an alternate lifestyle, and the breakdown of the nuclear family. We Christians might live in a political system which operates on human standards, but we are also supposed to be "set apart" which . . . is the root meaning of "holy."[6]

As I write this I am looking out my window at the neighbor's dog, a huge, white Great Pyrenees. In an attempt to keep him within his boundaries, his owners have put a heavy weight around his neck, attached by a chain. Even though the dog is determined to climb our stairs and onto our deck, the weight around his neck makes it difficult for him to ascend. In order for us to have accurate discernment in days ahead, God is going to liberate us from the weights that hold us back. He has put within us a desire to ascend and come into His presence through worship. The only way we can do this is by being holy and removing all the sins and weights that have so easily hindered us (see Heb. 12:1-2).

Holiness and humility are linked. As we become holy, we will be able to see God with much greater clarity. Seeing God for who He really is produces humility in us. Humility is a real strength under the subjection and control of a holy God. God will use humble, holy people to lead His kingdom in the coming days.

The Best Is Yet to Come

The Body has entered into a new *chronos* season and a *kairos* opportune time. In this new season we must gain our footing for the future. We cannot be so busy trying to *maintain* our lives—keeping everything done and in order—that we do not set aside time with the Lord to gain needed revelation. We are too often like Martha, distracted with the duties of serving (see Luke 10:40). We are often troubled and worried over many issues, and we want others to pity us for our burdens.

But we need to pull aside and spend the time with the Lord that it takes to gain revelation. Revelation establishes vision. Vision is linked with covenant favor. Covenant favor releases provision. The Lord is saying to you:

Pull aside and listen carefully! I have instructions that can adjust your course. I have strategies for your advancement. I have information that will cause you to grab hold of the best that I have for you.

Our future is linked with our expectations. Expectations are a function of desire. Desire is a function of the emotions. Therefore, to really embrace what God wants to do with us, we must be whole in our emotions. Our desires must be properly aligned with God's desires for us. "Delight yourself also in the LORD, and He shall give you the desires of your heart" (Ps. 37:4). Once our desires are linked with His desires, the *best* God has for us can be released in this new season.

Jesus saved the best for last at the wedding in Cana; He did this so that His glory could be revealed. Once again He has saved the best for last and so we are entering a season when His glory is going to be made manifest in new, tangible ways. This glory will overcome our unbelief, and by faith we will advance into His best!

Here are 10 principles for securing our future.

1. *To have a future, we must understand our past.* We must understand where we have come from, and we must be able to recognize sins and tricks the enemy has used to keep us from moving forward in days gone by. Once we break the cycles of sin in our past, we will be free to gain revelation for our future.

2. *To have a future, we must not be afraid of the broken places we see around us.* In Ezekiel 22, God reminded Ezekiel that the prophets had fallen into decay, the priests had violated God's principles, the princes had been corrupt, and the people had used all sorts of divination. However, if He could find one person who would stand in the gap for the nation, He could reverse the situation. Gaps are broken places that result from our sin. Many times we'd like to see the future released, but we must be willing to stand firm in prayer in the places where sin has removed the secure wall around us.

3. *To have a future, we must learn to stand.* When we are willing to make our stand in the place that God has asked us to stand, the demon forces that have been occupying that space must flee. We must rise up from the prostrate position we have been in and take our stand. If we do that, God will clothe us for the future with His favor and glory.

4. *To have a future, we must be willing to rebuild the wall that is torn down.* We must receive God's building strategy to rebuild what the enemy has tried to destroy. We must restore the wall. Restoration not only will get us back to the place where we were, but restoration will also unlock our future.

5. *To have a future, we must find our position on the wall.* Nehemiah and his people rebuilt the broken wall of Jerusalem in 52 days. The key to this effort was that, while most of the people were building, Nehemiah armed some with spears and positioned them to watch for the enemy's approach. We must each get positioned to do what we are called to do. Some are called to be watchmen, while others are called to be workers. All of us must be positioned properly to accomplish God's purpose.

6. *To have a future, we must endure the enemy's accusing and taunting.* While the devil will rise up to bitterly accuse those who are going forth and building the Kingdom, his accusations are really targeted against the Lord. I have found that when the world wants to accuse the Lord, they instead make accusations against one of His ambassadors. In Ezra we see a clear pattern of accusation stopping the building process. During the rebuilding of the Temple, the enemies first attempted to infiltrate, deceive and sabotage the building plans. After that plot failed, they resorted to discouragement and instilling fear in the people. When that also failed to stop the building process, they resorted to accusation. It was accusation that actually halted the building process for almost 14 years.

7. *To have a future, we must have an intimate relationship with the Lord that allows Him to communicate to us fresh strategies for victory.* A good example of this principle is found in the life of David. In 2 Samuel 5, David initially defeated the Philistines, but the Philistines regrouped and came against him once again. The Lord told David to listen for the wind in the mulberry trees and then attack, not by pursuing, but by coming upon the enemy from behind.

This was a different strategy from what had been used in the previous battle. You can't win today's battles with yesterday's revelation. If in his new battle David had used the same method that had previously brought him victory, he may well have been defeated.

8. *To have a future, we must honor those who have gone before us.* Honor is key. So many people never honor those who have paved the way for them to be positioned where they are presently. If you do not honor those who have mentored and parented, darkness will eventually overtake you. I believe this is why an Absalom spirit works in the Body trying to usurp authority. The Word tells us, "Honor your father and your mother, that your days may be long upon the land which the LORD your God is giving you" (Exod. 20:12). This passage ties the necessity of honoring to a prosperous future.

9. *To have a future, we must accept and have faith in the generation that is to follow.* When the Lord speaks about the future, He says to tell the next generation what is to come (see Deut. 6:20; Josh. 4:6,21). Therefore, we must have faith that those who are coming after us will be able to carry the standard and mantle of Christ into the next season.

10. *To have a future, we must have a testimony that will endure and overcome.* Your testimony is part of the overcoming strength of God on Earth. Not only do we have to stand, but we must also testify to the goodness of God. To testify, we must endure.

A Time for Prophetic Fulfillment

There is a relationship between obedience now and securing the future that a holy God has prepared for each of us. We need to understand the concept of *prophetic fulfillment.*

To prophesy is to communicate the mind and heart of God to a person, a group of people or a territory; therefore, prophecy is linked with the promise of God over our lives. God's promise is an announcement of His plan of salvation and blessing to His people. *A promise embraces both declaration and deed.* God's promise begins with a declaration by God and covers His future plan.

The promise of God focuses on the gifts and deeds that He will bestow on a few to benefit the many. Notice how God made His divine declaration, or assurance, first to Eve, Shem, Abraham, Isaac and Jacob—and then to the whole nation of Israel. This promise included:

1. He would be their God.
2. They would be His people.
3. He would dwell in their midst.

Land, growth and the call to bless the nations were all part of God's promise to Abraham (see Gen. 12:1-3). Added to these words of assurance was a series of divine actions in history that had to occur in order to bring fulfillment of the promise. These words and deeds of God began to constitute the continuously unfolding divine plan by which all the peoples and nations of the earth would benefit to this day. When a person becomes a believer, he or she is grafted into this plan.

A promise is like a promissory note on which to base one's confidence for the future. It is God's heart to fulfill His promise as He develops a relationship with us. When the gift of prophecy is in operation or a prophet is making declaration, this communication of God's heart is linked with the fulfillment of His promise.

God is sovereign. That means He has ultimate rule and say-so over the events of the universe. However, part of His sovereign design entails the human race's playing a part in the operation of the universe. In this plan are contingencies based on how the human race responds. If we respond properly, the fulfillment of His planned order in heaven can be seen on the earth. In His plan, He has built a way for His heart and mind to be communicated through the written Word and through prophecy.

Promises deliberately have a continuous fulfillment for generation after generation. Prophecy calls a generation to do its part now! Both the promise and prophecy of God are linked to our obedience.

God Remembers

God's promises apply to us individually and to our families, our churches, our ministries and the territories where we live. This is a time to hear the Lord saying, *"I long to remember My covenant promises for you. Because I will remember, I will advance you forward into a fulfillment of what I have spoken that was delayed."*

This is exciting!

The first time we see God "remembering," or enacting, His covenant is in Genesis 8:1. This is where the Lord remembered Noah's obedience to build the ark in preparation for a time of judgment. God sent a wind that passed over the earth, drying up the flood waters so that the human race could be reestablished and could perpetuate God's covenant plan. He also gave a sign in the heavens, the rainbow, signifying His love.

God also remembered Rachel, breaking a curse of barrenness and opening her womb (see Gen. 30:22). Perhaps one of the best examples is when the Lord remembered the Israelites in Egypt.

So God heard their groaning, and God *remembered* His covenant with Abraham, with Isaac, and with Jacob (Exod. 2:24, emphasis added).

The promises that had been dormant for 430 years suddenly began to stir in the heavenlies, and God sent a deliverer. God gathered His people. He made a way where there was no way. God propelled them forward toward something He had been longing to do for years.

We find this pattern recurring throughout biblical history, until finally, God the Father sent His Son so that one covenant season could be completed and a *new* covenant season begun. This new season gave each of us the opportunity to exchange our life for His and enter into a covenant destiny. The new promise still contained the law of God; only now the law became internalized, written on our hearts. This New Covenant still pledges that God will be our God and we will be His people.

Now the Spirit of God is moving on the earth and saying to the Church, "A new government is arising that will enforce the plan of the Son and fulfill the purpose of the Father!"

Entering into the Promise of God

If this is a time when God is remembering His covenant, then how do we enter into the promise?

- You must aspire and be motivated to say yes and amen to your promise (see 2 Cor. 1:20). Acknowledge Christ for who He was and who He is and is to come. He is near. Grab hold of the portion that He has for you by faith.

- The promise must be incorporated into the overall purpose and destiny of your life. Take that portion and focus on the place where God has positioned you. Let God purify your desires as He manifests His promise.

- To become successful in purpose we must receive prophecies that guide us into the fulfillment of our promise. Prophecy is powerful and keeps you in the Now of God. Do not despise it but, instead, receive it (see 1 Thess. 5:20).

- We enter our promise by warring with our prophecies (see 1 Tim. 1:18). We are God's army; we must develop an overcoming spirit. We must connect with others who are gifted in areas that we are not. Through its correct use, the word of prophecy is powerful to bind the enemy.

- Apostolic alignment and accountability are required for prophetic fulfillment. Authority brings your promise into unity with all of the Body of Christ. You are part of an apostolic sphere or function. Without proper alignment, many promises the Lord has willed for our generations will not be manifested. Understanding authority

releases faith. Faith overcomes. Remember, first apostles,
then prophets (see 1 Cor. 12:28).

- A persevering spirit is necessary for spiritual breakthrough.
  You must endure the process of time. The enemy—in the
  form of the flesh, the world and the devil—will attempt to
  stop the covenant promise of God from advancing in
  you. You must not resist change. Allow your spirit to be
  strengthened.

- Humility is key to entering into the promise. Humility is
  often misunderstood. Humility is strength and power
  under control and subjection. "I will dwell in the high
  and holy place, with him who has a contrite and humble
  spirit, to revive the spirit of the humble, and to revive the
  heart of the contrite ones" (Isa. 57:15). God resists the
  proud, and His promise resists pride. But a humble spirit is ripe to receive the promise of God.

Catching a New Wind for Your Future

"When the winds of change blow, adjust your sails." I love that saying! The wind is changing. Adjust! Advance! This wind is a whole
new wave of God's Spirit on the earth. Habakkuk 2:14 says, "For
the earth will be filled with the knowledge of the glory of the
LORD, as the waters cover the sea." Many say this wave will not be
like what we've seen in the past but rather more like a tsunami.

Brian Kooiman, my assistant at the World Prayer Center, had
a dream about this coming wave. He helped Rebecca and me while
we were working on this book. In his dream, Brian and Rebecca
were working on the book at a condominium near the ocean. They
could not see the beachfront since a high road (constructed to
protect the city) blocked their view. But Brian saw a huge wave the
size of a tsunami rushing toward shore. This wave crashed on the
shore, but only a misting of water came over the road and reached
the two of them. Then a second wave came and crashed against the

shore. They were not overtaken, but a heavier spray of water reached them. Finally, a third wave crashed on the shore. This one surged over the road barrier and came flooding into the first-floor room where Brian and Rebecca were working.

I believe this dream represents the next move of God. The move will come in a gradual progression, but it will eventually cut off the path we have been following in the previous season of the Church.

God is moving His Church into a new season. Arise, Church, receive the word of the Lord today! Let the wind of His Spirit blow upon you and advance you into a victorious future!

God's Unfolding Revelation: A Season of War and Harvest

In the midst of turmoil and war, God always has a people that rise up to reflect His character in the earth. That is just what is happening: Instead of bowing under the tumultuous times we are in, we are becoming strong. This strength is just as the Lord promises us in Daniel 11:33: "But the people who know their God shall be strong, and carry out great exploits" (*NKJV*). Because of this new strength, every mountain that has stopped your progress in the past will be beaten down and you will move forward on the path that the Lord has for you.

We must remember that He is with us at all times. Isaiah 41:10-13 says, "Fear not, for I am with you; be not dismayed, for I am your God. I will strengthen you, yes, I will help you, I will uphold you with my righteous right hand . . . those who war against you shall be as nothing . . . Fear not, I will help you!" This passage is in the prophetic context of changing identity and gaining strength. The Lord prophesies that Jacob—the people of Israel—will go from being a "worm" to "a new, sharp, threshing sledge with teeth" (vv. 14-15). This transformation is also for us today. The picture of threshing is used in the Bible to signify providential chastisement, judicial visitation and the labors of ministers, and each of these will play a part in what lies ahead. Key threshing floors in our areas must be uncovered this year. There is a new sound that is coming to the earth, linked with threshing. Much separation of the wheat and tares will occur.

After the first edition of this book was written, we began one of the most changing, challenging seasons in world history. The conflict between the Islamic world and the Judeo-Christian world began to intensify, but much of the revelation released in *The Future War of the Church* has helped the Body to adjust in this season. The government of God has matured to include all of the foundational gifts operating in the Body of Christ. However, anti-Semitism has increased and lawlessness has intensified. The tragedy of September 11, 2001, the terrorist attack that destroyed the World Trade Center and killed over 3,000 innocent individuals, changed the minds of people around the world about the concepts of war and peace. All war is terrible, but the war on terror is a different kind of war.

Get Ready for the Ride

When we began this season, I was speaking at Shekinah Christian Church in Ann Arbor, Michigan. When I stepped into the pulpit, the Lord said, "Get ready for the ride."

Then He showed me a bull and said, "This season will be like a bull ride." Bull riding is one of the most violent sports. We have entered into a season of violence. As we come to the close of this seven-year season, we can easily see how they have been violent years, much like riding a bull. But we are learning to ride! Day by day, we are learning to live in a tumultuous, violent environment. A tremendous learning curve is ahead for the Body of Christ. We must learn how to war and abound in this age (see 1 Cor. 2). Do not allow the fear of failure to keep you from experimenting and learning what God would have you learn—the righteous might fall seven times, but they will also get back up again (see Prov. 24:16). Fear not! Do not allow fear to overcome you. The economic structures of the earth are changing. Be willing to learn how to open up new supply lines.

We are living in a season called "the Beginning of Wars," which began on September 15, 2001, and will transition on September 29, 2008, at Rosh Hashanah. But we have no need to fear! We can be victorious and complete, confident of our secured future in Christ! These seven years of training and confrontation have caused God's remnant people to become aware of the conflicts surrounding them. With this new understanding, in the next seven years we will begin to do exploits!

The Watchman Anointing

We are developing eyes to see. We must continue to know whom we are watching after and with whom we are connected. We must also know who is watching after each of us. We are living in days when accountability is key. We must get our assignment quickly.

We are in a season of *watching*! The watchman anointing must mature in the Body of Christ. To "watch" means to look out, to peer into the distance, to investigate or get a new scope on something, to see an approaching danger (see 2 Kings 9:17-18) to warn those endangered, to review and evaluate your household (see Prov. 31:27) and to *see* so that we can guard our future! I see the Lord restoring the actual watches so that we can see things we have never seen before. God is reordering our days so that we can enter into His timeframe and experience the power of the watch. Let the Holy Spirit establish your watch!

In *Watchman Prayer*, Dutch Sheets shares on how a "watchman must 'beware'. . . be aware. If we are not aware, we are obviously unaware or ignorant . . . and this can give our adversary a distinct advantage. 'Wary' is also a word related to 'beware.' We must be wary regarding our enemy. Webster defines wary as 'on one's guard, on the lookout for danger or trickery.' We are not to fear our enemy, Satan, but we are to be aware of him and his subtleties."[7] Satan is very crafty and is constantly roaming to see who he may devour. Rebecca Wagner Sytsema and I wrote a book called *Prayers that Outwit the Enemy* that offers ways of communion that can help you watch for the enemy so that he does not get an upper hand in your life.

Declare that a *finishing anointing* will begin to work in your life and sphere of authority! This is a time to create a new beginning for yourself and your loved ones! Decree that those who have strayed from the path will return. Claim that all that is wayward or lost and that belongs to you will return under your authority! This is a season to receive new passion and be aroused! Break the spirit of apathy.

God Will Reveal His Glory and His Kingdom

We must learn to *interpret supernatural revelation*. Ask God for the gift of interpretation. The Lord will be releasing a new revelation in the earth realm so that we understand times and seasons. Dreams will become very significant. There will be a revival of the Spirit of God. We will once again begin to hear words of knowledge. Words of wisdom will begin to give us clear strategy for the words of knowledge being received.

The Body of Christ must once again understand *signs*. Signs are pointers that identify and uncover the godly, redemptive plan of God in the world. We must not miss our signs this year! We must not be afraid of the supernatural, and we must begin to enter into that dimension that will get us to our new "there." This will begin individually and work into a corporate demonstration.

We are moving into a season of understanding the kingdom of God. Kingdom has a culture, so in order to live according to God's culture, we will develop new ways to communicate and demonstrate God's power in days ahead. There is much dissatisfaction with traditionalism—people are seeking truth and power. Therefore, God will shift many into new places to reveal His glory and His kingdom.

The earth is the Lord's and the fullness thereof, and there are certain land-based curses that the Lord is ready to bring to an end. Land responds to the iniquity of man. Joel 2 is very important. Do not be afraid to face the curse that has hindered your progress. Decode the occult structure linked with the curse, evaluate its destruction and begin the rebuilding cycle for your future. The Promised Land was filled with curses, but the Lord told Joshua,

"Wherever your foot treads, I will give you that land" (Josh. 1:3). This is a time of *treading*. There are new paths ahead for each of us to walk. We will go to places we have not been before. The Lord will also begin to penetrate ungodly nations to bring His glory to places that have never experienced Him. This will be a season of pioneering into new places after judgment and wrath have occurred. This is the season to take dominion over the antichrist system. Fear not, and tread forth!

Heaven's Worship in the Earth Realm

We have entered a season when we will experience a different type of corporate worship. The Tabernacle of David is being reestablished (see Amos 9:11). Individual worship will turn into corporate worship, and corporate worship is a key to the transformation of our regions. I believe that the words I offer in *The Worship Warrior* are some of the most important concepts for God's people to embrace. The people of God always sing and worship before they understand things doctrinally.

There is a *roar* of the Lion of Judah developing in the House of God. The sound of God's people will become very distinguishable in days ahead. The enemy will roar loudly, but the Lion of Judah will roar louder. We must learn the Lion of Judah's sound. It is in us, and it must be drawn out of us.

Following is a word of prophecy spoken on Saturday, October 14, 2006, during our Feast of Tabernacles Gathering. On Sunday, October 15, 2006, an earthquake hit Hawaii and a flood overtook Houston, Texas.

Plant your feet! Ready yourself for change! We are entering a time of shaking and quaking! This time will be known as the Season of Holy Spirit Manifestation! This will be the season that the RIVERS will rise. Watch where heavens open and floods (physical) reach the earth, and document those places! Those are places targeted for a Holy Spirit invasion. Rising flood waters will cause you to move to higher ground. As the River of the Holy Spirit rises, you will find yourself moving to the high places. I will position My

people on the high places this year. As you worship, I will cause rul-
ing thrones of iniquity to topple. Like Dagon, their heads will fall
before My Presence! Get ready! I shake loose wicked structures.
Watch in the night and watch Me manifest in the light!

Finish Strong and Move into the Next Season Stronger!

In running our race, we must not let the devil keep us from finishing every assignment we receive with a powerful testimony. Too
many times, we see someone who is moving forward and having
great impact falter or get ensnared just seconds before they reach
the finish line. Don't let the devil get the victory! Instead, listen for
the Lord's voice and follow without fear. How do you enter in and
hear what the Lord has to say to you for the next season? *Remove all
distractions and listen for the wind of the Holy Spirit!* Resist your Martha
tendencies these next three months. Jesus said, "Martha, Martha,
you are so distracted." The Greek word for "distracted" means "to
drag around in circles." Do not let the enemy hold you captive in an
old circle of duty and miss the times the Lord has determined to
visit with you in the year ahead.

Let the Lord reorder your day! Evening comes before morning. Let
Him determine your hour of prayer. Invite a *new wave* of the Holy Spirit
to overtake your life and invade your region! This is the year of a Holy
Spirit Movement. Renounce and repent for quenching the Holy Spirit
in the past. *War with prophetic words that will unlock the seeds you have sown.*

This will release strategies for you to do *exploits!* I woke up this
morning and the Lord reminded me of Dr. George Washington
Carver and how he developed hundreds of uses for the peanut. That
is the concept of exploits. Pray to *unlock sounds* that will allow you to
advance past old worship systems and methods. Let the healing flow
of God burst forth! Open key portals for angelic hosts to lead you
to a new dimension of breakthrough. Press through and touch the
hem of His garment! Do not let trauma or infirmity from the past
season stop you from pressing out and touching the Lord to receive
virtue and power!

Trauma hides in your cells like a snapshot from a camera. The
picture of the trauma is stored deep in your brain. When not

processed and resolved, trauma will distort your world so that you perceive everything through that snapshot. The enemy tries to take advantage of us during traumatic times of loss or change. He uses trauma to create: (1) a failure mentality; (2) a confused perception of life; (3) a dullness, deadness, lost hope, or apathy in our spirit man; (4) blocked emotions; (5) a bitter root. Do not take bitterness with you into the next season. This will create roots that will entangle your feet and keep you from moving forward on your new path of success. But the Holy Spirit is ready to move in such a way that you are sovereignly delivered! This will give you a new perspective on life and the world around you. New vision will arise in you.

Do we have a great future ahead in the world of turmoil around us? Of course! We will possess our inheritance! That means that we will eventually rule in the midst of our enemies. Expect your end to be better than your beginning.

Here are seven issues that we must watch for and be aware of as we enter the next 21 years. These are fleshed out in *God's Unfolding Battle Plan*.

1. *Changing commerce and trade systems.* We must learn to overthrow trade iniquities that have never been overthrown (see Josh. 13:3-5; 19:24-31; 2 Kings 19; Ezek. 28; Rev. 19). We must understand Babylon. We must be aware of the dragon. We must understand China's role in the future, especially in the area of commerce. We must also watch Russia carefully.

2. *Breaking the fear of darkness.* We must learn to rule the night. The prayer movement will shift. From city to city, we will develop the night watch. This will not be done only in the Church but also in all spheres of authority.

3. *We must understand the concept of time and law.* Satan's strategy is to manipulate time and law. Be careful of attempts to overthrow "The Machine." Jesus threatened the system by doing what the Father said. Following

His example, we must not get caught up in the system trying to change the system. We must be a Kingdom people who obey our King and allow our obedience to change society.

4. *We will preach the power of the Blood!* The Spirit of God will begin to invade blood structures. We will return to an understanding of the power of His Blood. We will not preach a gospel with no power. This will result in gifts of healing and unusual workings of miracles.

5. *We must no longer just be attempting to build the Church.* We must understand God's kingdom plan for this hour. The season of fellowship is shifting into more decentralized fellowship. Our corporate gatherings will be filled with a new dynamic with worship and warfare. We will travail and gain strategy against the enemy's plans in the earth realm. God is releasing new strategies for us to govern in the spheres of authority that we have been assigned. The Church building plan of the future has changed.

6. *A dichotomy of good and evil is forming.* We are entering a season of polarization. We must understand God's covenant in these conflicts. Anti-Semitism is embedded in most national structures. When you blend nationalism with religious force, you get a dangerous dynamic in the world. We must watch the Middle East, a powder keg of religious force contending for territorial dominion.

7. *An unprecedented season of harvest is on the horizon.* This is a season to develop the strategies for the next major harvest of souls in the earth. To do this we must define our harvest fields, which are not the same fields from the last several decades. We must develop new

ways to plow the harvest fields. There is a new crop of souls ready to be harvested!

Mind-blowing changes are ahead for all of us who profess the name of the Lord Jesus Christ!

Endnotes

Introduction

1. C. Peter Wagner, *Destiny of a Nation* (Colorado Springs, CO: Wagner Publications, 2001), pp. 95-101.
2. Ibid., p. 97.
3. Chuck D. Pierce with John Dickson, *The Worship Warrior* (Ventura, CA: Regal Books, 2002), pp. 97-98.
4. Ibid., pp. 103-104.

Chapter One: Prepare for War

1. For more on the watchman anointing, see Dutch Sheets, *Watchman Prayer* (Ventura, CA: Regal Books, 2000).
2. For information on the World Prayer Center, call (719) 536-9100 or go to www.world prayerteam.org.

Chapter Two: Foundations for Future Victory

1. Graham Cooke, *A Divine Confrontation* (Shippensburg, PA: Destiny Image, 1999), p. 35.
2. John Eckhardt, *Leadershift* (Chicago: Crusaders Ministries, 2000), pp. 17-18.
3. C. Peter Wagner, *Warfare Prayer* (Ventura, CA: Regal Books, 1992), p. 61.
4. C. Peter Wagner, *Praying with Power* (Ventura, CA: Regal Books, 1997), p. 185.
5. Kevin Conner and Ken Malmin, *The Covenants* (Portland, OR: Bible Temple Publishing, 1983), p. 69.
6. John Dawson, *Healing America's Wounds* (Ventura, CA: Regal Books, 1994), p. 36.
7. Cindy Jacobs, *Women of Destiny* (Ventura, CA: Regal Books, 1998), p. 153.
8. Jane Hansen, *Fashioned for Intimacy* (Ventura, CA: Regal Books, 1997), pp. 13-14.
9. Dawson, *Healing America's Wounds*, p. 30.
10. Cooke, *A Divine Confrontation*, p. 285.
11. Harold R. Eberly, *The Complete Wineskin* (Yakima, WA: Winepress Publishing, 1997), pp. 1-2.
12. Ron Cantor, "The Most Hated People on Earth," *Israel's Restoration*, vol. 15, no. 11, p. 1.
13. Amiram Barkat, "Study: Anti-Semitic Acts Across Europe Rose Significantly in 2006," Haaretz.com, Feb. 21, 2007. http://www.haaretz.com/hasen/spages/818681.html (accessed May 2007).
14. "Gibson's Nondenial Denial," *THE WEEK*, December 29, 2006–January 12, 2007, p. 10.
15. "Ahmadinejad: What Holocaust?" *THE WEEK*, December 29, 2006–January 12, 2007, p. 19.

Chapter Three: The Third Day Church Arising

1. John Dawson, *What Christians Should Know About Reconciliation* (Ventura, CA: International Reconciliation Coalition, 1998), pp. 24-25.
2. Dick Eastman, "Angelic Activity in Spiritual Warfare," *The Spirit-Filled Life Bible* (Nashville, TN: Thomas Nelson Publishers, 1991) p. 1977.
3. C. Peter Wagner, *Churchquake!* (Ventura, CA: Regal Books, 1999), pp. 5-6.
4. C. Peter Wagner, *The New Apostolic Churches* (Ventura, CA: Regal Books, 1998), p. 20.
5. Bob Beckett, *Commitment to Conquer* (Grand Rapids, MI: Chosen Books, 1997), pp. 118-119.

6. C. Peter Wagner, *Apostles and Prophets* (Ventura, CA: Regal Books, 2000), p. 106.

7. Ibid., p. 89.

8. C. Peter Wagner, *Praying with Power* (Ventura, CA: Regal Books, 1997), p. 95.

9. C. Peter Wagner, *Apostles of the City* (Colorado Springs, CO: Wagner Publications, 2000), p. 43.

10. C. Peter Wagner, *Changing Church* (Ventura, CA: Regal Books, 2004), p. 12.

11. Ibid., pp. 14-15.

12. Ibid., p. 31.

Chapter Four: Dethroning Thrones of Iniquity

1. Bob Beckett, *Commitment to Conquer* (Grand Rapids, MI: Chosen Books, 1997) pp. 65-66.

2. *Random House Webster's College Dictionary* (New York: 1992), s.v. "sacrifice," definition #3.

3. C. Peter Wagner, *The Acts of the Holy Spirit* (Ventura, CA: Regal Books, 2000), p. 400.

4. Andy Butcher, "Inside the Cities of Darkness," *Charisma* (October 1999), p. 49.

5. John Suk, "What About Harry Potter?" *The Banner* (February 14, 2000), pp. 4-5.

6. This list was compiled from an article written by C. Peter Wagner, "The Josiah Declaration," *Prayer Track News* (April-June 1999), p. 15.

7. Chuck D. Pierce and Rebecca Wagner Sytsema, *Ridding Your Home of Spiritual Darkness* (Colorado Springs, CO: Wagner Publications, 1999), p. 23.

8. Dutch Sheets and Chuck D. Pierce, *Releasing the Prophetic Destiny of a Nation* (Shippensburg, PA: Destiny Image Publishers, Inc., 2005), pp. 46-51.

Chapter Five: Urgent, Fervent Prayer: How to Outwit the Devil

1. C. Peter Wagner, *Seven Power Principles That I Didn't Learn in Seminary* (Colorado Springs, CO: Wagner Publications, 2000), pp. 66-67.

2. *New Unger's Bible Dictionary* (Chicago, IL: Moody Press, 1988), s.v. "standard."

3. Cindy Jacobs, *Possessing the Gates of the Enemy* (Tarrytown, NY: Chosen Books, 1991), pp. 115-116.

4. Ibid., p. 116.

5. C. Peter Wagner, *Confronting the Powers* (Ventura, CA: Regal Books, 1996), p. 102.

6. This section is based in part on information found in "The Plagues of Egypt," *Lay Catholic Voice*. www.ih2000.net/catholicvoice/Lessons/ExodusPlagueLesson.html (accessed November 2000).

7. C. Peter Wagner, *Strategies for Church Growth* (Ventura, CA: Regal Books, 1989), p. 83.

8. Ibid.

9. C. Peter Wagner, "Looking Back to Surge Ahead," *Global Prayer News*, vol. 1, no. 3, p. 12.

10. For an in-depth look at the watch of the Lord, read my book *Reordering Your Day: Understanding and Embracing the Four Prayer Watches* (Glory of Zion International Ministries, 2006). I also recommend *Authority in Prayer: Praying with Power and Purpose* (Bethany House Publishers, 2006), *Intercessory Prayer* (Regal Books, 1996) and *Watchman Prayer* (Regal Books, 2000) all by Dutch Sheets, as well as *Praying with Authority* (Regal Books, 2003) by Barbara Wentroble.

Chapter Six: The Transference of Wealth

1. Jean Ziegler, *The Swiss, the Gold and the Dead* (New York: Penguin Books, 1997), p. 36.

2. Karin Laub, "A First: German President Addresses Israeli Parliament in German," *Associated Press: The Archive*, February 16, 2000. http://ap.pqarchiver.com/ (accessed November 2000).

3. Doris Wagner, *How to Minister Freedom* (Ventura, CA: Regal Books, 2005), pp. 260-262.

4. Brad Wolverton, "McDonald's Heiress Gives $1.5 Billion to Salvation Army," *The Chronicle of Philanthropy*, January 2004. http://www.philanthropy.com/free/update/2004/01/2004012001.htm (accessed May 2007).

5. Carol J. Loomis, "Warren Buffet Gives Away His Fortune," *Fortune*, June 25, 2006. http://money.cnn.com/2006/06/25/magazines/fortune/charity1.fortune/index.htm (accessed May 2007).

6. C. Peter Wagner, "Sophisticated Philanthropy for Apostolic Distribution," private letter dated April 22, 2006.

Chapter Seven: Lawlessness!

1. Matt Daniels, "United, We Fall," *World* (June 17, 2000), p. 65.

2. John Kelly, *End Time Warriors* (Ventura, CA: Renew, 1999), pp. 61-62.

3. John Cloud, "The Columbine Effect," *Time* (December 9, 1999), p. 51.

4. "Why We Need KidsNeedDads.Com," *KidsNeedDads.Com*, 1999. http://www.KidsNeedDads.com/thatswhy.htm (accessed December 2000).

5. "More Reasons We Need KidsNeedDads.Com," *KidsNeedDads.Com*, 1999. http://www.KidsNeedDads.com/morereasons.htm (accessed December 2000).

6. "Fatherless Males at Higher Risk for Jail," Reuters News Service, August 20, 1998. The article reports the results of a joint study by Cynthia Harper of the University of Pennsylvania and Sara S. McLanahan of Princeton University.

7. Roberts Liardon, *Spiritual Timing* (Tulsa, OK: Harrison House, 1990), p. 7.

8. The word to Baton Rouge in 2003 was "you will become a refuge city" (see Dutch Sheets and Chuck Pierce, *Releasing the Prophetic Destiny of a Nation* [Shippensburg, PA: Destiny Image, 2005]). In 2004, the word given in Baton Rouge was regarding purification coming to New Orleans. You can read this word at http://www.elijahlist.com/words/display_word.html?ID=2459.

9. "Chuck Pierce Calls for Emergency Prayer Against Lawlessness in Gulf Coast," The Elijah List, September 2, 2005. http://www.elijahlist.com/words/display_word/3379 (accessed May 2007).

10. Quoted by Joe Gyan, Jr., "Crime Surge Threatens Recovery," *The New Orleans Advocate*, Jan. 19, 2007. http://pqasb.pqarchiver.com/theadvocate/access/1197166411.html?dids=1197166411:1197166411&FMT=ABS&FMTS=ABS:FT&date=Jan+19%2C+2007&author=JOE+GYAN+JR.&pub=Advocate&edition=&startpage=4&desc=Crime+surge+threatens+recovery (accessed June 2007).

Chapter Eight: The Modern-Day "-Ites"

1. Dan Juster, from a message given at Glory of Zion Outreach Center in Denton, Texas, October 8, 2000.

2. Jim W. Goll, "Paradigm Shifts for the 21st Century," *Engage* (Fall 2000), p. 2.

3. Dan Juster and Kevin Intrater, *Israel, the Church and the Last Days* (Shippensburg, PA: Destiny Image, 1990), p. 121.

4. Marty Waldman, "Historic Issues: Jewish Roots of Christianity," *Pray for the Peace of Jerusalem* (vol. 2, no. 2), p. 4.

5. Rabbi David Levine, *In That Day* (Lake Mary, FL: Creation House, 1998), p. 83.

6. Jim W. Goll, *Kneeling on the Promises* (Grand Rapids, MI: Chosen Books, 1999), pp. 291-293.

7. C. Peter Wagner, *The Queen's Domain* (Colorado Springs, CO: Wagner Publications, 2000), pp. 23-25.

8. Ibid., p. 25

9. "The Rise of Islam in Mainstream America," *Christianity Today* (April 3, 2000), pp. 7, 40-53.

10. *Islamic Affairs Analyst* (August 2000), p. 3.

11. Ibid., p. 4.

12. "The Rise of Islam in Mainstream America," pp. 7, 40-53.

13. Victor Mordecai, *Is Fanatic Islam a Global Threat?* (Taylors, SC: V. Mordecai, 1997), p. 125.

14. Federal Bureau of Investigation, "Project Megiddo," November 2, 1999, p. 21. The report is available online at http://www.fbi.gov/library/megiddo/megiddo.pdf (accessed December 2000).

15. "Responses to Domestic Terrorism," *USA Today* (June 30, 2000), pp. A21, A22.

16. Federal Bureau of Investigation, "Project Megiddo," pp. 3, 4, 6, 8, 10.

17. The Ku Klux Klan is one such group. Several times in my ministry I have been confronted by the powers behind this secret society.

18. Selwyn Stevens, *Unmasking Freemasonry* (Wellington, New Zealand: Jubilee Resources, 1999), p. 29.

19. Ibid.

20. Kelley Varner, *The Three Prejudices* (Shippensburg, PA: Destiny Image, 1997), from the preface.

21. Peter Hirsch, "Anti-Israel/Anti-Jewish?" World Partner Special Partner Update, February 2007.

22. Prayer focus information adapted from personal communication from Martin and Norma Sarvis, who are part of Glory of Zion's ministry in Jerusalem, dated February 22, 2007.

Chapter Nine: Women Arising Now

1. Bruce I. Friedland, *The Dallas Morning News* (September 30, 2000), pp. 43A, 44A.

2. Bob Jones IV, *World* (June 17, 2000), pp. 28-30.

3. Judy Jacobs, "Warring in the Spirit," *SpiritLed Woman* (October/November 1999), pp. 42-46.

4. David Yonggi Cho, quoted in Kim Laurence, "Women: Our Most Untapped Resource," *Heartbeat of West Kentucky* (July 2000), p. 1.

5. Cindy Jacobs, *Women of Destiny* (Ventura, CA: Regal Books, 1998), pp. 271-272.

6. Jim David and Donna Johnson, *Redefining the Role of Women in the Church* (Santa Rosa Beach, FL: Christian International Ministries Network, 1997), p. 24.

7. Larry Kreider, *The Cry for Spiritual Fathers and Mothers* (Ephrata, PA: House To House Publications, 2000).

8. Cindy Jacobs, *Women of Destiny*, p. 173.

9. Leland Ryken, James C. Wilhoit, Tremper Longman III, gen. eds., *Dictionary of Biblical Imagery* (Downers Grove, IL: InterVarsity Press, 1998), pp. 64-65.

10. Merrill F. Unger, R.K. Harrison, eds., *The New Unger's Bible Dictionary* (Chicago: Moody Press, 1988), pp. 723-724.

11. John J. Davis, *Conquest and Crisis: Studies in Joshua, Judges and Ruth* (Grand Rapids, MI: Baker Book House, 1969), p. 110.

12. Herbert Lockyer, *All the Women of the Bible* (Grand Rapids, MI: Zondervan, 1988), pp. 41-43.

13. John H. Walton and Victor H. Matthews, *The Bible Background Commentary: Genesis Through Deuteronomy* (Downers Grove, IL: InterVarsity Press, 1997), p. 797.

14. J. G. Morrison, *Satan's Subtle Attack on Woman* (Kansas City, MO: Nazarene Publishing House, n.d.), n.p.

15. Barbara Yoder, *God's Bold Call to Women* (Ventura, CA: Regal Books, 2005), p. 8.

16. Barbara Wentroble, *Rise to Your Destiny, Woman of God* (Ventura, CA: Regal Books, 2006), pp. 21-22.

Chapter Ten: The Best Is Still Ahead: Pressing Toward Prophetic Fulfillment
1. For a more in-depth study on glory, see Chuck D. Pierce and Rebecca Wagner Sytsema, *Possessing Your Inheritance* (Ventura, CA: Renew Books, 1999), pp. 83-101.
2. Rick Joyner, *The Morning Star Prophetic Bulletin* (May 2000), pp. 1-3.
3. Cindy Jacobs, "The Righteous Revolution," *GI News* (vol. 9, no. 3), p. 1.
4. Barbara Yoder, *The Breaker Anointing* (Colorado Springs, CO: Wagner Publications, 2001), n.p.
5. Sergio Scataglini, *The Fire of His Holiness* (Ventura, CA: Regal Books, 1999), p. 36.
6. C. Peter Wagner, *Radical Holiness for Radical Living* (Colorado Springs, CO: Wagner Publications, 1998), p. 19.
7. Dutch Sheets, *Watchman Prayer* (Ventura, CA: Regal Books, 2000), p. 61.

Index

*For more information about Glory of Zion International
Ministries and other resources available from Chuck D.
Pierce, please write or call:*

*Glory of Zion International
P.O. Box 1601
Denton, Texas 76202*

*Phone: (940) 382-7231
Fax: (940) 565-9264
Email: plantern@aol.com
http://www.glory-of-zion.org*

What's Ahead for the Church in the Next 7 Years

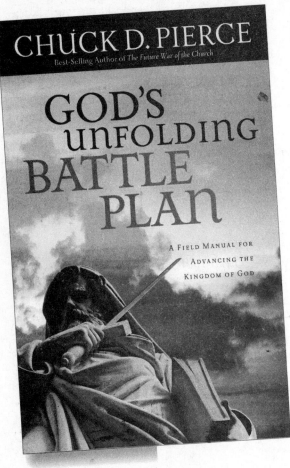

This new book from Chuck Pierce continues to empower Christians to face the exciting present (and future) for the Church that he began to lay out in *The Future War of the Church*. Yes, we are in the midst of a battle that will only increase in strength, but the victory has already been promised. Outlining the next 7-year period of spiritual war, 2008-2015, Pierce shows how God will advance His kingdom, causing the faithful to rise up and God's will to be done here on Earth as it is in Heaven. *God's Unfolding Battle Plan* offers a glimpse into what's ahead, as well as encouragement to triumph over the attending forces of lawlessness, hopelessness, and violence. Discover what God has said to Pierce about the upcoming period and learn how to prosper through strategic intercession, worship warfare, and a powerful new weapon of intercession, the four watches of the night. Remain hopeful knowing you are a part of God's unfolding battle plan, and the best is still ahead.

God's Unfolding Battle Plan
A Field Manual for Advancing the Kingdom of God
Chuck D. Pierce
ISBN 978.08307.44701

Available at Bookstores Everywhere!
Visit **www.regalbooks.com** to join **Regal's FREE e-newsletter.**
You'll get useful **excerpts from our newest releases** and **special access to online chats with your favorite authors.** Sign up today!

Regal
God's Word for Your World
www.regalbooks.com